D1186940

BRITISH CAVALRY UNIFORMS
Since 1660

BRITISH CAVALRY UNIFORMS
Since 1660

Michael Barthorp

Illustrated by
Pierre Turner

BLANDFORD PRESS
POOLE · DORSET

First published in the U.K. 1984 by Blandford Press,
Link House, West Street, Poole, Dorset, BH 15 1LL.

Copyright © 1984 Blandford Press Ltd.

Distributed in the United States by
Sterling Publishing Co., Inc.,
2 Park Avenue, New York, N.Y. 10016.

British Library Cataloguing in Publication Data

Barthorp, Michael
  British cavalry uniforms since 1660.
  1. Great Britain. *Army*—Uniforms—History
  2. Great Britain. *Army*—Cavalry—History
  I. Title
  357'.188   UC485.G7

ISBN 0 7137 1043 8

Typeset 10/11 pt Linotron Plantin
by Polyglot Pte Ltd, Singapore

Printed in Singapore by Toppan Printing (S)

Frontispiece: *The last days of horsed cavalry: the 7th
Queen's Own Hussars.*

CONTENTS

Preface

The aim of this book is to trace the development of the dress of the British Cavalry, Household and Line, from the establishment of the Sovereign's standing army in 1660 to the present day, in peace and war, in temperate and tropical climates. The term *dress* embraces not only uniform—full dress, undress, service or combat dress—but also the equipment worn by officers and men and their weapons. As far as the accoutrements of the cavalryman's horse are concerned, the largely decorative furniture and the more functional equipment receive consideration, but discussion of bridles and saddlery has had to be omitted for reasons of space. (Nor is the subject of cavalry standards and guidons dealt with in detail.) The treatment is entirely confined to the Regular Army since the cavalry element of the Reserve forces, the Yeomanry, is a subject in itself.

Each chapter deals with a century and is divided into sections, all but the first of which corresponds to the major dress changes. The first section of each chapter is a brief consideration of the organisational developments in the century that follows. The succeeding sections are subdivided into the various types of cavalry: Household, Horse, Dragoons, and later Hussars and Lancers. In order that the subject may be related to its correct context, the text begins with a Chronology of Campaigns fought by Regiments as Horsed Cavalry, followed by an Introduction which summarises the subject up until 1660.

The regiments of the British Army have always been noted for their individual dress distinctions and in an Arm like the Cavalry—where the uniforms of each type have differed markedly, particularly in later periods—it is impossible, when trying to compress the dress worn over three centuries into one volume, to be as detailed as the subject deserves. It has therefore been necessary in the text to treat the subject in a fairly broad way. However, much regimental detail can be found in Appendices 1–9. Even so, there are bound to be one or two omissions and inadvertent inaccuracies for which the author must crave the indulgence and forgiveness of any who feel themselves slighted.

The descriptions of uniform in the text are complemented by a large number of contemporary paintings, watercolours, prints and photographs in black and white, and enhanced by thirty-two coloured plates, executed by the masterly hand of Pierre Turner from information supplied by the author. Though some of the figures in these plates are displayed mounted—as cavalrymen should be—the majority are not, so as to permit the illustration of more figures in the space available.

For the first eighty years of this survey, 1660–1741, the evidence, both documentary and pictorial, is relatively slight. The scale of clothing for a soldier is documented but the details of what it looked like are much harder to ascertain. The problem is aggravated by the considerable licence enjoyed by regimental colonels over the clothing of their men, which therefore might alter, at least in detail, according to the whims of successive colonels. Furthermore, since the very existence of a standing army was, at best, only tolerated by the nation, and since military costume differed little in its cut from prevailing civilian fashions, there was scant incentive for artists to record the dress of military men, particularly that of the ordinary soldier. Officers' portraits from this early period are scarce and those that do exist can only be regarded as reliable for the particular officer portrayed, since officers' dress at this time was much less regulated than later on. Not until George II diminished the colonels' powers by instituting a system of clothing regulations backed by Royal authority does the path of the uniform student become easier, aided by a growing increase in military portraiture and illustration of ordinary soldiers' dress.

In the nineteenth century the regulations became more detailed, large numbers of military paintings and prints appeared and, by the time of the Crimean War, uniform was being recorded by camera. Personal records of men serving overseas often yield documentary and pictorial evidence of what was actually worn in the field, while further evidence of this nature can be gleaned from the work of war artists and correspondents sent out to cover the many colonial campaigns of the second half of the nineteenth century. At home, the demand for military illustration, much of it for boys' books but none the less valuable, grew apace in the 1880s and 1890s, resulting in the prolific output of such artists as Harry Payne and Richard Simkin. In the twentieth century, of course, there are few military activities which have not been captured by the camera. For the latter half of this survey, therefore, the evidence is far more plentiful than the first, but against this the dress changes have been more frequent and the variety of clothing worn more extensive. The seventeenth-century soldier had just the one suit of clothes he was issued with; his modern counterpart has a dozen different orders of dress.

In the course of researching this subject over a number of years, and in the preparation of this book, the assistance of many institutions and individuals has been sought. Among the former, the author gratefully acknowledges the help given by the staffs of: The Lord Chamberlain's Office; the Royal Library, Windsor; the National Army Museum; the Imperial War Museum; the Scottish United Services Museum; the Armouries, H M Tower of London; the British Museum, Department of Prints and Drawings; the Victoria and Albert Museum; the Scottish National Portrait Gallery; the India Office Library; the Ministry of Defence (Army) Library; the Army Museums Ogilby Trust; the Courtauld Institute of Art; the Parker Gallery; the Royal Pavilion, Brighton; Sotheby, Parke, Bernet & Co; Wilton House. Also the headquarters or museums of several regiments, old and new, in particular those of: the Household Cavalry; 1st The Queen's Dragoon Guards; 4th/7th Royal Dragoon Guards; Royal Scots Dragoon Guards; Royal Hussars; 14th/20th King's Hussars; 17th/21st Lancers. The author is also indebted to the following individuals who have helped either in a private or professional capacity: Douglas Anderson; Major-General J B Akehurst; W Y Carman; Michael Chappell; Major R M Collins; Andrew Festing; Major J A Friend; Mrs Marion Harding; R G Harris; R J Marrion; Colonel P S Newton; Lieutenant-Colonel H M Sandars, Queen's Own Hussars; Miss J M Spencer-Smith; Captain R C G Vivian.

A particular word of gratitude is due to John Mollo, whose book this would have been but for prior commitments, and who generously made available the results of much of his own researches into the subject. A special debt must be acknowledged to all contributors, past and present, to that invaluable source of information, the Journal of the Society for Army Historical Research. Lastly the author must thank Pierre Turner, for his friendly co-operation and skill with the plates, and for bringing to the task his own knowledge and feeling for the subject, and Barry Gregory for his encouragement and forbearance.

M J B
Jersey, C I

Chronology of Campaigns fought by Regiments as Horsed Cavalry

The abbreviations of regiments listed below can be found on page 177. Up to 1755 H = Horse; from 1803 H = Hussars.

1661–84
Tangier campaigns against the Moors: Tangier Horse (1 D)

1685
Monmouth's Rebellion: RHG, KING'S H, 4 H, 1 D

1689–97
Jacobite Rebellions in Scotland & Ireland: RHG, KING'S H, QUEEN'S H, 4 H, 6 H, 7 H, 8 H, 1 D, 3 D, 4 D, 5 D, 6 D, 7 D

1689–97
WAR OF THE GRAND ALLIANCE: HG, KING'S H, QUEEN'S H, 4 H, 5 H, 6 H, 7 H, 8 H, 1 D, 2 D, 3 D, 4 D, 5 D, 7 D

1702–13
WAR OF THE SPANISH SUCCESSION: KING'S H, QUEEN'S H, 4 H, 6 H, 7 H, 8 H, 1 D, 2 D, 3 D, 4 D, 5 D, 7 D, 8 D

1715
Jacobite Rebellion: QUEEN'S H, 4 H, 1 D, 2 D, 3 D, 4 D, 6 D, 7 D, 9 D, 11 D, 13 D, 14 D

1719
Jacobite Rebellion: 2 D

1742–48
WAR OF THE AUSTRIAN SUCCESSION: HG, RHG, KING'S H, 8 H, 1 D, 2 D, 3 D, 4 D, 5 D, 6 D, 7 D

1745–46
Jacobite Rebellion: QUEEN'S H, 4 H, 3 D, 10 D, 11 D, 13 D, 14 D

1755–63
SEVEN YEARS WAR: RHG, 1 DG, 2 DG, 3 DG, 6 DG, 7 DG, 1 D, 2 D, 6 D, 7 D, 10 D, 11 D, 15 LD, 16 LD, 17 LD

1775–83
WAR OF AMERICAN INDEPENDENCE: 16 LD, 17 LD

1790–92
Third Mysore War (India): 19 LD

1793–1801
FRENCH REVOLUTIONARY WAR: RHG, 1 DG, 2 DG, 3 DG, 5 DG, 6 DG, 1 D, 2 D, 6 D, 7 LD, 8 LD, 11 LD, 12 LD, 13 LD, 14 LD, 15 LD, 16 LD, 17 LD, 18 LD, 20 LD, 21 LD

1799
Fourth Mysore War: 19 LD

1803
First Mahratta War (India): 8 LD, 19 LD

1803–15
NAPOLEONIC WAR: LG, RHG, 1 DG, 3 DG, 5 DG, 1 D, 2 D, 3 D, 4 D, 6 D, 7 H, 9 LD, 10 H, 11 LD, 12 LD, 13 LD, 14 LD, 15 H, 16 LD, 17 LD, 18 H, 20 LD

1812–14
American War: 14 LD, 19 LD

1814–16
Gurkha War: 8 LD

1817–19
Pindari & Mahratta War: 8 LD, 17 LD

1825–26
Bhurtpore Campaign (India): 11 LD, 16 L

1837–39
Canadian Rebellion: 1 DG, 7 H

1838–42
First Afghan War: 3 LD, 4 LD, 16 L

1843
Sind and Gwalior Campaigns (India): 9 L

1845–46
First Sikh War: 3 LD, 9 L, 16 L

1846–47
Seventh Kaffir War: 7 DG

1848–49
Second Sikh War: 3 LD, 9 L, 14 LD

1850–53
Eighth Kaffir War: 12 L

1854–56
CRIMEAN WAR: 1 DG, 4 DG, 5 DG, 1 D, 2 D, 4 LD, 6 D, 8 H, 10 H, 11 H, 12 L, 13 LD, 17 L

1856–57
Persian War: 14 LD

1857–59
Indian (or Sepoy) Mutiny: 1 DG, 2 DG, 3 DG, 6 DG, 7 DG, 7 H, 8 H, 9 L, 12 L, 14 LD, 17 L

1860
Third China War: 1 DG

1868
Abyssinian War: 3 DG

1878–80
Second Afghan War: 6 DG, 8 H, 9 L, 10 H, 15 H

1879
Zulu War: 1 DG, 17 L

1881
Transvaal (or First Boer) War: 1 DG, 6 D, 14 H

1882
Egyptian War: LG, RHG, 4 DG, 7 DG, 19 H

1884–85
First Sudan War: 5 L, 10 H, 19 H; detachments of LG, RHG, 2 DG, 4 DG, 5 DG, 1 D, 2 D, 3 H, 4 H, 5 L, 7 H, 10 H, 11 H, 15 H, 16 L, 18 H, 20 H, 21 H (all for Camel Corps)

1898
Second Sudan War: 21 L

1899–1902
SOUTH AFRICAN (SECOND BOER) WAR: all (less 4 DG, 11 H, 15 H, 21 L)

1914–18
WORLD WAR 1 (OR THE GREAT WAR): all

Introduction

From the Norman Conquest until the thirteenth century European warfare was dominated by the mounted man-at-arms, the armoured knight on his heavy horse, equipped with lance, sword, shield and dagger. Armed combat was the prerogative of European chivalry. Not until the fourteenth and fifteenth centuries did the dominance of the mounted warrior begin to decline due to the re-emergence on the battlefield of bodies of foot-soldiers—drawn from the ordinary people—to supplement and eventually overcome the knightly array. In particular, the English archer with his long bow and the Swiss pikeman, who formed with his peers a solid mass of 16–ft pikes, were spectacularly successful. Against the bristling hedgehog of the latter, knights were powerless, while to counter the former the mounted man-at-arms could only increase his armour and thereby his weight, consequently limiting his mobility. In any case, his horse, as much a part of his fighting entity as himself, remained vulnerable despite attempts—largely unsuccessful—to armour it, and once dismounted the capacity of a man-at-arms for shock action was lost and he became valueless.

The widespread adoption of firearms in the sixteenth century further increased the vulnerability of the armed horseman, but any superiority that foot musketeers might have attained was lessened by their vulnerability due to the unreliability and slow rate of fire of their muskets, necessitating the protection of pikemen, who in turn became vulnerable when the horsemen's lances were replaced by portable firearms, or when the horsemen were closely supported by their own musketeers. The shock action of the mounted charge by armoured lancers gave way to a drill perfected in Germany known as the 'caracole', in which volleys of pistol fire were delivered by successive ranks of horsemen formed in a square formation. However, the mounted man's speed of advance became reduced to little more than a walk, due either to the slow, deliberate movements of the caracole if the fire was to be effective, or to accommodate the accompanying musketeers.

In addition to pistol-armed cavalry and foot-soldiers, a third type of warrior evolved in France from the middle of the sixteenth century: one who was mounted for movement but fought on foot, armed with a short musket or carbine known as a 'dragon', from which he acquired the designation of dragoon.

Thus by the seventeenth century the mounted elements of an army comprised both the armoured cavalrymen—armed chiefly with pistols and sword and known as Horse—who, due to the relative inefficiency of the infantrymen's firearms, were still relied upon to effect a decision on the battlefield, and the more lightly equipped dragoons, whose tasks ranged from escorting artillery and baggage to patrols, outposts, the seizure of tactical features during an advance and even heading storming columns at sieges. In the Thirty Years War, Gustavus Adolphus of Sweden sought to exploit the musketeers' weaknesses by reverting to shock action with his Horse after previously softening up the enemy with artillery and musketry. He abandoned the slow-moving block formations of the caracole in favour of a controlled charge (probably at little more than a trot), by Horse in three or four ranks who, after firing a single volley with their pistols, would then attack with their swords.

In England, where no standing military forces were maintained, the Civil War saw armies hastily raised from scratch and, with those most accustomed to horsemanship gravitating mainly to the King's cause, the Royalist Horse under Prince Rupert gained an early ascendancy. Suffering a dearth of firearms and inadequately-trained men, Rupert adapted Gustavus' methods by cutting out the pistol volley and relying entirely on the shock effect of the charge at speed, sword in hand; those who had pistols were to use them only after they had come to close quarters with the enemy. In the early battles, Rupert's Horse carried all before them but their tactics contained a fatal flaw: their inability to rally and reform after a charge.

This lack of discipline was quickly perceived by Oliver Cromwell, then commanding a troop of Parliamentary Horse, who determined to raise a regiment whose discipline would maintain it as a formed and effective body from the first onset to the final rout of the enemy. He adopted the

Armour, buff coat, accoutrements and weapons of a
mid-seventeenth century trooper of Horse.

triple-rank formation with the sword as the primary weapon but relied for his shock effect, not on speed, but on the weight and mass of a controlled advance at a smart trot. By 1643 his regiment totalled 14 troops, each of four officers, three corporals, two trumpeters and some 60 troopers, and in 1644 his methods and skill as a cavalry leader were fully proved at Marston Moor.

When Parliament raised the New Model Army in 1645, the first standing force of its kind in England, Cromwell's regiment, now split into two, provided the prototype for its Horse. This consisted of ten, later eleven, regiments, each of six troops of 100 men including corporals and trumpeters but excluding officers of which a troop generally had four: a captain, lieutenant, a cornet who carried the troop standard, and a quartermaster. Besides the Horse, there was a regiment of Dragoons, 1,000 strong and, reflecting its semi-infantry character, formed in ten companies, each with the same number of officers as the Horse, but with sergeants and drummers instead of corporals and trumpeters.

In the earlier stages of the Civil War attempts had been made by both sides to achieve a measure of uniform appearance among their men, at least within regiments. It was a feature of the New Model that it should be uniformly clothed in red, a colour which, at least since Tudor times had had English associations, and which had been used by both Royalist and Parliamentary regiments. For the Foot the upper garment was a 'cassock' of Venice red, a hip-length coat, which was later worn longer, lined with contrasting colours for different regiments, worn with 'breeches of grey or other good colour', stockings and a broad-brimmed felt hat. This costume was most probably shared by the Dragoons, though with riding boots. Whether the Horse had similar red coats is uncertain as their outer garment in the field was the stout buff leather coat, worn with breeches and long thigh-length boots. Their armour consisted solely of the lobster-tailed helmet, with neck and ear guards and sometimes a single or triple-barred face guard attached to the front peak, a back-and-breast cuirass, and perhaps a bridle gauntlet worn on the left or rein hand and forearm. In the early years of the New Model the arms of a trooper of Horse were a pair of pistols carried in holsters attached to the saddle and a broadsword slung from a buff leather shoulder belt, but later a carbine was added for which a second shoulder belt was necessary. Dragoons were accoutred and armed like the Foot, with a bandolier, or collar of cartridges, a sword and a musket, the latter preferably a flintlock which, unlike the more common matchlock of the Foot, could be fired from the saddle. The sword was slung from a shoulder belt but the musket probably had a sling.

After Charles II was restored to his throne by General George Monck, the Cromwellian standing army was to be disbanded. But the disturbed state of the capital suggested that the King's safety required a permanent body of guards, Horse and Foot. During his exile in Holland, Charles had been guarded by two troops of Royalist Horse, his own and the Duke of York's, and a regiment of Foot, all of which arrived in England. This was not thought to be a large enough force, so when Monck paraded his own Foot regiment (later Coldstream Guards) on Tower Hill in February 1661 to lay down its arms, it was immediately ordered to take them up again in the service of the King. Also affected by this ceremony was Monck's own troop of cavalry, known as the Lord General's Life Guard of Horse. In due course this troop was added to the King's Guards but had to yield precedence to the two other Royal troops which had come from Holland. These three troops subsequently formed the regiment still known today as the Life Guards but, as will be seen, this title would not be assumed for more than a hundred years.

Among the soldiers escorting Charles II on his first procession through London in 1660 were some Commonwealth regiments of 'Army Horse'. These were disbanded, but one, formerly Colonel Crooke's, was taken over by the King and designated the Royal Regiment. This too was disbanded in December 1660 but the uncertainties of the times led to it being reformed a month later under the Earl of Oxford's command. Thus, with the three troops of Royal Guards and this regiment of Horse, was begun the mounted branch of the Sovereign's standing army.

The 17th Century

Background

The King's mounted guards were known as the Horse Guards, as distinct from his two regiments of Foot Guards, and from 1661 were designated the 1st or King's Troop, the 2nd or Duke of York's Troop, and the 3rd or Duke of Albemarle's Troop (as Monck had become). When Albemarle died in 1670 his Troop became the 2nd or Queen's, and the Duke of York's the 3rd Troop. A 4th or Scots Troop was raised in Scotland but did not come south until after 1707. The subsidiary titles were dropped in 1685. The 200 men of each troop of Horse Guards were not ordinary soldiers but 'private gentlemen'. However, in 1678, when a new type of soldier, the grenadier, was added to regiments of Foot, it was decided to form troops of Horse Grenadier Guards trained as dragoons for attachment to each troop of Horse Guards; the men for these were recruited in the same way as the rest of the rank and file of the Army. The senior troop had 80 grenadiers, the other two 60, each with three

officers and two each of sergeants, corporals, drummers and hautbois.

The Earl of Oxford's Regiment was initially the only one of Horse, consisting of eight troops, each of the same strength as the Horse Grenadiers' troops; by 1684 the troop strength, excluding the four officers, was three corporals, two trumpeters and 45 men. This was the regiment better known in recent times as the Royal Horse Guards (Blues), receiving the title of Royal Regiment of Horse Guards in 1687 though ranking not among the Horse Guards proper, but as first of a number of regiments of Horse raised from 1685 by James II and William III. Some were disbanded but, by the end of the century, the number of regiments which were to have a continued existence thereafter totalled eight. The number of troops per

The Duke of York's Troop of Horse Guards at the Coronation of Charles II, 1661, led by a kettle-drummer and five trumpeters. Engraving by Wenceslas Hollar.

13

regiment varied between six and nine, each having the same complement of officers[1], corporals and trumpeters as Oxford's regiment, but with the number of troopers fluctuating from 50 in war to 36 in peace.

The need to garrison Tangier, which formed part of Catherine of Braganza's dowry on her marriage to Charles II, led to the raising in 1661 of the Tangier Horse. When Tangier was abandoned in 1684, the regiment was converted into the senior regiment of English Dragoons with the designation 'King's Own Royal'. Meanwhile some independent troops of Scots dragoons raised from 1678 were regimented in 1681 as the Royal Scots Dragoons, with six companies each of 60 men, which later took precedence after the Royal Dragoons. To these two regiments more were added by James II and William III but not all survived into the next century; those that did took precedence as the 3rd–8th Dragoons, the 5th and 6th being styled Royal Irish and Inniskilling respectively.

Gradually the Dragoons, though not losing their mounted infantry role or the infantry ranks, weapons and accoutrements that accompanied it, were transformed into cavalry, as witnessed by an order of 1684, which required that in the field they were to take place among the Horse but in garrison among the Foot. Whereas the NCOs of Horse all ranked as corporals (as they still do in the Household Cavalry), Dragoons had sergeants and corporals as did the Foot, with drummers and hautbois instead of the Horse's trumpeters. A dragoon troop, of which six to eight formed a regiment, had three officers, a quartermaster, a sergeant, two corporals, one drummer, one hautbois and between 36 and 60 dragoons, according to whether it was peace or war.

Dress 1660–1700

Horse Guards and Horse Grenadiers

The first pictorial evidence of the dress of the King's Horse Guards comes from the engravings by Wenceslas Hollar of Charles II's Coronation in 1661, which shows the Duke of York's Troop riding six abreast in eight ranks, preceded by a kettle-drummer and five trumpeters with one officer at the head of the Troop and another at the rear. According to Sir Edward Walker's account of the procession the hat feathers were red, white

[1] Quartermasters in the Horse Guards and the Royal Horse Guards were commissioned officers; in the Horse they were not.

and black for this Troop but red and white for the King's. Walker stated the King's Troop wore buff coats but Hollar shows what appear to be hip-length cloth coats, presumably scarlet, with slashed, laced and be-ribboned sleeves. The cuirasses were apparently painted black in the Duke of York's but were polished in the King's and the waist scarf or sash was red. The full breeches, terminating in knots of ribbons, can be seen on those riders who have pushed down the wide tops of their thigh-length boots. The private gentlemen in the ranks (see Plate 1) were armed with carbines (for which a belt was slung over the left shoulder) and swords, apparently suspended from a waistbelt under the sash. The officer's sword hung from an embroidered baldrick over the right shoulder. All ranks had a pair of pistols attached to the saddle. The drummer and trumpeters were dressed similarly but wore no cuirasses and their coats had false sleeves hanging from the shoulders. They were armed with swords suspended from baldricks but had no pistols. Their drum and trumpet banners were embroidered with a shield bearing the Royal coat

PLATE 1: 1660–1700

1. **Gentleman, Duke of York's Troop of Horse Guards, 1661 (later 1st Life Guards).**
2. **Officer, Royal Regiment of Horse, 1680 (later Royal Horse Guards).**

Figure 1 is based on Wenceslas Hollar's engraving of Charles II's Coronation and Sir Edward Walker's description of the procession, which noted for this Troop the black-painted cuirass, the tri-coloured hat feathers and belts trimmed with the yellow of the Duke's livery. The elaborate dress is typical of the fashions the King brought from France in reaction to the austere clothing of the Commonwealth. At this date the ranks of the Horse Guards troops were filled with gentlemen, though each was armed as an ordinary trooper with sword, carbine and pistols. Figure 2 is taken from a portrait by Kneller of Captain Thomas Lucy who served in this, the senior regiment of Horse, between 1679–1684. Although he is depicted in a buff leather coat, some of his troopers appear in the picture wearing the red-faced blue coats, which have ever been peculiar to this regiment, and the same grey felt hats with black feathers. Military hats were by now generally black, and the jacked black leather boot had replaced the supple buff type of Figure 1. Rank is indicated by his shoulder knot and fringed red sash. The buff coat, as a protective garment, was still being worn by some of the Horse as late as 1696.

1. Gentleman, 2nd Troop, Horse Guards, 1661.

2. Offr, Royal Regt of Horse, 1680.

of arms within the garter surmounted by the crown.

An account written in 1669 described the King's Troop as having 'red jackets faced with blue richly ornamented with gold lace' and white feathers in the hats. York's and Albemarle's Troops had the same jackets without the lace, and the latter's hats were adorned with crimson ribbons instead of feathers.

By the 1670s the hats were made of black felt, were lower in the crown and had the brim turned up on one side. The coat skirts had lengthened and the cuffs were turned back to reveal the facing, or lining colour. The long boots with wide tops, formerly buff, were now of black, stiffened or jacked leather—hence the term jack-boots. A portrait of an officer of the lst Troop, Randolph Egerton, c 1672, shows the following developments: a full-skirted red coat, embroidered in gold with blue cuffs and lining, worn over a buff, gold-embroidered waistcoat of similar length, the sleeves of which show between the coat cuffs and the buff leather gauntlets. A crimson and gold sash is worn over the right shoulder as a mark of rank. The sword belt is beneath the coat, the hilt emerging through a slit in the skirts. Whether the waistcoat is of buff leather or cloth is uncertain, but a trooper in the background, whose hat feather and sash also signify the 1st Troop, is dressed in a buff coat under a polished steel cuirass; others wear the same but with lobster-tailed helmets.

After Albemarle's death the coats of the re-numbered 2nd and 3rd Troops remained red faced blue for all, but each Troop was distinguished by its velvet-covered carbine belts, holster caps and housings: the 1st having blue belts laced with gold and silver but red holsters and housings, the 2nd green belts laced gold and the 3rd yellow belts laced silver; in the two junior troops the holsters and housings matched the belts, and all bore the Royal cypher and crown. These distinctions were all noted at a review in 1684 at which features of the attached troops of Horse Grenadiers were also recorded. Their coats had lace loops at the buttonholes in the troop colours with yellow tufts at the ends. Their headdress was described as 'Grenadier caps lined the same' (i.e. blue) and 'a blew round mark on the outside'.

These Horse Grenadiers were armed and equipped as dragoons, each having a musket with a sling, a bayonet, grenade pouch, cartouch box with girdle, waistbelt and sword, with two pistols on the saddle. Each troop had two drummers and

the sergeants and corporals carried partisans and halberts respectively as a mark of rank.

A fuller description of the Horse Guards and their Grenadiers appeared in the account of James II's Coronation by the herald, Francis Sandford. The officers of the 1st Troop wore coats either 'of Crimson Velvet Imbroidered with Gold or Silver, or both intermixed'. Their waist scarves were either of 'Gold or Silver Network, or Crimson Taffeta, richly fringed with Gold or Silver on the Edges, and a deep Fringe of the same at the Ends'. These variations of coat and scarf may have been a sign of officers' respective ranks. Their cloaks were scarlet, embroidered on the collars and down the front in gold or silver or both, and their hats had white feathers. The holsters and housings were of crimson velvet, similarly embroidered, and the manes, tails and cruppers of the horses bore knots of blue ribbon.

There is no mention of blue facings to the officers' coats but the scarlet coats and cloaks of the private gentlemen were faced with blue shalloon, the cuffs also laced with a 'Figured Galoon of Silver (edged with Gold) two inches broad', and silver buttons. Each had a 'good Buff Coat', worn presumably as a waistcoat, and buff gauntlets. Their hats were black, edged with silver lace, turned up on one side, and with knots of blue ribbon which also adorned the horses' heads. The gentlemen were armed with a broadsword suspended from a buff shoulder belt, a carbine clipped to a shoulder belt five inches broad and covered in blue velvet with the same lace as appeared on their cuffs, and a pair of pistols whose holsters matched the scarlet of the housing, both being embroidered with the Royal cypher and crown within a border of foliage.

The 1st Troop of Horse Grenadiers had red coats (not scarlet) faced blue, with blue lace loops as before but edged and tufted with black and white. The description of their grenadier caps seems to suggest that these consisted of a pointed red bag cap, the top of which fell to the rear where a blue roundel or grenade showed, with stiffened triangular turn-ups in front and behind faced with blue plush. There is no mention of any device on the caps, but since the cypher and crown appeared on the grenadier caps of the 1st Foot Guards at this date, it seems unlikely that the Horse Grenadiers would have lacked them. Their arms and accoutrements were as described earlier. Their holster caps and housings were the same as for their Horse Guards Troop but in red and with scalloped edges.

The distinguishing colour of green for the 2nd Troops of Horse Guards and Horse Grenadiers appeared on their housings, holsters, ribbons and carbine-belts, and the cypher on the two former was within a border of Royal badges. The lace on hats, cuffs and carbine-belts was gold edged with silver. The Horse Guards' coats were faced blue like the 1st Troop's, but the Grenadiers continued the green distinction in the facings of their caps and coats, which also had gilt buttons and green lace loops with black and white tufts and edging (see Fig. 3, Plate 2).

Both 3rd Troops were in all respects similar to the 2nd but with yellow distinctions instead of green. The gentlemen's lace was silver, the Grenadiers' yellow with the same black and white additions and silver buttons.

The cuirasses seem to have been laid aside by now and the private gentlemen's hats have lost their feathers. However, the latter were re-

James Scott, Duke of Monmouth, Colonel of the 1st (King's) Troop of Horse Guards, c 1670. The red coat had increased in length since 1660, and was now worn over a long buff waistcoat.

introduced by William III in 1699, in white, red or green for the different troops.

The dress of the Horse Guards' trumpeters contained features that can still be seen today in the State Dress worn by Household Cavalry musicians. For example, from 1678 black velvet caps were listed in addition to the more usual hat, which was laced with gold and silver. Their crimson velvet coats, faced blue, were laced all over with gold and silver, and from 1690, a gold twist or chain was introduced, between the bands of lace, which is still worn. From 1696 all narrow and silver lace was abolished, leaving only the broad gold and the twist. In the reign of William and Mary the conjoined Royal cyphers and crown were embroidered on the front and back of the coats. From 1678 breeches were blue, changing to crimson in 1696. Trumpeters' waistbelts, for the sword, were also laced, the white type worn from 1678 with silver, the buff from 1696 with gold. Cloaks were crimson with a blue collar laced with gold and silver and lace loops down the front. The kettle-drum and trumpet banners were embroidered with the Royal arms and supporters, fringed with gold and silver, and tied with blue ribbon. The trumpet cords, at first gold and silver, changed in 1696 to crimson, blue, gold and buff. The drummers of the Horse Grenadiers had infantry drums like Dragoons, not kettle-drums which were the prerogative of Horse. They and the hautbois at first had red coats faced blue, blue breeches and hats, not grenadier caps. From 1689 their dress became more assimilated to the Horse Guards' trumpeters, though with variations in the lace. Their belts were purple leather, laced.

Horse

Since the Earl of Oxford's Royal Regiment of Horse Guards was not part of the Household Cavalry at this period, evidence of its appearance is neither so detailed nor so prevalent as the Horse Guards proper. However, at the afore-mentioned review in 1684, the regiment was described as 'Coated and Cloaked Blew, lined Red', a reverse of the Royal livery worn by the Horse Guards which has continued until the present in this regiment, which will therefore be described hereafter by its later, popular name of the Blues, to avoid confusion with the Horse Guards troops. Their carbine-belts were 'laced with Gold upon Buff with a Red edging', and the buff colour also distinguished their waistcoats and breeches. The housings and holster caps had the Royal cypher embroidered on blue.

The red facings applied only to NCOs and men, for orders issued by the Earl of Oxford in 1686 stated that officers' coats were to be faced blue, the captains having gold lace 'laid double upon every seam and slit with a gold foot between the two laces'. Their buttons were of gold thread and 'a gold fringe around the sleeves, under which must be laid the same lace as down the sleeves'. The lieutenants' and cornets' coats had single broad lace and no fringe. Quartermasters had gold edging down the front, at the pockets, slits and round the sleeves, the latter also having a broad lace like the subalterns. Officers' hats were black, edged with gold and with a white feather, their trimming and the cravat strings yellow. In the

portrait of Captain Thomas Lucy, on which Fig. 2 Plate 1, is based, he is shown with a grey hat with black feather. The same hats are worn by a blue-coated detachment in the background, but the painting was executed six years before the order stipulating black was issued.

The Tangier Horse appear in a painting of a review of that garrison in 1683 shortly before it was abandoned. Although the officers wear hats, the troopers are all in black lobster-tailed helmets with face guards, black cuirasses over red coats and long black boots; they are armed with carbines and presumably swords, though the latter are not visible. The kettle-drummer and trumpeters wear hats and red coats with a sleeveless garment over the top, possibly a buff coat.

Cuirasses and helmets ceased to be issued from 1689, although an iron skull cap for wearing under the hat on service continued in use. Horse regiments had carbines as well as swords and pistols from 1677, so that the two shoulder belts

---

PLATE 2: 1660–1700

3. **Grenadier, 2nd Troop, Horse Grenadier Guards, 1685, (later 1st Life Guards).**
4. **Officer, Queen's or 2nd Regiment of Horse, 1689 (later King's Dragoon Guards).**
5. **Dragoon, Royal Regiment of Scots Dragoons, 1697 (later 2nd Dragoons).**

All wear the full-skirted coat, waistcoat, breeches and long boots which, with various modifications, clothed the cavalryman until well into the next century. Figure 4 has the crimson coat of the Horse, in contrast to the Dragoons' red, and his rank is signified by superior materials and embroidery, and by the sash, worn at this time round the waist. His coat has regimental facings, a practice by no means then universal among officers. Figure 3, which is based on Sandford's description of James II's Coronation, has the coat buttonholes decorated with distinctive lace in the fashion peculiar to grenadiers. Over his left shoulder is slung a pouch for grenades while a smaller pouch on the waistbelt is for cartridges. His accoutrements and those of Figure 5 reflect the semi-infantry character of a dragoon, further underlined by the carriage of both plug-bayonet and sword. A hatchet attached to the pouch can be seen on Figure 5; this would probably have been carried also by the grenadier. The wood work of all firearms at this time was painted black. Since a dragoon had to fight on foot, his boots were of supple leather, not jacked like those of the Horse. All three figures, being based primarily on documentary rather than pictorial evidence, are to some degree speculative.

3. Grenadier, Horse Grenadier Guards, 1685.

4. Offr, Queen's Horse, 1689.

5. Pte, Royal Regt of Scots Dragoons, 1697.

A troop of Horse, with its standard carried by a cornet, at the funeral of Queen Mary in 1694. Note the hats turned up in front and the crossed sword and carbine-belts of the troopers. The swords, held at the 'carry', have the blades pointing slightly forwards as was the practice until 1759.

crossing on the chest became a distinctive feature of the Horse.

Another distinction was their crimson coats, as can be seen from a clothing list dated 1696. This states that corporals' coats were to be of superior cloth, and also includes the following items for each man: cloak of red cloth, hat edged with silver, sword and shoulder belt, carbine belt, cloth waistcoat, pair of buff gloves, embroidered housings and holster caps, pair of jack-boots, and a cartridge box. There is no mention of breeches though these are noted in similar lists for Dragoons and the Foot. Nor are they mentioned in Sandford's very detailed description of the 1685 Coronation. Colonel Clifford Walton in his *History of the British Standing Army, 1660–1700* believed that the Horse mostly had 'tawny leather' breeches which, being more durable than cloth, did not have to be included in the periodical clothing lists. Furthermore, if they were universal among the Horse, commentators like Sandford might not have thought them worth mentioning. The crimson waist sashes worn earlier by every trooper seem to have been discontinued. The coats were long, with full skirts, no collars, deep cuffs turned back to show the facing colour, and a large quantity of buttons down the front, on the cuffs, on the pocket flaps in the skirts, and down the slits at side and back. The facings in 1686 were as follows: the Queen's Regiment yellow (Fig. 4, Plate 2); Lord Peterborough's red, changed to buff in 1694; Lord Plymouth's green, with grey waistcoats from 1692; Lord Arran's white; Lord Shrewsbury's buff, changed to white in 1689; and the Queen Dowager's green[2]. In 1688, a regiment ranked as 10th Horse (later 8th and eventually 7th Dragoon Guards) was clothed

[2] By 1690 these six regiments were numbered 2nd–6th and 8th Horse. They eventually became the 1st–6th Dragoon Guards.

in blue, lined white, but two years later the universal crimson was adopted.

The kettle-drummers and trumpeters of the Blues and Queen's Horse wore the same Royal livery of crimson, blue and gold as the Horse Guards. There is no information as to trumpeters of other regiments but the practice of wearing coats in reversed colours (i.e. of the facing colour lined crimson) which was soon to become common may have begun in the seventeenth century.

Dragoons

As for the Horse, pictorial evidence of Dragoons at this period is almost non-existent, but there is considerable documentary information from clothing lists and the like. The independent companies of Scots Dragoons raised in 1678 had stone-grey coats and bonnets, presumably the blue type common all over Scotland. They were armed with broadswords, a pair of pistols and firearms—variously described as carbines, firelocks of different types or short muskets—for which slings and buckets were issued. The grey coats continued after the companies were regimented in 1681 as Royal Scots Dragoons, but when the regiment moved to England in 1685 the coats changed to red, lined blue, each coat having no less than 120 'tin buttons'; by 1692 the buttons were reduced to about 90 per coat and were made of brass (see Fig. 5, Plate 2).

When the Tangier Horse was converted into the Royal Dragoons in 1684 the regiment was 'coated and cloaked red lined blue' with the holster caps and housings 'embroidered with blue and yellow upon red with the Royal cypher'. Although there are references to crimson coats for dragoon officers, even sergeants, the men's were red. However, by 1699, all ranks of the Royal Dragoons had crimson coats like the Horse, worn with blue waistcoats and breeches; the two

latter were also worn by the 3rd Dragoons. A corporal had broad gold lace round the cuffs while a sergeant had additional lace, broad and narrow, on his sleeves, coat flaps and belt. A clothing list for a regiment of Dragoons published in 1696 shows that while all non-commissioned ranks received cloaks and boots of the same quality, the sergeants' headdress, clothing, swords, belts, housings and holsters were all superior; a sergeant, for instance, had a cravat instead of a dragoon's neckcloth. Suits for corporals, drummers and hautbois were more expensive than for a dragoon, but they had the same quality hats, caps, neckcloths, waistbelts, swords and horse furniture. Dragoons had caps as well as hats, the former probably being a bag cap with fur surround. Dragoon boots were considerably cheaper than the Horse's jack-boots; in view of their dismounted role, this may have meant that they were not stiffened and perhaps were shorter.

Besides the pistols carried on the saddle, a dragoon was armed and accoutred with a snaphance musket fitted with a sling, a waistbelt with frogs for sword and bayonet, a cartouch box slung from a shoulder belt, and a hammer-hatchet; all belts were of buff leather. Bayonets and cartouch boxes were not issued to sergeants, corporals, drummers or hautbois. In 1690 there is reference to grenade pouches for a Grenadier company of the 4th Dragoons, but by the end of the century grenades were discontinued. Sergeants were armed with halberts and in 1684 corporals of the Royal Dragoons had partisans, but as dragoons became increasingly transformed into cavalry these weapons were dispensed with. In 1699 sergeants and privates of the Royal Dragoons were to have carbine-belts like the Horse for their muskets, which seems to have been peculiar to this regiment. As to dragoon swords, it is impossible to be precise since there was no regulation

pattern—nor would there be for another century. The only references are to 'broadswords', which the colonel of the 6th Dragoons required, in 1691, to have three-barred hilts.

There is little evidence of officers' dress in this period but a clothing list for the 6th Dragoons reveals that they had beaver hats, crimson coats lined with shalloon of the same colour, and ash-coloured waistcoats. The captains' coats had gold loops and buttons, their waistcoats gold lace, and their belts gold fringe, the subalterns having silver; a total of 216 buttons were required for each coat and waistcoat. The housing and holster caps for a colonel were described as embroidered and fringed, the remainder's being cloth and laced, either in gold, or silver for the junior officers. In 1684 dragoon officers were to be distinguished by the same gorgets worn by the Foot: captains to have gilt, lieutenants black with gilt studs, and cornets silver; how long this practice continued for Dragoons is not known. The other mark of an officer, both Horse and Dragoons, was a scarf or sash, of crimson silk and gold or silver fringe, worn, in this century and for some years of the next, round the waist.

The remarks made earlier on trumpeters' dress also applied to drummers and hautbois of Dragoons: Royal livery for Royal regiments, reversed coats for others.

Although not strictly concerned with uniform, it might be noted that while it would be many years before the Scots Dragoons had the colour of their horses officially included in their title as Royal Scots Greys, in 1694 the regiment was observed at a review in Hyde Park as 'all mounted on white or gray horses'. The Horse Guards were all mounted on blacks, a colour which was becoming common, though not yet universal, for all troop horses. Trumpeters, drummers and hautbois were usually mounted on greys.

The 18th Century

Background

The eighteenth century, so much of which was taken up with war against France, saw a considerable expansion of the British Cavalry, though not all the new regiments survived the peace following the particular campaign for which they were raised. It also witnessed numerous changes in organisation and designation, and a new type of cavalry.

To deal first with the Household Cavalry, the three troops of Horse Guards were joined, after the Act of Union, by a 4th Scots Troop. In 1746 the 3rd and 4th Troops were absorbed into the 1st and 2nd. The former attached troops of Horse Grenadiers had been regimented in 1693 as one troop, Horse Grenadier Guards. A similar troop raised in Scotland in 1702 came south after the Union, whereupon the English troop was numbered 1st and the Scots 2nd. In 1788 the 1st Troops of Horse Guards and Horse Grenadier Guards were regimented as the 1st Life Guards, while the 2nd Troops of each became the 2nd Life Guards. Thereafter no grenadiers featured in the two regiments. Just prior to this reorganisation the Horse Guards seem to have degenerated from the days of being a 'corps d'élite', with the ranks filled with men of social position, for the Duke of York pronounced them to be 'most useless and unmilitary... a collection of London Tradespeople', although he found the Horse Grenadiers 'were to a degree soldiers'.

In 1750 the Blues ceased to be styled Royal Regiment of Horse Guards, becoming Royal Horse Guards (Blue). They continued to enjoy a position which was outside the Household Cavalry but superior to the Cavalry of the Line, as the regiments of Horse and Dragoons came to be known.

As Dragoons increasingly lost their mounted infantry function, so did the difference between them and the Horse disappear. Since a dragoon was cheaper to maintain than a trooper of Horse, it was decided in 1746 to convert the three senior regiments of Horse after the Blues into Dragoons. To compensate for the loss of pay and prestige, they were given a more dignified designation and so the 2nd, 3rd and 4th Horse were re-styled 1st, 2nd and 3rd Dragoon Guards. The remaining four regiments of Horse were re-numbered 1st–4th. In 1788 they too were converted into the 4th–7th Dragoon Guards and the old title of Horse disappeared.

Extra dragoon regiments were added to the existing eight for the War of the Spanish Succession and the 1715 Jacobite Rebellion, of which six were retained thereafter, being numbered 9th–14th. A regiment raised for the 1745 Rebellion as Kingston's Light Horse was retained as 15th Dragoons but disbanded after the War of the Austrian Succession.

The number of troops per regiment continued to fluctuate between six and nine as did the number of men in them. In the regiments converted to Dragoon Guards, drummers took the place of trumpeters, but from 1766 the latter were ordered for all Dragoon Guards and Dragoons.

The dearth of light cavalry for outpost and reconnaissance duties as performed by such troops of Continental armies, notably the Hungarian hussars of the Austrian service, led to the attachment, in 1756, of specially equipped light troops to three of the Dragoon Guards regiments and eight of the Dragoons (see Appendix 3). Each consisted of a captain, a lieutenant, a cornet, a quartermaster, two sergeants, three corporals, two drummers and 60 dragoons, including a farrier. Three years later a complete regiment of light cavalry was raised as the 15th Light Dragoons, of six troops each of the same strength as the light troops, plus one hautbois. The latter and the drummers were abolished in favour of trumpeters from 1764. This experiment was followed by the raising of six more such regiments. At the end of the Seven Years War three of these and the eleven light troops raised in 1756 were

Thomas Wentworth, Earl of Strafford, Colonel of the Royal Regiment of Dragoons, 1711. His coat bears the garter star with its riband over the left shoulder. His officer's sash is now worn round the waist and the sword is suspended under the coat. Painting by Leygebe.

disbanded, leaving the 15th–18th Light Dragoons on the establishment. This type of cavalry was further increased in 1768, 1775 and 1776 by the conversion of the 12th, 8th and 14th Dragoons respectively. In 1783 the 7th, 9th, 10th, 11th and 13th followed suit.

During the War of American Independence, although only the 16th and 17th Light Dragoons of all the Cavalry served across the Atlantic, light troops were again added to the heavy regiments, but were then transferred to form three new regiments. Two more were newly raised, but at the peace all were disbanded except the 23rd Light Dragoons, re-numbered 19th in 1786, which became the first British cavalry regiment to serve in India, remaining there from 1782–1807. In 1792 a new regiment, numbered 20th, was raised for service in the West Indies.

On the outbreak of the French Revolutionary War the Cavalry, apart from the Life Guards and the Blues, stood at seven regiments of Dragoon Guards, six of Dragoons (1st–6th), and fourteen of Light Dragoons (7th–20th). In the expansion of the Army that followed, the number of heavy cavalry regiments was not increased, and indeed was reduced by the disbandment for mutiny of the 5th Royal Irish Dragoons in 1799, but thirteen new regiments of Light Dragoons were raised. The 30th–33rd had a very brief existence, but the 22nd, 23rd, 24th and 28th continued until disbanded after the Peace of Amiens in 1802, whereupon the remaining new regiments after the 21st were renumbered 22nd–25th. Thus, when war was renewed in 1803 the Cavalry of all types mustered 34 regiments.

Dress 1701–1741

General
There is a paucity of evidence, especially pictorial, for the reigns of Queen Anne and George I. With the accession of George II, who concerned himself with the clothing of his Army, the picture begins to become a little clearer, though not fully so until the next period. However, it is clear—from such sources as the Blenheim Tapestries and the Laguerre paintings of Marlborough's victories, though no specific regiments are shown—that the dress of the mounted arm remained essentially as in the two previous decades: the broad-brimmed black felt hat, now turned up on all three sides to form a tricorne, the full-skirted long coat, waistcoat, breeches and jack-boots.

Horse Guards
An eyewitness account by a German visitor of a review of the Horse Guards in 1710 gives an incomplete description of their dress, mentioning only that, while all troops wore red uniforms, the 2nd and 3rd's were laced gold and the 4th's silver; of facings, only the 2nd's of green are noted. The 1st Troop had black cockades in their hats, the 2nd white feathers, and the 3rd green and white feathers. The Horse Grenadiers were on parade but no details of their dress were noted.

A wall painting of a trooper of the Horse Guards c 1712 shows him in a gold-laced hat with black cockade and a red coat, faced blue and laced in gold on the seams and around the cuffs; its buttons are apparently set on either side of the opening, connected vertically by lace giving the effect of lapels, each button having a lace loop, as do those of the pocket flaps. The waistcoat and breeches match the facing colour which also appears on the gold-laced carbine-belt and housings, which suggests the 1st Troop, although the distinguishing colours on these accoutrements were to change later.

A portrait of an officer of the 4th Troop some twenty years later shows a very plain all-crimson coat without lace, worn unbuttoned over buff waistcoat and breeches. The holster caps are blue, laced and fringed with silver. The dress however has an almost civilian air about it and may be some form of undress. The full dress coat of an officer of the same troop in about 1740 is scarlet with a small turned-over step collar revealing the blue lining, laced gold down either side of the front opening and round the cuff slashes. The rows of buttons in pairs on either breast of the coat have a width of lace above and below each button which is looped over at the end from which a small tassel falls; the same decorates the cuff buttons. The waistcoat is buff with gold lace and loops. The breeches are not visible in the portrait but are probably also buff. A private gentleman of the 4th Troop in 1740 is shown in Fig. 8, Plate 3.

Horse
Although Prince Eugene remarked in 1704 that the British Cavalry was the 'best appointed and finest' he had ever seen, specific evidence as to its

Captain Richard Gifford, 4th Troop of Horse Guards, c 1730. His plain crimson coat without contrasting facings or lace may be some sort of undress garment. Waistcoat and breeches are buff. Painting by B Dandridge.

dress in this, and the following two decades, is confined to a few scanty descriptions of clothing issued. In 1700, for example, the red coats of Lord Arran's 6th Horse had pewter buttons and white facings and waistcoat, but by 1711, when it had become Lord Cadogan's, the description of a deserter quoted: 'a Hat with Silver Lace, a red Coat faced with Green, and broad Silver Lace on the Sleeves, and Sleeves and Pockets bound with narrow (silver), green Wastecoat and green Shag[3] Breeches' (see Fig. 6, Plate 3). The same notice mentions a green housing and that the man wore a wig in a hairbag, an item also recorded as issued to Bland's 3rd Horse in 1713. Cuirasses had been abolished for the Horse in 1689 but were re-issued in 1707, during the War of the Spanish Succession, though without the back pieces. The breast plate appears to have been worn under the coat. In 1714 they were withdrawn.

In default of any regulations it is impossible to be precise about officers' dress, though obviously it followed the general cut of the men's but was manufactured from richer materials. A portrait of an officer of the 2nd Horse in 1722 shows a silver-laced hat, a plain red coat with deep cuffs turned back to the elbows, also red, yellow or buff waistcoat and breeches. The waistcoat's silver lace loops are enclosed within vertical strips of lace, none of which appears on the coat. No sash is worn, signifying that he is not on duty, but by this date it was becoming the practice for cavalry officers to wear their sashes over the left shoulder instead of round the waist. This regiment had been faced yellow prior to 1714, changing to blue on becoming 'King's Own', but troopers in the background of the painting still have yellow facings. However no coloured facings show on the officer's coat, and indeed the practice of officers displaying their regimental facings was not general until about the middle of the century.

From the accession of George II a more centralised control over dress enforced a greater degree of uniformity upon regimental colonels. In 1727 the King required a 'fixed clothing' for each regiment, distinguished from others only by its facings, and which, once fixed, was not to be changed by successive colonels. In the same year all Horse were to have cross-belts of plain buff, rather than having them ornamented with lace as was the custom in some regiments. Two years later it was ordered that every trooper of Horse was to be supplied every second year with 'a new

cloth coat, well-lined with serge; a new waistcoat; a new laced hat; a pair of large buff-coloured gloves with stiff top (gauntlets)'. His housings, holster-caps, horse furniture, boots, cloak, and belts were to be supplied 'as they may be wanted', an interval more strictly fixed in 1736.

There is no indication that the men's coats had lapels in this period, but clothing lists dated 1729 and 1737 for the 8th and 7th Horse show that their officers had velvet lapels, in black and yellow respectively, the former having gold lace, the latter silver. The 7th's list also refers to grenadier caps, for which oil cloth covers were supplied.

Dragoons
A schedule of clothing and accoutrements for the 8th Dragoons when fighting in Spain in 1706–1707 gives information for this type of cavalry during the War of the Spanish Succession. Their hats were laced, with gold for sergeants and corporals, probably with yellow worsted for dragoons. From 1707 iron skull caps were provided for wear under the hats by all Dragoons in Spain.

PLATE 3: 1701–1741

6. Private, Cadogan's or 6th Regiment of Horse, 1711 (later 5th Dragoon Guards).
7. Officer, Cathcart's or 8th Regiment of Dragoons, 1731.
8. Private Gentleman, 4th Troop, Horse Guards, 1740 (later 2nd Life Guards).

The hats have now assumed the tricorne shape. Figure 6, based on a *London Gazette* description, is typical of Marlborough's Horse and wears a cuirass, re-issued in 1707, under the by now red coat, and the crossed sword- and carbine-belts which remained a feature of the Horse's accoutrements for another eight decades. Figure 7, based on a portrait, wears a lapelled coat, with the facing colour only on the cuffs, and the lapels buttoned over. A silver shoulder knot hangs behind the right shoulder and his officer's sash has moved from the waist to the left shoulder. The sword belt is worn under the coat. Officers' dress still lacked uniformity, both amongst themselves and with their men, whose coats, at this period, had no lapels. Figure 8 is taken from a set of paintings of this Troop, showing the motions of carbine drill; here the ramrod is about to be inserted in the muzzle. The cuffs of the gold-laced coat have acquired a slash and the skirts are buttoned back to reveal the lining. The gold-laced carbine-belt has the blue stripes distinguishing this troop. In 1746 it was absorbed into the 2nd Troop, which at this date had white stripes.

---

[3] Worsted cloth with a velvet nap on one side.

6. Pte, Cadogan's Horse, 1711.

7. Offr, Cathcart's Dragoons, 1731.

8. Pte Gentleman, 4th Troop, Horse Guards, 1740.

Sergeants' and corporals' coats were laced with gold on the sleeves and pocket flaps, and were further distinguished by sergeants' coats being crimson while the corporals' lace was narrow. The waistcoats and breeches matched the coat lining; whether this was yellow as worn by 1735 is uncertain. Drummers' hats were gold-laced and their coats were listed simply as 'laced', while hautbois had 'coats for liveries, laced as the Sergeants', which suggests they were in reversed colours, with superior lacing to the drummers. The clothing for all was completed by cravats, shirts, stockings, gloves, boots, spurs and spur-leathers.

Accoutrements included 'carbine-belts or broad cross-belts for muskets, waist-belts large and strong to carry basket-hilted swords, with cartridge-box belts, laced; cartouch-boxes or pouches, housings and holster caps, buckets with straps'. (The straps were to secure the muzzle of the musket when strapped to the saddle.) A sculpture on the monument to Brigadier Killiegrew, Colonel of the Regiment, shows the pouch to be large and square, with a double-headed eagle badge covering the flap and a belt three inches wide. Drummers had 'drum-slings, or carriages, and waist-belts, laced'; hautbois had, 'waist-belts suitable to the coats, laced as the Sergeants'. Items of horse furniture were listed as 'headstalls, reins, breast-plates and cruppers, bits, bosses, collars and cloak-straps; saddles with skirts and furniture with straps, with girths, stirrup-leathers and irons'. Weapons for NCOs and dragoons were a 'large, full-bored musket' with socket bayonet and 'Highland Scotch broadswords'. Drummers and hautbois merely had swords.

Since officers were responsible for the provision of their own uniforms there is seldom evidence of their clothing in such lists. However, correspondence relating to the 1st Royal Dragoons, also in Spain, reveals that in 1709 the officers of that regiment had their clothing made up locally. This included 'a plain red coat and breeches, lined with canvas, a canvas waistcoat embroidered with gold'. A grey feather was worn in the hat. The housings and holster caps were red, laced with gold and embroidered with the crown and cypher. In the same year the dragoons of the regiment had to make do with some 'ill-made' clothing sent out from England for another regiment with orange facings, but the colonel had them altered to be 'faced blue with a slashed sleeve and a cape (collar)'.

Whereas Horse suspended their swords from a shoulder belt, Dragoons generally used a waist-belt like the Foot. Nevertheless this did not always apply as a list of equipment for the Royal Scots Dragoons in 1706 mentions 'buff shoulder sword-belts'. The 8th Dragoons also had such belts, retaining them for many years in memory of the Battle of Almenara in 1710, where they had equipped themselves with the shoulder belts of a regiment of Spanish Horse they had defeated and taken prisoner.

Later in the century the Scots Dragoons were to be distinguished by the universal wearing of grenadier caps but the 1706 list makes clear that this was then confined to the actual grenadiers, each regiment of Dragoons having such a troop, the rest of the men wearing hats. How long grenadiers were retained is uncertain, but a scale of clothing published in 1708 states that grenadier caps were to be provided 'as long as the Grenadiers shall be continued', which suggests that their retention in mounted regiments was under consideration. Strangely a clothing contract for the Scots Dragoons in 1715 contains no mention of grenadier caps at all.

In the same document there appears the first reference to shoulder-knots, an ornamental plaited cord with metal points attached to a button on the shoulder, usually the right, similar to an aiguillette. This would remain a feature of mounted regiments' coats until 1764 and was worn by all, though in different quality for each rank. In 1735, for example, the officers and sergeants of the 8th Dragoons had theirs of silver, and the corporals of silver and yellow mixed.

The regulations instituted by George II for the Horse from 1727 applied equally to Dragoons, the chief difference between the two types remaining as before in the accoutrements: Dragoons continuing to have a waistbelt for the sword 'with a place to receive the bayonet' and a sling for the musket, instead of the Horse's sword belt and carbine-belt over each shoulder. The attempts by George II and the Duke of Cumberland to regularise the uniform of the Army were to culminate in the first illustrated document to show the authorised dress for each regiment, as will be seen in the next period, but the cut and style depicted therein had clearly been developing for some years before its actual publication in 1742.

An officer of Horse, 1744, possibly of the Royal Regiment of Horse Guards. The sword belt is worn over the waistcoat, under the coat, which is unlaced and lapelled to the skirts. The sash is again worn over the shoulder. Painting by Stephen Slaughter.

Dress 1742–1750

General

The 1742 document, *Representation of the Cloathing of His Majesty's Household and all the forces upon the Establishments of Great Britain and Ireland*, commonly called the Clothing Book, is the first pictorial evidence for the dress of a trooper or dragoon of each cavalry regiment as sanctioned by Royal authority. The four Troops of Horse Guards are represented by the same basic figure, coloured differently according to the distinctions of each troop. Another figure is used for the two troops of Horse Grenadier Guards. The Blues and the seven regiments of Horse are illustrated by two alternative mounted figures, one firing a pistol, the other drawing his sword. The 1st, 3rd, 5th and 7th Dragoons are represented by a mounted figure with musket slung across his back, the remaining eight regiments, less the 2nd and 8th, by a dragoon in the 'Port Arms' position. The 2nd Dragoons have the same

figure as the Horse Grenadier Guards and the 8th are represented by a dismounted dragoon standing at his horse's head.

The distinguishing features of each regiment, as recorded in the Clothing Book, are tabulated at Appendix 1 for the Horse Guards and Horse Grenadiers, at Appendix 2 for the Horse—including the Blues—and the Dragoons. The alterations to the dress of the 2nd, 3rd and 4th Horse on their conversion to 1st, 2nd and 3rd Dragoon Guards in 1746 will be considered under the next period.

The figures in the Clothing Book appear to have their hair cut short, but it is more likely that it was tied back and turned up under the hat, or tucked under the coat collar as was the practice in the Foot. Except for the Horse Grenadier Guards and 2nd Dragoons (styled Royal North British since the Act of Union) who are shown in grenadier caps, all wear the black hat, laced and turned up on three sides with the black Hanoverian cockade secured by a button and loop on the left side; a full-skirted red coat (except for the Blues) without lapels—worn open and having a low, $1\frac{1}{2}$-inch collar, deep cuffs with a buttoned flap or slash—with the facings showing on a small collar patch, the cuffs and the turned-back skirt linings; a waistcoat; gauntlet gloves; and breeches, which were protected from the blacking on the long boots by pieces of white cloth or canvas buttoned over the knees. According to an order dated 1746, all cavalry were to wear black linen gaiters when performing dismounted duties. Besides these generalities there were other differences in detail which must now be considered.

Horse Guards and Horse Grenadier Guards

The hats of the Horse Guards were laced gold and their hair was powdered. Their scarlet coats had buttons in pairs set on gold lace loops down each side of the coat front, with similar loops on the pocket flaps and cuffs which were also laced round. The Horse Guards do not appear to have had shoulder knots. The figures in the Clothing Book have a roughly square-shaped piece of blue cloth laced all round just below the collar, but this does not feature on the series of drawings of a man of the 4th Troop on which Fig. 8, Plate 3 is based. The buff waistcoats were also laced round the edges.

The accoutrements included the gold-laced carbine-belt with two stripes of each troop's colour and a buff waistbelt with frog for the sword, laced on the outer edges and through the centre, which was worn under the coat. The sword was straight, with a basket hilt, and when the carbine was carried on the horse its butt rested in a bucket strapped to the saddle to hang below the off-side holster while the stock was steadied by another strap attached to the front of the saddle. The cloaks were rolled and strapped to the back of the saddle. As can be seen from Appendix 1, each troop was distinguished solely by the different colours on carbine-belts, housings and holster caps.

The caps worn by the Horse Grenadiers acquired the tall mitre shape during the second decade of the century. The bag was drawn up from within its turn-up and attached behind the top of the pointed front, which had a little flap at its base. The front was embroidered with the Royal cypher within the garter surmounted by the crown. The device on the little flap at this date is uncertain but in 1751 it was a grenade for the 1st Troop, a thistle for the 2nd. The caps were red and blue but varied between each troop (see Appendix 1 and Fig. 11, Plate 4).

The coats of the Horse Grenadiers were similar in cut to the Horse Guards but in red and with only white worsted lace. They did not have the piece of material at the neck but did have white shoulder cords. The buff waistcoat had the same lace loops as the coat.

The buff leather accoutrements consisted of a waistbelt for the sword and bayonet worn under the coat and a grenade pouch slung over the left shoulder. Resting on the top of the pouch was a powder flask, whose cord, in different colours for each troop, was fastened all round the pouch belt. The musket was furnished with a sling but, when the grenadier was mounted, was secured by the same bucket and straps as in the Horse Guards.

Horse

The hats of the Horse were all laced yellow or white, gold or silver for officers. Their coats had buttons down each side of the front opening, but it is difficult to say whether these had loops as much of the coat front was concealed by the broad cross-belts. The latter were retained by plain shoulder straps. The waistcoats and breeches matched the facings (Appendix 2), except for the 8th Horse who had buff and the Blues who had blue breeches. The cloaks matched the coats, with linings in the facing colour, the 8th again having buff.

The carbine-belt had a flask cord attached as described for the Horse Grenadiers and was worn over the sword shoulder belt. The cord was

generally in the facing colour but there were exceptions in the four junior regiments. The housings and holster caps of the three senior regiments were red, the remainder having yellow or white, and the devices thereon for the Blues, the King's or 2nd Horse and the 5th Horse differed from the other regiments. Among the latter the 4th and 7th had a leaf design as a border instead of a scroll pattern and the 4th were further distinguished by a red binding to the housings and holsters. Each trooper was armed with a basket-hilted broadsword, a pair of pistols and a carbine carried, when mounted, in the way already described. A trooper of the 8th Horse is shown in Fig. 9, Plate 4.

Black leather was used for all saddlery, bridles and so on. The horses were black, from $15\frac{1}{2}$ hands and had docked tails, a practice which had been in force for cavalry horses since 1703.

No officers appeared in the Clothing Book nor was their dress regulated by general orders. While

---

PLATE 4: 1742–1750

9. Private, Ligonier's or 8th Regiment of Horse, 1742 (later 7th Dragoon Guards).
10. Officer, Royal Regiment of Dragoons, 1748 (later 1st Royal Dragoons).
11. Grenadier, 1st Troop, Horse Grenadier Guards, 1742 (later 1st Life Guards).

This and Plate 5 are representative of the War of the Austrian Succession and illustrate George II's attempt to impose Royal authority over regimental clothing by the issue of the 1742 Clothing Book. Figures 9 and 11 are based on this document. In the Horse, the waistcoat and breeches generally matched the facings and linings, the 8th Regiment here being an exception, having these garments and the coat lining in buff instead of black. Officers' dress was not governed by the 1742 book and an officer of the 8th Horse appears in the next plate, wherein the differences between officers' dress and the men's can be seen. A similar comparison can be made between Figure 10, based on a portrait of General Hawley, Colonel of the Royal Dragoons, and the ordinary dragoon (though of a different regiment) in the next plate. Although this officer's breeches are red like his men's, he has a buff waistcoat edged blue, instead of all blue. His lace loops, with crowsfoot ends, are more ornate. Figure 11 shows how the Horse Grenadiers' dress has developed from that in Plate 2, the cap having assumed the mitre shape and the coat being much the same as a dragoon's. The two Troops differed in the colours of their caps and flask-cords. Note the neckcloth of former times has given way to a white stock.

9. Pte, Ligonier's Horse, 1742.

10. Offr, Royal Regt of Dragoons, 1748.

11. Grenadier, Horse Grenadier Guards, 1742.

Right: *Private, the King's Regiment of Horse, 1742 (from 1746, 1st King's Dragoon Guards). Facings, waistcoat and breeches are blue, the holsters and housings red with yellow and white embroidery. The flask cord on the carbine-belt is blue. From the 1742 Clothing Book.*

Opposite, left: *Private, 2nd Royal North British Dragoons, 1742, in the grenadier cap worn by this regiment. The coat is faced blue, the holsters, housings and flask cord are red. The musket is held upright in its bucket in the 'advance your firelocks' position used when marching past. From the 1742 Clothing Book.*

Opposite, right: *Private, Kerr's Regiment of Dragoons (later 11th), 1742. Note the infantry-type pouch carried by dragoons. In contrast to the Horse's sword shoulder belt, the dragoon sword belt went round the waist under the coat. The coat is faced white, with buff linings matching the holsters and housing. Waistcoat white, breeches red. From the 1742 Clothing Book.*

the cut of their coats followed the men's, the skirts were not looped back and their lace was either gold or silver. The colour of their waistcoats and breeches did not necessarily conform with the men's nor did their coats always display the regimental facings. The sash was now customarily worn over the left shoulder and the sword belt under the coat, or even under the waistcoat. The housings and holster caps were of richer materials and bore, not the devices on the men's furniture, but a trefoil knot and tassels. At Fig. 12, Plate 5 is an officer of the 8th Horse, adapted from a portrait of Lord Ligonier, Colonel of the Regiment from 1720–1749.

Dragoons

Dragoon hats were the same as in the Horse, except for the grenadier caps of the 2nd Dragoons. On the evidence of the Clothing Book it seems likely that this headdress was now worn by all ranks of the regiment. This included officers, judging by an extant cap which is apparently of this period. However, hats were worn on less formal occasions. The cap had a red front, edged yellow with an embroidered border of roses and thistles in yellow, green and pink. The central device was the St George's cross within the garter, superimposed on a yellow cross and a

white saltire or St Andrew's cross. The little flap was blue, edged yellow, with a thistle below a scroll with the motto *Nemo Me Impune Lacessit*. The bag was red, piped yellow and the turn-up blue, edged yellow. The officers' caps were similar but in velvet with gold and silver embroidery.

Evidence of the dragoon coat in the Clothing Book is supplemented by an actual coat of the 2nd Dragoons of this period, preserved in the Scottish United Services Museum. The coat has twelve buttons down either side of the open front, each with a narrow white thread loop, the buttons being at the outer extremity of the loop. These loops also go round the buttons placed on the facing patch on the collar, on the four cuff slash buttons, and six vertical buttons closing the pockets in the skirts where the loops form a chevron. Four loops without buttons have been sewn either side of the skirt's back slits. Another button without loop has been sewn at the top of each pleat in the skirts, and two more again without loops, lower down to which the skirts were turned back. The (53 in total) buttons on the 2nd Dragoons coat are in pairs, but this arrangement may not have been common to all regiments. On the left shoulder, to retain the pouch belt, is a plain red strap fastened by a button (thus accounting for the odd number in the total) and on the right a white shoulder knot

stitched to the cloth with one loop and two tasselled ends hanging free. The 1st Royal Dragoon figure in the Clothing Book has a yellow knot at the left shoulder, while the 8th Dragoons' coat has much wider loops than other regiments.

In the majority of regiments both waistcoat and breeches matched the facings, but four had red breeches (see Appendix 2) and in the 13th and 14th Dragoons both garments were white. Owing to the pose of the Clothing Book figures, the waistcoat details are none too clear. A reconstructed waistcoat accompanying the 2nd Dragoons coat has white loops, like on the coat, all down the front on either side but only one row of buttons; the 2nd Dragoons figure in the Clothing Book, which shows the waistcoat more clearly than other figures, appears to have two rows of buttons, as on the coat. The cloak and its lining matched those of the coat.

Dragoon accoutrements were similar to those described for the Horse Grenadiers, thus continuing the former practice of suspending sword and bayonet from a waistbelt, by now always worn under the coat. In the Clothing Book all the belts are buff except for white in the 2nd Dragoons. The five regiments with a Royal title—1st, 2nd, 3rd, 5th and 7th—all had flask cords on the pouch-belts. The 8th Dragoon figure wears a shoulder belt for the sword, thus continuing the tradition mentioned in the previous period, but he also has a waistbelt under the coat, probably to support the bayonet.

The holster caps and housings, which had rounded corners, matched the facings in most but not all cases, and the five Royal regiments had different devices from the others (Appendix 2). Each dragoon was armed with a basket-hilted sword, a pair of pistols, and a musket with a sling and a bayonet. His horse, at 15 hands, was slightly smaller than those of the Horse but was also black, except in the 2nd Dragoons where greys prevailed. Docked tails were common to all.

The variations in dress that existed between officers and men of the Horse applied equally to the Dragoons. For example, a portrait of the colonel of the Royal Dragoons has him in a buff waistcoat (see Fig. 10, Plate 4) whereas his men's were blue. His coat shows the regimental blue facings, but in another portrait, of a cornet of the 10th Dragoons, the coat is all scarlet, laced silver, showing none of the yellow facings of that regiment. In the former, the sword is a light weapon, unlike the men's broadswords, and the sword belt is apparently worn under the waistcoat. Both these officers wear their sashes over the left shoulder.

There is nothing in the 1742 Clothing Book about the dress distinctions of NCOs, trumpeters or drummers but these were to be regularised in the next period. It is known that sergeants of the Horse Grenadiers and Dragoons wore sashes like the Foot, possibly with a central strip in the facing colour; these were worn round the waist from 1745.

One regiment that had a short existence in this period but which does not appear in the Clothing Book was that raised as the Duke of Kingston's Light Horse for the 1745 Jacobite Rebellion. Disbanded in 1746, it was immediately re-embodied as the Duke of Cumberland's or 15th Dragoons. As the latter, it is portrayed in one of David Morier's paintings as having the usual dragoon uniform (but without buttonhole loops), housings with pointed corners and what appears to be a lighter type of boot; its facings, etc are

Private, Duke of Cumberland's or 15th Dragoons, 1747, formerly Kingston's Light Horse. The first regiment of light cavalry to be raised, it was disbanded in 1748. Coat red, faced green, buff waistcoat and breeches. The hat has a field sign of oak leaves, as worn in the War of the Austrian Succession. Painting by David Morier.

given in Appendix 2. As Kingston's, the regiment's carbines were shorter than those of the Horse and their accoutrements and harness were of a light pattern, all of which were continued after re-embodiment. Its horses, too, were lighter, being $14\frac{1}{2}$–15 hands; the horse in the Morier painting is chestnut and not the more usual black. At the close of the War of the Austrian Succession this first regiment of Light Horse was disbanded, and it was to be another ten years before such was seen again in the British Cavalry.

Dress 1751–1767

General

Although the dress did not change greatly in this period, it must nevertheless be considered separately because at the beginning of this period the Royal Clothing Warrant of 1751 was published which did make certain alterations of detail and, for the first time, promulgated regulations affecting officers, NCOs and musicians. The evidence of this important document is further supplemented by the series of paintings made by

PLATE 5: 1742–1750

12. Officer, Ligonier's or 8th Regiment of Horse, 1745 (later 7th Dragoon Guards).
13. Private, King's Own Regiment of Dragoons, 1742 (later 3rd Dragoons).

Figure 12, based on a portrait (and compared with Figure 9) shows that despite differences, like the coat lapels and the scarlet breeches, officers' dress was gradually conforming with the men's, as can be seen from the regimental facing colour on the cuffs. The lapels reaching to the base of the skirts would become a feature of the coats of all ranks of Horse in the next period. The cut of the men's coats for Horse and Dragoons was still broadly similar in this period, the chief difference in their overall appearance being the accoutrements. The housings and holster caps of both types of Cavalry also varied in their devices, of which there were two basic designs for both Horse and Dragoons: either a Royal badge or a trophy. Figure 13, based on the 1742 Clothing Book, has the Royal cypher and garter, shared with the 1st, 2nd, 5th and 7th Dragoons, though with variations in the ground colour and embroidery. The shoulder knot, just visible behind the man's right shoulder, was another Dragoon peculiarity not worn by the Horse. Below the off-side holster can be seen the bucket for the butt of the firelock. All troop horses had docked tails until 1764.

13. Pte, King's Own Dragoons, 1742.

12. Offr, Ligonier's Horse, 1745.

Lieutenant-General Onslow, Colonel of the 1st Troop, Horse Grenadier Guards, with officers of the troop, followed by its standard, grenadiers and drummers (in black caps), c 1750. The standard at this time was carried by an officer, ranking as a 'guidon'. The Horse Grenadiers acted as dragoons to the troops of the Horse Guards. Painting attributed to J Wootton.

David Morier under the patronage of the Duke of Cumberland, which serve to illustrate the warrant, showing, for the Cavalry, a mounted soldier from each troop of Horse Guards and Horse Grenadier Guards, and each regiment of Horse, Dragoon Guards and Dragoons. Morier also included a trumpeter of the 1st Troop, Horse Guards, a kettle-drummer of the 1st Horse and a

farrier of the 11th Dragoons. The period is also important, since it saw the introduction, on a permanent basis, of light cavalry, first as Light Troops of selected regiments, followed by the raising of complete regiments of Light Dragoons, whose appearance was also captured by Morier. In this period, therefore, many details that were unknown or uncertain henceforth become clearer and the variety of cavalry dress widens[4].

In general, the headdress, clothing and accoutrements remained much as before in cut, colour and the manner of wearing, but the coats of some regiments acquired lapels and the waistcoats

---

[4] Regimental distinctions for all Horse, Dragoon Guards and Dragoons under the Warrant are given in Appendix 3.

and breeches matched the facings with one exception, as will be seen. The hats of all had gold or silver lace with the black cockade and were worn with the front cock over the left eye and the left cock tilted up slightly. The Clothing Warrant also mentions a watering or forage cap for all Cavalry in red, turned up with the facing colour and bearing the number of the regiment; this was probably like a simplified grenadier cap without the upright front. Except in the Household troops, the men's hair was unpowdered and tied back in a kind of knot which rested level with the upper edge of the collar.

The warrant did not cover the Household Cavalry but since its provisions regarding officers, NCOs and musicians were applicable to all Horse, Dragoon Guards and Dragoons, they will be considered here to avoid repetition later. Officers' coats were to be made to the same pattern as the men's and the warrant specifically mentioned that they were to display the regimental facings, which hitherto had not always been done. The buttons were to be set on in the same way and the button-holes to have narrow gold or silver lace or embroidery. The waistcoats and breeches were also to match the men's. The housings and holster caps were to be of the facing colour with gold or silver lace, in the middle of which was to be a velvet stripe of the same colour ordered for the men. The trefoil knots and tassels continued though not mentioned in the warrant. Officers' rank was indicated by the crimson sash over the left shoulder and, of course, by the superior quality of their clothing; there were no special insignia to distinguish one rank from another. Their shoulder knots were in gold or silver but, since these were worn by all ranks except in the Horse, they were part of the uniform rather than a rank distinction. The sword knots crimson and gold, striped; the sword belt not usually visible being worn round the waist under the waistcoat.

Theoretically, therefore, officers' dress was brought into line with the soldiers' but to what extent officers actually complied with the regulations is uncertain. For example, on a surviving coat of an officer of the 3rd Horse (formerly 7th) the embroidery is far more ornate than stipulated in the warrant, and the lapels are of the type ordered for Dragoon Guards.

As for NCOs, quartermasters were to wear crimson sashes round their waists and dragoon sergeants worsted sashes in the facing colour with a stripe matching the housings' lace. Corporals of Horse were to have narrow gold or silver lace on

Private, 1st Troop of Horse Guards, 1751. The carbine-belt stripes and the ground of the housing are red, in contrast to the 2nd Troop's blue. Waistcoat and breeches are buff. The rolled cloak shows blue. Painting by David Morier.

the shoulder straps, dragoon sergeants having gold or silver shoulder knots; both had the same lace on the lapels, cuffs and pockets. Dragoon corporals had yellow or white silk shoulder knots and narrow gold or silver lace only on cuffs and shoulder strap. (The term 'dragoon' here embraces both Dragoon Guards and Dragoons, and the cuffs varied between Horse and all Dragoons, as will be seen.)

The coats of kettle-drummers and trumpeters

(of Horse) and dragoon drummers and hautbois were, for non-Royal regiments, to be of the facing colour, lined and turned up with red, and laced with the same as on the housings; waistcoats and breeches were to be red. Royal regiments were allowed the Royal livery, i.e. red coats, lined and turned up with blue, laced with a Royal lace, and worn with blue waistcoat and breeches. All coats were to have false sleeves hanging from the shoulders and fastened at the waist. According to Morier's kettle-drummer of the 1st Horse, such musicians wore hats, but dragoon drummers wore caps, similar to grenadiers' though lower: the front and turn-up at the back in the facing colour, the former having either the badge of the regiment or a trophy of guidons and drums, the latter a drum and the number of the regiment; the little flap in front was red, with the white horse of Hanover and motto *Nec Aspera Terrent*, and the bag was also red with a white tassel falling behind.

The kettle-drums of the Horse were carried on either side of the drummers' mounts and covered by banners in the facing colour with the badge or regimental number in the centre. Their trumpet banners were of the same colour, with the Royal cypher and crown and the number underneath. Dragoon drums were slung from the drummers' right shoulders and were made of brass, the front being painted in the facing colour and emblazoned with the regimental badge or number. All such numerals were in gold or silver Roman figures on a crimson ground within a wreath of roses and thistles.

Horse Guards and Horse Grenadier Guards
Although the four remaining troops of Household Cavalry do not feature in the 1751 Warrant, all were depicted by Morier. There is little difference between the Horse Guards 1751 uniform and that shown in the 1742 Clothing Book, except that the piece of blue cloth below the collar has disappeared and the gold lace loops in pairs on the coat have acquired pointed ends. A gold shoulder knot at the right side is visible in the painting of the 1st Troop but the pose for the 2nd prevents this being shown. The 2nd Troop's former white distinctions have changed to the blue of the old 4th Troop (see Appendix 1).

The Horse Guards accoutrements continued to be the carbine-belt, as used by Horse, and the sword waistbelt, as used by Dragoons, both laced. Morier shows differently-hilted swords, the 1st Troop's being barred and in gilt or brass, the 2nd's a basket hilt in steel.

It is clear from Morier's painting of a negro trumpeter of the 1st Troop in a State coat that, apart from the hat, the different cypher, the breeches and boots, there has been little change since then to the State Dress still worn today by musicians of the Household Cavalry (see Fig. 19, Plate 7). Trumpeters' housings and holster caps were the same as the troop's and, as was then customary for all cavalry trumpeters and drummers, their horses were greys, a tradition maintained by the modern Household Cavalry.

Morier's Horse Grenadiers display little change in uniform from those given in the Clothing Book but more detail is visible, particularly in a rear view of a dismounted grenadier of the 1st Troop. The latter clearly shows that the bag with its white tuft at the back of the cap was not fastened up to the pointed front, as shown in the Clothing Book, but allowed to fall back. The caps were still coloured differently for each troop (see Appendix 1), and the device on the little flap was a grenade with motto *Dieu et Mon Droit* for the 1st Troop and a thistle with *Nemo Me Impune Lacessit* for the 2nd, while the turn-up at the back appears to have had either a drum or a grenade, flanked on either

---

PLATE 6: 1751–1767

14. **Officer, 11th Dragoons, 1759.**
15. **Drummer, 15th Light Dragoons, 1760.**
16. **Private, 2nd The Queen's Dragoon Guards, 1751.**

This and Plate 7 illustrate the 1751 Clothing Warrant and are typical of the Seven Years War period. This warrant required officers' dress to conform with the men's, and Fig. 14, based on a Reynolds portrait of Cornet Winter, illustrates this trend, though the lacing on cuff-slash and pockets is at variance with Morier's private of the 11th. Officers tended to wear their sword belts under the waistcoat. The waist-length lapels which distinguished Dragoon Guards from Dragoons can be seen on Figure 16, as can the shoulder knot worn by all ranks of both types until 1764. The Horse now had lapels to the base of the skirts and no knots. Figure 16's waistbelt supports bayonet and sword but his firearm is not shown. The 15th's drummer has his regiment's special cap, but a coat reversed from its red, faced green (see black and white illustrations) and heavily laced with red on white lace. From 1766 the infantry-type drums were replaced in all Dragoon regiments by trumpets as formerly used only by the Horse. The white, unlaced waistcoats, white breeches and lighter boots of the Light Dragoons were adopted by all Dragoons from 1764.

14. Offr, 11th Dragoons, 1759.

15. Dmr, 15th Light Dragoons, 1760.

16. Pte, 2nd Dragoon Guards, 1751.

Private, Royal Horse Guards (Blue), 1751. The carbine-belt with red flask cord and flask is clearly shown, as is the method of carrying the firelock in the butt bucket. The housings match the red facings of the blue coat. Waistcoat and breeches are buff. Painting by David Morier.

side by crossed swords and muskets, all in white. The hair is shown powdered and, in the fashion of grenadiers, plaited and turned up under the cap. The coats are of the dragoon pattern described under the last period, the narrow white button loops being set on the cuff and pocket flaps to form a chevron. There is no collar patch in the facing colour. The shoulder strap retaining the pouch belt is sewn on behind the left shoulder, while behind the right the white knot falls in two loops and two ends with points.

Quartermasters were, by now, no longer com- missioned officers—instead they held a rank which was similar to a combination of the modern warrant officer and staff sergeant—and Morier's quartermaster of the 1st Troop is shown dressed like the grenadiers, except for a broad white or silver lace round the cuffs and pocket slash.

The dress for officers of the Horse Grenadiers is shown in a painting attributed to Wootton (but possibly by Morier) of Lieutenant-General Onslow and the 1st Troop, Horse Grenadiers of which he was Colonel from 1747–1760. All the troop officers wear gold-laced hats, not caps, and their scarlet coats have blue tabs on the collar and blue cuffs, the latter having button loops and embroidery all round in gold wire. The front openings of the coat are similarly embroidered as are the buttons, set one-two-one on either side, and the pockets. The skirts are not turned back, a gold aiguillette shows at the right shoulder, and all, save one, have sashes over the left. The waistcoats are white, embroidered with gold, and the breeches are scarlet. Gold-embroidered waistbelts, for the sword, are worn over the waistcoats. The hous- ings and holster caps are blue with much gold embroidery, while the harness is red leather with gilt ornaments. The painting includes mounted grenadiers as already described, and also three drummers on greys in black jockey caps, scarlet coats, faced blue and richly laced in gold, and red breeches.

Horse

After 1746 the Horse was reduced to the Blues and the four regiments renumbered 1st–4th, the latter taking precedence after the three regiments of Dragoon Guards. The Clothing Warrant of 1751 required their coats to have lapels in the facing colour from the neck to the bottom of the skirt, these being fastened back with buttons. The sleeves had small square cuffs in the facing colour which were buttoned horizontally without flap or slash. All buttons, whether on lapels, cuffs or pockets, were set on in pairs with buttonholes of very narrow yellow or white lace; from 1764 the buttonholes began to be plain. No shoulder knots were worn but a cloth strap of the coat colour was sewn on each shoulder to retain the cross-belts. The coat lining, which showed on the turned- back skirts, matched the lapels and cuffs, except in the 4th Horse which had buff linings. The waistcoat (with buttons and loops as on the coat) and the breeches also matched the facings, the 4th Horse again being the exception with buff. The knee-pieces were white.

Officer, 1st (King's) Dragoon Guards, formerly 2nd Horse, 1762. Dragoon Guards' coats were now lapelled to the waist. Officers' uniform has been brought more into line with the men's by the 1751 warrant, though the horse furniture is more ornate. Painting by J Schaak.

Dragoon Guards and Dragoons

The conversion of three former regiments of Horse to the 1st–3rd Dragoon Guards changed their dress, accoutrements, arms, ranks and horses to those of Dragoons. In appearance, therefore, they were virtually indistinguishable, except for one important difference. The coats of Dragoon Guards had lapels to the waist in the facing colour; Dragoons had no lapels (see Fig. 16, Plate 6 and Fig. 17, Plate 7). Both had buttons in twos or threes and narrow yellow or white lace loops at the buttonholes. The Dragoons' coats were described as 'double breasted', which meant they could have buttons and holes on both sides of the open front, or, buttons only on one side but holes on both. For a time the 2nd and 3rd Dragoons adopted the former arrangement but from 1753 all were to have holes on both sides and buttons only on the right. Dragoon Guards having lapels of course had buttons on both sides. The cuffs, described as 'slit sleeves turned up with the colour of the facings', were secured in place by a row of six vertical buttons with loops arranged in chevrons, the same serving to close the 'long pockets'. Although the men's cuffs no longer had the flap, or slash, the latter are still shown in two paintings of officers of the 11th Dragoons (see Fig. 14, Plate 6). All had yellow or white shoulder knots until 1764 when they were abolished for officers and men in favour of an epaulette on the left shoulder. Waistcoats and breeches of all regiments matched the facings but from 1764 white was ordered, and the waistcoat lace dispensed with. At the same date 'boots of a light sort' were also ordered.

The gold or silver-laced hats were common to all, except for the 2nd Dragoons whose grenadier caps were sanctioned by the 1751 warrant. These had altered since 1742 and now had a blue front with the thistle within the circle of St Andrew, the little flap red with the white horse of Hanover and *Nec Aspera Terrent*, the bag red and the turn-up blue with the thistle embroidered between 'II D' (Fig. 17, Plate 7).

Details of housings and holster caps are listed with other regimental distinctions at Appendix 3, but a point not mentioned in the warrant, though shown by Morier, is that whereas the rear corners of the housings were rounded for most regiments, in the 1st, 4th, 6th, 7th and 11th Dragoons they were pointed. Bearskin flounces covered the pistols and the red cloaks were rolled at the back of the saddle with the lining colour outwards.

The accoutrements for all regiments remained

The broad cross-belts for carbine and sword continued as before, with a red flask cord for the Blues only. Belts, gauntlet gloves and sword knots were all of buff leather. Details of the housings and holster caps are given with the other regimental distinctions at Appendix 3, and the butts of the pistols were covered by brown bearskin flounces. In 1758, when ordered to Germany for the Seven Years War, the Blues were issued with cuirasses, not worn since Marlborough's day, and iron skull caps for the hats. Two years later the 3rd and 4th Horse were similarly equipped.

as they had been for Dragoons in 1742, but the Royal regiments which had then had flask cords on their pouch-belts no longer had them. The swords shown by Morier all have basket hilts with buff leather knots, and the muskets are fitted with slings although a butt bucket attached to the saddle was also provided. In 1760 'Camp Necessaries' for all Dragoons were listed as: 'Haversacks 20 in. long, 22 in. broad, flap 4 in., strap 36 in. long and 2 in. broad. Canteens, hempen strap to run through side of lid. Frocks [an undress garment]. Pickets 4 ft 4 in. long, staple and ring at top, ash.'

The horses portrayed by Morier are all blacks, with docked tails, except for the greys of the 2nd Dragoons and a bay for the 2nd Dragoon Guards, a colour that became traditional in this regiment, resulting many years later in the title 'The Queen's Bays'. Some other paintings, of the 11th Dragoons, show brown horses. After 1764 the docking of tails was discontinued.

Though not referred to in the warrant, the dress for regimental farriers is shown by Morier in a figure of the 11th Dragoons. The headdress is similar to a low grenadier cap, with red bag and tassel at the back but a brown fur front; in place of the little flap is a white-edged red plate with a horseshoe between a hammer and pincers in white. The normal dragoon coat is blue (a colour still worn in full dress by farriers of the Life Guards), faced red, lined buff, with white button-holes. Waistcoat, breeches and gloves are all buff. A brown leather apron is worn tucked up round the waist under the coat. The farrier holds an axe in his right hand for which a black case is suspended over his left shoulder by a buff strap. The housings are as for the other ranks, but in place of the holsters is a leather container, covered by a grey fur flounce, for the tools of the man's trade. Another painting, of the 11th's farrier of a few years later, shows him with a sword, but from 1766 it was ruled that 'neither firelock, pistols nor swords to be accounted for' for farriers. The same ruling allowed drummers a sword and one pistol.

Light Troops and Light Dragoons
In 1756 a Light Troop was added to those regiments of Dragoon Guards and Dragoons noted in Appendix 3. The men were to be 'light, active young men', between 5 ft 6½ in. and 5 ft 8 in. in height. Their horses were to be not less than 14¾ hands, 'well-turned nimble road horses, as nigh to the colour of the horses of the regiment as can be got'.

The clothing and cloaks were not altered but 'light jockey boots with small stiff tops' were ordered and caps instead of hats. The caps were 'jockey caps ornamented in front with HM's Cypher and Crown in brass and the number of the regiment. The crest is likewise to be covered with brass, out of which is to be a tuft of stiff horse-hair, coloured half red, and the other half of the facing.' This cap had a rolled-up flap at the back to protect the neck, which was later replaced by a turban rolled round the whole. Made of strong black, jacked leather this cap appears in a Morier painting of the 11th Dragoons Light Troop, which clearly shows the black skull surmounted by a brass crest, with a turned-up red front bearing the devices mentioned and edged with brass; the tuft, which looks white, appears to be fixed on the left side, just behind the front. The pockets and cuffs seem to have only three buttons and there is no shoulder knot.

An officer's cap of the 2nd Dragoons Light Troop also has a leather skull and crest without

---

PLATE 7: 1751–1767

17. Private, 2nd Royal North British Dragoons, 1755.
18. Private, 17th Light Dragoons, 1759.
19. Trumpeter, 1st Troop, Horse Guards, 1751 (later 1st Life Guards).

Figure 17 wears the coat without lapels ordered for Dragoons by the 1751 warrant. Prior to 1753, this regiment and the 3rd Dragoons had buttons on both sides but were then ordered to conform with other regiments by having buttons on one side only. This private also has the grenadier cap peculiar, in the Cavalry, to this regiment and to the Horse Grenadier Guards. Another peculiarity was the whitening of the belts and pouches, other regiments having theirs buff. Figure 18 shows a variation of the Light Dragoon helmet and the shorter coat but with lapels like the Dragoon Guards. As stated in the text the accoutrements differed slightly between Light Dragoon regiments, and it is not clear from the Morier painting of the 17th, on which this figure is based, where the cartridge pouch was carried, unless it was attached to the carbine-belt in the manner that later would become universal. Note the short gloves, light carbine and sword of these regiments. Apart from the hat, netherwear and cypher, the dress of the trumpeter in Figure 19 differs little from the State Dress of Household Cavalry musicians today. Negroes were popular as trumpeters in the eighteenth century in both Household and some Line Cavalry.

1751-1767

17. Pte, 2nd Dragoons, 1755.

18. Pte, 17th Light Dragoons, 1759.

19. Tptr, 1st Troop, Horse Guards, 1751.

REG.ᵗ OF HORSE

brass, but has an upright cloth front similar to their grenadier caps though more rounded at the top, and cloth turn-up at the back. The colours of the cloth parts are the same as the grenadier cap, and the embroidery and edging in gold and silver. On the left side is a falling blue, white and red horsehair plume.

Housings and holster caps were of the same pattern but smaller in proportion to the size of the horse. The accoutrements were entirely different, being all of tan leather: one belt, $3\frac{3}{4}$ in. wide, worn over the left shoulder, with a spring and swivel for attachment to the sliding ring on the carbine; another, $1\frac{1}{2}$ in. wide, suspending a cartouch-box containing 24 cartridges just below the shoulder blades; and a waistbelt under the coat for sword and bayonet. The carbine was 4 ft 3 in. long, the sword and bayonet blades 34 in. and 17 in. respectively, the former having a barred hilt. Only one pistol was carried on the horse, on the off side, while on the near was a churn, holding a spade and axe or bill. The saddle was of the jockey type, to which was fitted a butt bucket and a pipe for the horse-picket.

The success of these light troops on the French coast in 1758 led to the raising of the first regiment of Light Dragoons, numbered 15th, in 1759, for whose appearance evidence is plentiful: in particular two series of paintings by Morier of the regiment, one in the Royal Collection, the other at Wilton House. These show a number of differences from the Light Troop costume.

The cap or helmet was copper, enamelled black, with a silver metal fluted crest from which flowed a red horsehair mane, and a dark green turban round the base tied in a knot at the back with two white tassels. At the front was a turned-up, pointed plate, with the crown above the cypher flanked by the initials 'LD'. In some of the paintings at Wilton a red and green rosette is fastened to the left side of the helmet; one commentator has suggested that this may be the mark of a recruiting party. A black stock was worn, with the white shirt collar showing above. The coat was red, with a white epaulette on each shoulder and faced green which showed on the

Private, 7th Queen's Own Dragoons, 1751. The breeches were listed in the warrant as matching the white facings but in this painting they are red. Note the oak-leaf field sign and the absence of lapels. Painting by David Morier.

round cuffs, on the lapels to the waist and on the turned-down collar, of a type not seen before on cavalry coats. The buttons were white metal with white loops, each lapel having eight, in pairs, and each cuff and pocket flap three vertically. The skirts, shorter than usual, were lined white and turned back. One of the Wilton figures has a white edging to his collar, lapels and cuffs, possibly the mark of an NCO. The unlaced waistcoat and breeches were white, worn with light boots.

The accoutrements, although in tan leather, differed from the Light Troops' in that the sword belt was worn over the right shoulder but under the coat, and a waistbelt, also under the coat, supported a tan leather pouch placed centrally; the carbine-belt was as described above. The weapons were a light carbine, two pistols and a sword with a simple guard. Housings and holster caps were replaced by a dark green saddle cloth or

Private, 1st Regiment of Horse (formerly 5th Horse, later 4th Dragoon Guards) 1751. The coats of Horse differed from those of the Dragoon Guards by being lapelled to the base of the skirts, and by having shoulder straps, no shoulder knots and different lacing on the cuffs. This regiment had pale blue facings, waistcoat and breeches. Painting by David Morier.

Farrier, 11th Dragoons, 1751. Coat linings, waistcoat, breeches and housings are of the regimental buff, but the coat is blue, faced red. His special farrier's cap is of brown fur with a red frontal. A looped-up leather apron is worn round the waist and the holsters are replaced by a churn containing the farrier's tools. Painting by David Morier.

shabraque edged with a red stripe between white lace; at the front was the crown above the cypher and at the rear a red patch bearing 'LD' in white within a wreath of roses and thistles. Flounces of light yellowish fur covered the pistols and the red cloak was rolled with the white lining outwards. The harness was black leather.

Drummers wore the same caps but reversed coats, without lapels and laced with red-striped white worsted (see Fig. 15, Plate 6). The coat had the customary false hanging sleeves at the back but these were not fastened in to the waist, instead they terminated in white tassels. In the Morier paintings a straight sword appears in one picture, a curved one in another. Two versions of the drum carriage are also shown: one plain black leather, the other dark green and laced on the edges. Yet another uniform appears in the Wilton paintings, a French hornist, of which each troop

had two in addition to its two drummers. The cap is the same but with a red turban. The coat is green with red epaulettes, but the collar, cuffs, lapels and waistcoat are all light grey[5], the two former edged with red, which colour also serves for the narrow loops on the lapels and cuffs. His sword belt is the same as for a private. Both the drummers' and the hornists' horses are grey, their manes plaited with red ribbons and with red and green rosettes at the brow band.

No officers are shown in the above paintings but a later work by Morier, also at Wilton, depicts Lieutenant Floyd in about 1765 when the 15th, after distinguishing itself in the Seven Years War, particularly at Emsdorf, was granted that battle as an honour (the first battle honour to be officially approved in the Army), and the additional designation of 'The King's', which altered the facings to dark blue. The uniform is generally of the same style as the men's, with the addition of a button and loop on the turned-down collar. The lace, loops and fringed epaulettes are silver, and the waistcoat, breeches and skirt lining, though logically white, appear as buff, again possibly due to discolouration of the paint. The front of the helmet is edged silver and bears the King's crest (lion over crown) within the garter, all crowned and in silver, with below the word 'Emsdorf' in gold on a green oval label. Either side of the central device, also in gold on green labels, are the words 'The' and 'King's'. The shabraque is dark blue, edged with scarlet-striped silver lace, and bearing the usual officer's silver knot and tassel. The flounces are of leopardskin. Figure 22, Plate 8 shows an officer of the 15th ten years later, in a uniform almost identical to that worn by Floyd.

The other new regiments of Light Dragoons, 16th, 17th and the short-lived 21st or Royal Foresters, were also portrayed by Morier and, though broadly similar in appearance to the 15th, had certain differences, particularly in their caps.

[5] It is possible that they were originally white, but have faded with the age of the picture.

Private, 16th Light Dragoons, c 1760. The helmet differs from that of the 15th, and the black-faced coat has no lapels. The sprig of leaves in the helmet may have been a temporary field sign, rather than a permanent device. Painting by David Morier.

fur flounces, for the 17th, red, edged white and black with white fur flounces, for the 21st, white goatskin with no edging. The 16th had housings and holster caps like ordinary dragoons, but the 17th and 21st had saddle cloths like the 15th. Instead of the more usual devices the 17th had their special badge, as on their caps, at both ends, while the 21st had a hexagonal piece of blue cloth embroidered with the cypher and their number on the forepart only. The badge for officers of the 21st had the initials 'RF' embroidered in silver, surrounded by criss-crossed double silver lace giving a saw-tooth effect. Their officers' helmets also differed slightly from the men's, having a brown fur edging to the frontal. This regiment was disbanded in 1763.

The 16th's had no mane, a black fur turban and a sprig of oakleaves. The 17th's had a brass skull and crest, white mane, a red frontal with a white death's head above the motto 'Or Glory', and a fur band encircling the base and over the frontal (see Fig. 18, Plate 7). The 21st's had a red skull, white metal crest, green mane, black or blue turban, and an asymmetrical black frontal, edged white with the crown and cypher. The coats were similar to the 15th's, but the 16th had no lapels until 1766 when their facings were changed from black to blue on being made Royal, and the 17th's had the collar and shoulder strap of the ordinary dragoon coat. Both the 16th and 21st wore red stocks. The accoutrements differed, all being of buff leather, with the 16th and 17th suspending their swords from waistbelts, the 21st from a shoulder belt over the coat. The horse furniture was not, as usual, in the facing colour but, for the 16th was white, edged red and black with white

Dress 1768–1795

General

In 1768 a new Clothing Warrant was published. More comprehensive than the 1751 document, it incorporated certain trends in dress which had been appearing before its issue. The uniforms prescribed, however, represented a development, rather than any radical change, and those features of the Light Dragoons' costume already noted were adopted for all cavalry. Because the Light Dragoons were the leaders in cavalry fashions, their dress underwent less alteration in the first decade or so of this period, until 1784, when their appearance broke away entirely from that of the red-coated cavalry, both in cut and colour.

The Household and Heavy Cavalry, except for the Horse Grenadiers and 2nd Dragoons, continued to wear the hat throughout this period, but the front cock gradually became more upright until it virtually disappeared in the 1790s, turning the hat into a bicorne. The coat, with or without lapels, became closer fitting, with permanently turned-back skirts falling to the rear, rather than the sides, and fastened across the chest, either with hooks and eyes or by buttoning the lapels over; though pictures indicate the latter tended to be confined to officers. Turned-down collars of the type already adopted for Light Dragoons became universal and towards the end of this period began to be turned up. The reduction of

An officer, possibly of the 1st Troop of Horse Guards, in the late 1760s. The shoulder knot has now been replaced by an epaulette.

the old turned-back cuff to a small, neat round cuff, also pioneered by the Light Dragoons, was ordered in the new warrant, though still in the facing colour. Stocks were to be universally black, and waistcoats and breeches plain white (or buff for regiments faced with that colour and four others), without lace or braid. Hair was worn in the style known as clubbed and was powdered until 1795 when the practice was abandoned. From 1768 all accoutrements were to match the waistcoats, white or buff. Another innovation was the placing of the regimental numeral on the buttons, except in the three regiments of Dragoon Guards, who respectively bore the additional titles

of King's, Queen's and Prince of Wales's and thus bore the initials of these designations, e.g. K.D.G. This use of initials, combined with the numeral, was later extended to all Royal regiments, for example 'L$^K_{15}$D'. The boots for all cavalry were henceforth to be 'round-toed and not of a heavy sort', and were also described as having 'folded tops'; black gaiters were issued to the men for dismounted duties. The men's cloaks remained red but with only the collar in the facing colour, the linings being the same as the coat linings, all now white or buff; at the top were clasps upon loops of the same colour as the housing lace.

The most obvious mark of an officer, besides the use of gold or silver lace, remained the crimson silk sash, which was now to be worn round the waist, under the coat. The entire uniform for all officers was to be made up in the same manner as the men's. Other distinctions, together with those of NCOs, musicians and farriers, will be considered under the different types of cavalry.

The distinctions of the Horse Guards and Horse Grenadier Guards until 1788 are given in Appendix 1; for the 1st and 2nd Life Guards thereafter, see Appendix 6. For the Blues and all Line Cavalry in 1768, see Appendix 4; for the Blues and all Heavy Cavalry from 1788, Appendix 6. For the Light Dragoons from 1784, see Appendix 5.

A new warrant and other regulations appeared in 1796 but as their use continued until 1812, they will be considered under the next century.

Household Cavalry
Since the Household troops were not included in the 1768 warrant, information about their appearance is not so plentiful, although pictures show that their clothing followed the general style of the Line Cavalry.

A mounted figure of the 2nd Troop, Horse Guards in 1767 has a coat with blue lapels to the waist, edged all round with gold lace and with buttons in pairs with gold loops. The low collar of the former coat is laced all round without the blue patch, and the sleeves have small round blue cuffs with four buttons in pairs arranged vertically with gold chevron loops, the same arrangement closing the pockets. The waistcoat and breeches are white. The accoutrements are unchanged, the colour of the carbine-belt and housings continuing to distinguish each troop. The housings now have pointed corners, and white fur flounces over the pistols.

A portrait of an officer of the same troop c 1780 displays a similar uniform but with a turned-down collar with button and gold loop, and blue epaulettes on both shoulders, laced all round with gold and with a fringe. The lapels are narrower, in keeping with the prevailing fashion, and are without the lace edging. The sword is suspended from a white shoulder belt worn under the coat and the sash is around the waist. Another painting shows a 1st Troop officer similarly dressed but with the lapels buttoned over at the chest only. There are, however, other portraits which show the old stand-up scarlet collar and which reveal a variety of lace patterns and button arrangement (see Fig. 24, Plate 9).

A major change instituted by the warrant was the replacement of the embroidered cloth grenadier cap by a new pattern of black bearskin with a red top at the back and a metal plate in front. It would appear, from a portrait of an officer dated 1763, that the Horse Grenadiers already had such

---

PLATE 8: 1768–1795

20. **Private, 1st Royal Dragoons, 1768.**
21. **Officer, 15th The King's Light Dragoons, 1775.**
22. **Grenadier, 1st Troop, Horse Grenadier Guards, 1787 (later 1st Life Guards).**

The dress of Figure 20, from a Morier painting (as worn in the year the new clothing warrant was published) retains some features of the former period while displaying characteristics of the next, such as the coat collar, the black stock, the epaulette on the left shoulder, the small cuff, and the white waistcoat, breeches and accoutrements. Under the 1768 warrant the Dragoons' coats still had no lapels, while those of Dragoon Guards and Light Dragoons continued to be lapelled to the waist, as can be seen from the officer of the 15th, based on a portrait of Lord Ferrers by Reynolds. Light Dragoons had epaulettes on both shoulders, Dragoon Guards only on the left, until 1787, when they also received two. The facings of the 15th changed from green to blue in 1766 on being designated 'The King's', a title also embossed on the helmet either side of the garter surrounding the Royal crest; the flags to right and left represented the French colours taken at Emsdorf. The sword with lion's head grip and simple cross-guard was peculiar to the 15th, and was carried by all ranks in a shoulder belt, as was customary for Light Dragoons. Figure 22, in the last year of this regiment's existence, wears a coat in the Dragoon style, as it had developed under the 1768 warrant, with two epaulettes, and the new bearskin grenadier cap, worn only by the Horse Grenadiers and the 2nd Dragoons.

1768-1795

20. Pte, 1st Royal Dragoons, 1768.

22. Grenadier, Horse Grenadier Guards, 1787.

21. Offr, 15th Light Dragoons, 1775.

Sir Henry Pigot, 3rd (Prince of Wales's) Dragoon Guards, 1782. The hat's front cock is now more upright and the coat has the turned-down collar and narrower lapels prescribed by the 1768 warrant. Facings, waistcoat and breeches are all white. Painting by Francis Wheatley.

caps some time previously. The metal plates— gilt for officers, white metal for the grenadiers— displayed the Royal arms and gold or white tassels hung at the right side.

The coat for grenadiers continued to follow the dragoon style, with white loops down either side of the coat front but no lapels; white fringed epaulettes on both shoulders; blue facings showing on the turned-down collar and round cuffs, which had four buttons in pairs with chevron loops; and white linings, waistcoat and breeches. The accoutrements, pouch belt and sword waistbelt worn under the coat, were all white, as was the pouch itself (see Fig.22, Plate 8).

An officer of the 2nd Troop, Horse Grenadiers, c 1787, has a somewhat different coat with a low gold-laced, turned-up blue collar, scarlet lapels with gilt buttons in pairs and narrow gold loops,

indented blue cuffs edged with gold lace and three buttons above with narrow chevron loops. Unlike the officers of the Horse Guards, his shoulder belt for the sword is worn over the coat, and bears a silver star-shaped breast plate, a device then coming into fashion throughout the Army which derived from the original belt clasp or buckle. With the formation of the 1st and 2nd Life Guards in 1788, the unique costume of the Horse Grenadiers disappeared and henceforth the only grenadier caps in the Cavalry were those of the 2nd Dragoons.

The uniform of the two regiments of Life Guards was broadly similar: gold-laced hat, scarlet coat lapelled in blue and laced gold, white waistcoat and breeches, jack-boots. Pictures of officers towards the end of this period show the minor differences. The 1st Regiment had a white-over-red hat feather, the 2nd black. Both had a scarlet collar laced all round, despite an order for the 1st Regiment's to be blue. The lace loops of the latter were square-ended and set on the cuffs and pockets in chevrons, while the 2nd Regiment's were pointed and so broad that very little of the facing colour showed on the lapels; their cuffs had four vertical buttons but with the loops only pointing forwards. The shoulder-belt plate of the 1st Life Guards was oval, in gilt with the crown and cypher in silver, the 2nd's being rectangular with the same device, all gilt. These belts were now worn over the coat.

As will be seen, 1788 marked the introduction of regulation pattern swords for Line Cavalry but as the Household Cavalry were outside such general regulations the swords chosen did not apply to them. As far as is known the swords of the Life Guards in this period were of the same basic pattern as the Heavy Cavalry, having long, straight blades and basket guards of brass or iron bars.

Heavy Cavalry

Other than the Blues (whose uniform will be considered separately after this section) the Horse ceased to exist as such during this period and, since their appearance under the 1768 warrant became more assimilated to that of the Dragoon Guards, which they were to become in 1788, they will be discussed with the latter and the Dragoons under this heading.

The hats of all, (except the 2nd Dragoons), continued to be laced gold or silver until 1794, when the lace was abolished and only a yellow or white loop retained with a button to hold the cockade in place. In about the last decade of this period, feathers began to be worn behind the cockade. According to an order book of the 2nd Dragoon Guards (1795) hats were to be worn well forward and over the right eye, 'not too much on one side but in such a manner that the front cock comes about in a perpendicular line over the left eye ... those of officers and quartermasters not so much across'. The 2nd Dragoons kept their grenadier caps but did not receive the new bear-skin pattern, with the circle of St Andrew on the metal plate, until 1778. These caps were reserved for more important occasions, hats being worn at other times.

The coats of both Horse and Dragoon Guards were now to have lapels to the waist, three inches wide and in the facing colour (Appendix 4). Dragoons continued to have no lapels but buttonholes on both sides, buttons only on the right. Towards the end of this period the hooks at the top of the front opening and opposite the third button were to be hooked through the shirt, with the $1\frac{1}{2}$ in. shirt frill showing between. All coats had a turned-down collar in the facing colour with one or two buttons and loops, and the sleeves were turned up in the same colour to make a small indented cuff. Buttons were arranged regimentally with narrow yellow, white or buff braid loops for Dragoon Guards and Dragoons, plain twist for Horse, the loops on cuffs and pockets being in chevrons. Horse had plain red shoulder straps, Dragoons Guards and Dragoons an epaulette on the left shoulder (on both from 1787) in the facing colour, with white or yellow edging and fringe.

For the carriage of pouch and sword the Horse and 8th Dragoons continued to wear cross-belts, the remainder a shoulder belt and a waistbelt. The shoulder belt was $4\frac{1}{2}$ in. wide, the waistbelt, worn under the coat, $2\frac{3}{4}$ in. From 1787 all dragoons were to wear their sword belts over the right shoulder, to retain which the extra epaulette was added, and to render the appearance of the two belts more uniform the width of the pouch-belt was reduced to 3 in. From 1793 the pouches, formerly white, were to be of polished black leather. The housings and holster caps were largely as before.

Hitherto the type of sword carried by any one regiment had been a matter for its colonel but from 1788 there were to be regulation patterns. The weapon selected for Heavy Cavalry had a half-basket iron hilt with a straight blade 39 in. long, carried in a black leather scabbard with iron chape. The firearm carried by Dragoons had

Cornet Parkyns, 15th (The King's) Light Dragoons, 1780. This shows the red Light Dragoon uniform four years before it changed in style and colour to blue. The 15th's facings altered from green to blue after the grant of the Royal title in 1766. Painting by John Boultbee.

for many years been the Short Land musket with 42-in. barrel, but in 1770 a new pattern was issued, of the same length but with carbine bore and a side bar and ring for attachment to the swivel on the pouch-belt.

For officers, lace or embroidery on their coats was optional in Horse and Dragoon Guards but, if the colonel so chose, it was to be gold or silver, as stipulated for Dragoons. All officers were to have an embroidered or laced epaulette with fringe in gold or silver on the left shoulder (on both from 1787). Officers of the 2nd Dragoons had two epaulettes from 1784. Crimson sashes were tied round the waist on the left side under the coat. Officers of Horse were to have their sword belts over the right shoulder but under the coat, officers of Dragoons wore their's round the waist. From 1787, the latter were to conform with the men, the belts going over the shoulder outside the coat when on duty, under it when off. Their sword knots and belts matched the colour of the waistcoat, and the belt clasps matched the metal of the buttons. When the regulation sword was introduced for the men, officers had a similar pattern, but when dismounted or off-duty they usually carried a lighter weapon. Their housings and holster caps were as the men's but with gold or silver lace, and the tassels and knots as before.

Quartermasters' uniforms had no lace or embroidery but their coat had gilt or silver buttons and an epaulette in the same. They wore crimson waist sashes and their housings were like the officers' but without tassels.

Corporals of Horse and sergeants of Dragoons were distinguished by gold or silver buttonholes, a narrow lace round the collar, and gold or silver lace round the shoulder straps or the epaulettes, the latter's fringe matching the lace. Sergeants were to have pouches like the men and a crimson waist sash with central stripe in the facing colour. Corporals of Dragoons had narrow gold or silver lace round the turn-up of the sleeves and their epaulettes edged and fringed with yellow or white silk. The epaulette strap for dragoon sergeants and corporals was in the facing colour. After the conversion of the remaining regiments of Horse to Dragoon Guards, the rank of corporal only equated to sergeant in the Household Cavalry and the Blues (as it does to this day with the rank of corporal-of-horse).

The kettle-drummers of Horse were to wear black bearskin caps, each with a metal plate bearing the King's arms and trophies of Colours and drums and the regimental numeral on the back. All trumpeters were to wear hats with a feather matching their facings, except the 4th Dragoons who had negro trumpeters in 'Moorish turbans', a headdress also permitted for any black kettle-drummers in the Horse. The distinctive colouring of trumpeters' coats continued as before with certain exceptions (see Appendix 4) but the hanging sleeves were discontinued. Swords with scimitar blades were ordered for all musicians. The banners of kettle-drums were in the facing colour, with regimental badge or numeral in the centre, and were 3 ft 6 in. deep and 4 ft 8 in. long, exclusive of the fringe. Although such drums were the prerogative of the Horse, the 3rd and 5th Dragoons were also permitted them. The cords of the brass trumpets were crimson mixed with the facing colour, the latter also showing on the banners, 12 in. deep and 18 in. long, with the King's cypher and crown above the regimental numeral.

All farriers' coats, waistcoats and breeches were to be blue, with blue lapels, and collars and cuffs in the facing colour (red in Royal regiments). The buttonholes were as the men's. The headdress was small black bearskin cap with a black metal plate bearing a silver horseshoe. Farriers had leather aprons and churns for their tools.

The 1768 warrant's description of the forage or watering cap is the same as in the 1751 warrant, while stable dress is described in standing orders of the 2nd Dragoon Guards as a white woollen double-breasted jacket with metal buttons and edging in the facing colour. Trousers of brown Russia duck, buttoning up the sides, were worn over the breeches.

Royal Horse Guards (Blue)

This regiment was not yet formally part of the Household Cavalry (though sharing many of the

---

PLATE 9: 1768–1795

23. Private, Royal Horse Guards (Blue), 1790.
24. Officer, 1st Troop, Horse Guards, 1788 (later 1st Life Guards).
25. Sergeant, 10th Prince of Wales's Own Light Dragoons, 1790.

Figure 23, from a painting by Morland, has the coat and cross-belts of the style worn by the regiments of Horse before they were discontinued, except for the Blues, in 1788. The front cock of the hat is now more upright and the hair is clubbed. The buff waistcoat, breeches and belts were also worn by red-coated regiments faced buff. Figure 24, after a painting by Byron, shows an officer's uniform just before the troops of Horse Guards and Horse Grenadier Guards became the two regiments of Life Guards. There seems to have been some variety in the coats of Horse Guards' officers at this time. Figure 25, based on the Stubbs painting, displays the entirely new blue uniform adopted for the Light Dragoons from 1784, with Tarleton helmet, looped under-jacket and sleeveless shell. The helmet feather, which at first matched the facings, became a universal white-over-red after 1794. The white leather breeches were buff for regiments faced with that colour. Chevrons to indicate rank would not be officially authorised until 1803, and the two worn here by the sergeant, together with his sash, were a purely regimental device. The sword was suspended by slings from a shoulder belt which also carried a bayonet. The carbine, not shown, was either carried on the horse or attached by its side bar to the swivel on the pouch-belt.

23. Pte, Royal Horse Guards, 1790.

24. Offr, 1st Troop, Horse Guards, 1788.

25. Sgt, 10th Light Dragoons, 1790.

duties), nor was it listed with the other regiments of Horse in the 1768 warrant. However, contemporary pictures reveal that the uniform of this regiment followed that of the Horse, as already described; its blue coats faced and lapelled red and lined white, although the waistcoat and breeches, which logically should have been white, remained buff as before. A painting by Morland of a trooper in St James's Park, c 1790, shows the broad cross-belts formerly worn by Horse, with a flask cord on the carbine-belt, and a small black leather pouch attached on the front of a waistbelt worn under the coat (see Fig. 23, Plate 9). This figure has a laced hat but a drawing made during the Flanders campaign of 1793 indicates a plain hat with a red-over-black plume; while the cross-belts are narrower and have a shoulder-belt plate. For this campaign the Blues were issued with iron skulls and cuirasses but owing to the age of these items they were returned to store. While on the Continent a plainer uniform without gold lace was served out.

A portrait of an officer in 1775 shows a similar uniform and makes clear that the buttons and gold loops—concealed in Morland's trooper by his cross-belts and his pose—were in pairs on the lapels, one each side of the collar and four on the cuffs, with chevron loops, the lowest being on the red facing (a similar arrangement appears on the skirts). There is one scarlet and gold-fringed epaulette on the left shoulder and the lapels are unbuttoned. A crimson waist sash is tied over the waistcoat on the right side and the sword belt, with gilt buckle, is worn over the right shoulder under the coat. In another portrait dated 1780 the belt buckle has been replaced by an oval gilt plate bearing the crown and cypher, and the gold loops are much narrower. In the earlier portrait the housings are scarlet with gold lace and the usual tassels, but in the later the crown and garter star have replaced the tassels.

Light Dragoons (1768–1783)

The headdresses for all ranks of Light Dragoons were described in the warrant merely as 'helmets'. Though there were regimental variations of detail, the general pattern was that described in the last period: leather or metal skull, a crest with a gorgon's head in front on top with a mane or plume, a turned-up frontal plate, and a turban secured with chains. The regimental devices appeared on the frontal, e.g. the King's crest for the 15th, the Queen's cypher for the 16th, both within the garter with the crown and scrolls, the

Colonel Sir John Burgoyne, 23rd Light Dragoons, in the short-lived green jacket worn by this regiment, c 1782. His cloth cap is also predominantly green with silver lace and black plume. Painting by Romney.

death's head of the 17th. Turbans were variously red, blue, black or fur, the 17th having white; in the American War the latter were of sheepskin.

The coats, waistcoats and breeches conformed with those of the Dragoon Guards but an epaulette was worn on both shoulders by all ranks. The rank distinctions also conformed. The shoulder belt for carbine and waistbelt for sword were narrower, being $2\frac{1}{2}$ in. and $1\frac{3}{4}$ in. respectively. A painting of a 16th private, c 1770, shows a small black pouch on the front of the waistbelt. According to Hinde's *Discipline of the Light Horse*, by

Officer, 12th (Prince of Wales's) Light Dragoons, in the new blue uniform, faced yellow, adopted from 1784. The Tarleton helmet (on the wall) has a yellow turban and silver regimental crest on the side. The lace is silver.

1778 Light Dragoons were using a shoulder belt for their swords (as their officers had from 1768), except in the 16th who retained their waistbelts but carried their pouches on the left side suspended by a belt over the right shoulder. The housings and holster caps followed the same principles as the rest of the cavalry, with the usual regimental distinctions and exceptions to the general rule of being in the facing colour (see Appendix 4). The officers of the 12th and 16th had special designs: respectively, black cloth with stripes of white goatskin and silver lace, and leopardskin with silver fringe. All officers had black or white bearskin flounces covering their pistols. The arms of a Light Dragoon were described by Hinde as a carbine with 29-in. barrel, with or without a 12-in. bayonet, two pistols, a sword with 37-in. blade, either curved or straight according to regiment, and a hatchet.

The regulations for Light Dragoon trumpeters were the same as for other Dragoons including the wearing of hats with feathers, although the 17th's were noted as wearing helmets in 1768. According to Hinde one trumpeter also carried a curved bugle-horn. Farriers' dress conformed with those of the Dragoon Guards.

During the war in America the exploits of Lieutenant-Colonel Banastre Tarleton's British Legion, a loyalist corps of light cavalry and infantry, demonstrated the value of dark clothing. The Legion cavalry wore short, dark green jackets, with a helmet thought to have been devised by Tarleton himself, since it was always described by his name: a leather skull with a turban round the base, bearskin crest passing over the top from front to rear and a projecting peak. A similar helmet, though with turned-up peak, was worn by the short-lived 22nd Light Dragoons (1779–1783), with a green jacket and pelisse, or slung jacket as used by continental hussars. A green uniform was also briefly worn by the 23rd Light Dragoons, raised in 1780 by Sir John Burgoyne. A red coat faced green was originally ordered, but a portrait of Burgoyne and notices for deserters immediately prior to the regiment's departure for India in January 1782 reveal a green uniform which may have been worn in India until May 1784, when the regimental order book stated 'the men will very soon wear their red dress'. Burgoyne's portrait shows a very plain, hip-length dark green coat with silver fringed epaulettes worn open over buff waistcoat and breeches. The low, stand-up collar and round cuffs are green, outlined in silver piping, the buttons in pairs are

without loops, and the turnbacks are white. His cap has a turned-up front and back, edged with double silver braid, a black feather at one side, a rosette at the other. The shoulder belt is black leather with a silver tip engraved 'XXIII LD'.

Despite this brief manifestation of green as a cavalry colour, it was not pursued and, when the Light Dragoon dress was entirely altered in 1784, dark blue was chosen for the new uniform.

Light Dragoons (1784–1795)

From this date the dress of the light cavalry began to differ markedly from that of the heavy regiments and, except for a brief period in the next century when the colour red would be resumed, would continue to do so for as long as full dress was worn.

After the American war, the Light Dragoons started to adopt the Tarleton helmet and, in 1788, it was officially ordered for all. Apparently the 15th were reluctant to give up their old helmet and a portrait of a cornet, dated 1789, shows the obsolete pattern still in use. The new headdress, described as a 'cap', was made of japanned leather, had a peak over the eyes (bound with silver plating), a turban, usually in the facing colour folded round the base of the skull and fastened with chains, and a black bearskin crest. Above the peak was a band of plated silver with the regimental title. On the left side of the skull was an upright feather in the facing colour unless the latter was white when it was mixed with red; on the right-hand side was any crest to which the regiment was entitled, e.g. the Prince of Wales's feathers for the 10th, the Royal crest, cypher and garter with 'Emsdorf' for the 15th, and others too numerous to list here[6]. After 1794 all feathers were white over red.

Hitherto all uniform coats had revealed part of the waistcoat, but in the new Light Dragoon costume the waistcoat, made of flannel, was entirely concealed by a blue jacket which was closed down the front as low as, if not just below, the waist. Over the jacket went a shell, a sleeveless coat in the same colour without lapels, which curved away from below the shirt frill to fall behind in hip-length skirts turned back on their forward edges. The standing collar and pointed cuffs of the jacket and collar of the shell were red for Royal regiments, in the facing colour for

[6] Given in full in *Metal regimental badges on Light Cavalry helmets*, LE Buckell, Journal of the Society for Army Historical Research, Vol XX, pp 72–84.

others, and the linings were white except for buff-faced regiment (Appendix 5). The jacket had three vertical rows, each of 13 buttons, down the front, each horizontal row of three connected by white cord loopings. Three more buttons, also looped, were placed horizontally at the top of a slit at each hip. The collar and cuffs were edged with white cord, which also went all round the garment and the cuff opening, which was closed by three buttons. The shell had similar loopings and edgings but only two rows of buttons in front, arranged in pairs, with another button at each hip, to which the front skirts were looped back showing a heart-shaped ornament. The central vent at the rear was edged with white cord terminating in a trefoil at the top, on either side of which was another trefoil whose cord descended in a spray of three lines, each with a tassel at the base. The shell had white-edged shoulder straps in the facing colour to retain the belts, and its armholes were furnished with a small piped wing

'The Encampment at Brighton', showing men of the 16th The Queen's Light Dragoons, c 1790. The plumes and facings are scarlet, the turban black, the housings and rolled cloak lining white. Note the bayonet attached to the sword belt. The men's outer jacket, or shell, being sleeveless has a small wing covering each armhole. Painting by Francis Wheatley.

to give a neater appearance where the jacket sleeves emerged (see Fig. 25, Plate 9).

Breeches were of white or buff leather. When mounted, knee-length boots with cuffed tops were worn, when dismounted, black gaiters. Under the 1768 warrant the latter were to be half-gaiters for Light Dragoons, and these are shown in Stubbs' well-known painting of the 10th Light Dragoons, c 1793. However, in a series of watercolours of the same regiment, in about 1787, possibly by Edmund Scott, the gaiters are knee-length. From 1786 the old red cloaks were altered to blue in conformity with the shell and jacket.

The accoutrements consisted of a carbine-belt with swivel, a shoulder belt with frog for the bayonet and two rings to which the sword was attached by slings, and a cartouch box. In the 1787 pictures of the 10th the latter is shown as white, quite long, and attached to the front of a waistbelt worn over the jacket but under the shell. In Wheatley's painting 'The Encampment at Brighton', executed at about the same time, his arrangement of figures of the 16th Light Dragoons does not permit a sight of the pouch, but the Stubbs picture makes it clear that by then it was attached by means of buckles to the carbine-belt which passed underneath it, a system that would continue for all types of cavalrymen for some seventy years. Both shoulder belts were $2\frac{1}{2}$ in. wide and from 1793 the pouches were to be of black leather. The housings were unchanged and the flounces were of black bearskin.

A short carbine with 28-in. barrel, designed by General Eliott, Colonel of the 15th from 1759–1790, was chosen as the regulation pattern for all regiments in 1786 from a number of weapons with barrels of varying length. This carbine was carried on the horse with the butt uppermost and the muzzle in a bucket hanging below the off-side holster, a reversal of past practice. The regulation Light Dragoon sword or sabre approved in 1788 had a 36-in. curved blade, a straight knucklebow guard, in steel or wrought iron, furnished with a white leather knot, and a scabbard of the same metal painted black and fitted with two rings.

The 1784 regulations laid down two uniforms for officers and quartermasters: a dress uniform, with the coat in the 1768 style but in blue with regimental facings (Royal regiments having scarlet), and a field uniform of the same cut as the men's but with sleeves fitted to the shell, and the loopings in silver, except for the gold of the 13th. Their fringed epaulettes, worn on both shoulders,

varied between regiments: the 10th, for example, had metal scales on theirs, while the 11th had two stripes of blue on their silver lace, a 12-pointed star and a crescent bearing the regimental title. From 1785 officers of the 16th were permitted to wear a pelisse, lined with leopardskin, instead of the shell but three years later this was forbidden.

Sergeants were distinguished by silver or gold cord loopings, changed in 1790 to a narrow silver lace, and a waist sash as before but in blue, with stripe in the facing colour. In the 1787 pictures and the Stubbs painting the 10th's sergeants have two yellow chevrons edged white on the right upper arm, but such rank badges were not to be authorised officially until 1803. Corporals had a silver or gold cord round the collar and cuffs.

Trumpeters had a jacket and shell in the facing colour with lace loopings instead of cord and lace on the seams. From 1792, black bearskin caps were ordered instead of hats. The cap shown on the 10th's trumpeter in the painting by Stubbs resembles a large hussar busby in shape, and has a peak, a yellow feather at the left side and white cap-lines terminating in tassels on the right (cap lines will be increasingly met with in the uniform descriptions for the nineteenth century. They consisted of cords, with decorative ends, attached to the cap and secured round the neck or body, to prevent loss of the headdress when mounted). The lace on his yellow jacket and shell is also yellow, possibly gold, but white on the red collar and cuffs. Edging the front of the shell is blue lace with a yellow border, which also forms chevrons up the sleeves, these being further decorated with white tufting; the same appears on the outer edge of the red wings. The sword belt is red, edged with blue and yellow lace and a white diamond and oval pattern running down the centre. The brass trumpet has blue and yellow cords but no banner.

The 19th Century

Background

In 1805, the 7th, 10th and 15th Light Dragoons were designated Hussars, a type of light cavalry long familiar in Europe but never seen before in the British regular cavalry except for some foreign or emigré regiments in the British service during the French Revolutionary War. Two years later, the 18th Light Dragoons followed suit and when this regiment was disbanded in 1821, the 8th Light Dragoons took its place as hussars. These changes, however, only affected dress, not role or organisation, and these regiments were still formally designated Light Dragoons until 1861, the word 'Hussars' being confined to parentheses in their title.

The Household Cavalry, to which the Royal Horse Guards (from 1819 'The Blues' instead of 'Blue') would be formally admitted in 1820, and the Heavy Cavalry of the Line, Dragoon Guards and Dragoons, remained unchanged throughout the Napoleonic War. In 1818, the 3rd and 4th Dragoons were converted into Light Dragoons which, though reducing the Dragoons to the 1st (Royal), 2nd (Royal North British) and 6th (Inniskilling), in part compensated for the disbandment between 1818–1821 of the 18th–25th Light Dragoons.

Two of these higher-numbered regiments, the 19th and 23rd, had, in common with the 9th, 12th and 16th, been converted into Lancers in 1816, in emulation of a type of cavalry widely used by European armies during the Napoleonic War. Following the disbandment of the 19th and 23rd, in 1821 and 1817 respectively, the three senior Lancer regiments were joined by the 17th, in 1822. Although this brought a new weapon and yet another new uniform into the ranks of the cavalry, the four regiments of Lancers, like the Hussars, continued to be designated primarily as Light Dragoons.

However, this title, once a source of pride and distinction in the eighteenth century, was now losing favour. The 11th became Hussars in 1840, dispensing with the older title altogether, and in 1858 a new 18th was re-raised as Hussars while the old 5th Dragoons was resurrected as a lancer regiment, assuming its former title of Royal Irish. Three years later the last four regiments dressed as Light Dragoons, the 3rd, 4th, 13th and 14th, all became Hussars and the former title disappeared entirely. In the same year, three regiments of European light cavalry from the now defunct Honourable East India Company's forces were taken into the Cavalry of the Line as 19th, 20th and 21st Hussars. The last-named was converted to Lancers in 1897. Thus by the end of the century, besides the three regiments of Household Cavalry, the mounted arm mustered seven regiments of Dragoon Guards, three of Dragoons, twelve of Hussars and six of Lancers; 31 in all.

Despite this diversity of regiments and the classification of the Household Cavalry and all Dragoons as heavy cavalry and the others as light, the differences between the types were almost entirely of dress, size of men and horses and, to a lesser extent, of armament. Compared with other armies, the British Cavalry was always few in numbers and consequently, while shock action or the charge had traditionally been the role of heavy cavalry and the duties of outposts and reconnaissance that of light horse, British regiments, be they heavy or light, had been compelled to undertake both roles. This had been the case in the Napoleonic War, if not before, and was officially recognised in Queen's Regulations of 1844 which stated that 'it is of the utmost importance ... that both the Heavy and Light Cavalry should be equal to the charge in line, as well as to the duties on outposts.'

Some time after the Crimean War the Cavalry was classed as heavy, medium and light, though this was a reflection of the weight carried by the horse; the weights were, respectively, about 19 stone 10 lb, 19 stone 5 lb, and 18 stone 5 lb. The heavies included, besides the Household Cavalry, 4th and 5th Dragoon Guards, and the 1st and 2nd Dragoons, all of whom recruited a bigger man. The other Dragoon Guard regiments, 6th Dragoons and all the Lancers were medium, while the Hussars were light. This classification ironed out the anomaly of the 6th Dragoon Guards (Carabiniers) who, prior to sailing for India in 1853, had been ordered to convert to light

cavalry, thus acquiring a Light Dragoon uniform but retaining the headdress and title of Dragoon Guards. By 1890 the heavies had been reduced to the Household Cavalry and the 1st and 2nd Dragoons only, but in 1897 the medium classification was dropped and all regiments except Hussars were classed as heavy.

During the Napoleonic War a regiment generally had eight troops. Although after Waterloo the numbers of men in each troop were progressively reduced, the eight-troop organisation continued until 1822 when the troops were reduced to six, except for regiments in India. At that date a troop of a home regiment had one captain, one lieutenant, one cornet, a troop-sergeant-major, two sergeants, three corporals, a trumpeter, a farrier and 47 privates. This, with a regimental headquarters staff of ten officers and five NCOs, gave a regimental strength of 363. By contrast a regiment in India had a total strength of 745. The Crimean War and the Indian Mutiny revived the eight-troop organisation for all, which was maintained thereafter, but the number of privates in each continued to fluctuate between about 40 to 70, according to whether a regiment was at home or abroad, in peacetime quarters or on active service.

Since the seventeenth century two, three and even four troops of cavalry had been grouped into squadrons for battle, but the troop remained the administrative sub-unit of the regiment. In 1869, a regiment's eight troops were grouped into four squadrons for all purposes, but, owing to the loss of their commands by the four junior captains, the change only lasted for a year. However the four-squadron organisation was finally adopted in 1892, though modified in 1897 for all regiments at home and abroad except India, to three service squadrons and one 'reserve' squadron; in India all four squadrons were 'service'.

Dress 1796–1811

General

In 1796 cavalry dress was reviewed by a board of officers whose recommendations led to the publication of a new warrant, the provisions of which

A senior NCO of the 2nd Life Guards, Troop Quartermaster Ransom, c 1800. The coat is now worn fastened down to the waist, as ordered from 1796, and the blue lapels are buttoned across except at the top. The hat has assumed the upright shape, as worn by all Heavy Cavalry. Painting by De La Bère.

were to govern the appearance of the Cavalry through much of the French Revolutionary and Napoleonic Wars.

In this period the practice of displaying the waistcoat, already discarded in the Light Dragoons, was discontinued in all regiments as the coat became closed down to the waist. Despite this change, the Household and Heavy Cavalry continued to have an eighteenth century flavour to their dress, since, after 1800, they were the only part of the Army to retain the black hat for all ranks, though by now this was of bicorne shape[7]. In contrast to such conservatism, a new uniform appeared in the British Cavalry, that of the hussar; a costume originally of Hungarian origin, but one which had long been familiar in Continental armies. Elements of hussar dress, which had been emerging in the Light Dragoons uniform in the preceding period, were now to become more pronounced in such regiments, though not to the same degree as in those designated Hussars in 1805. The regimental distinctions, which by now had become fixed, are given for this period in Appendix 6 for Household and Heavy Cavalry, at Appendix 5 for Light Cavalry.

One change common to all cavalry ranks in 1796 was the method of dressing the hair. Powder had been abolished the year before and now the club was done away with. Instead the hair was to be bound in a queue, or pigtail, the binding to extend for nine inches from just below the upper edge of the collar, with one inch of hair showing at the bottom of the binding. In 1804 the queue was shortened by an inch and from 1808 the hair was to be cut short. Hussars may not have complied with this last order immediately, as three years later privates of the 10th Hussars were observed with long hair, including one with 'long ringlets'. Hussars were also noticeable in a clean-shaven Army by their cultivation of drooping moustaches.

Household Cavalry

The hats of the Life Guards were gold-laced in full dress but bound in black when the frock uniform (a type of undress) was worn, and had a white-over-red feather above the black cockade, the latter being secured by a gold cord loop for the men, a scale loop for officers.

The blue lapels of the long-skirted coat were edged round with gold lace and had the same loops as before but were now closed up with

[7] Hats continued to be worn in this period by infantry, artillery and engineer officers and by light cavalry officers on certain occasions.

Cavalry officers, 1808. From left: 20th Light Dragoons, 7th Queen's Own Light Dragoons (Hussars), (rear) 12th (Prince of Wales's) Light Dragoons, Royal Horse Guards, (rear) 14th Light Dragoons, 10th Prince of Wales's Own Hussars, (rear) 16th The Queen's Light Dragoons, General officer of Hussars, 15th (The King's) Light Dragoons (Hussars), (rear) 17th Light Dragoons, 1st (Royal) Dragoons, (rear) 8th (King's Royal Irish) Light Dragoons, 9th or 11th Light Dragoons, 13th Light Dragoons, 18th King's Light Dragoons (Hussars). Watercolour by Robert Dighton the younger.

hooks and eyes down to the waist. The stand-up collar was also laced round, the 1st Life Guards' all blue, the 2nd's scarlet, with a blue patch in front. The cuffs were blue but were generally concealed by white gauntlet gloves, the buttons being arranged in pairs, as they were on the skirts, with loops in chevrons. The edges of the white turn-backs were finished with gold lace. The epaulettes appear to have been blue, edged gold and with a short gold fringe. White breeches were worn with jack-boots.

The accoutrements consisted of two white cross-belts: over the left shoulder, the carbine-belt with swivel and black leather pouch attached to the belt; over the right, the sword belt with bayonet scabbard and two rings to which the sword slings were attached. The horse furniture

of the 1st Regiment continued as scarlet, gold-laced with the garter star. A print after Atkinson of a trooper of the 2nd Regiment in 1807 shows a blue shabraque which suggests the perpetuation of one of the old distinguishing features of the two former troops of Horse Guards. Another print of the 2nd Regiment displays a white goatskin instead of a cloth shabraque.

In 1796 the Household Cavalry and the Blues were ordered to adopt a new sword but this seems to have been the pattern then authorised for the Heavy Cavalry, as will be described. In the same year, the latter were to have a carbine with 26-in. barrel but the firearm in the Atkinson print appears to be the longer weapon with 42-in. barrel.

The officers' full dress coats were of the same style as the men's, each epaulette having a gold-laced strap, a crescent enclosing the garter star and a bullion fringe about 3 in. long. The frock uniform of the 2nd Life Guards is shown by Robert Dighton as of the same cut but much plainer, only the cuff and skirt buttons having loops, the lapels scarlet, and the scarlet collar unlaced with one button on the blue patch. Cross-belts were worn but without the swivel, the left shoulder belt suspending a pouch bearing the Royal arms. Both regiments had rectangular belt plates, the pattern for the 1st Life Guards with cut corners. The crimson waist sash was worn over the coat and belts, and was tied in the middle at the back.

When on duty, mounted or dismounted, officers were, from 1796, to carry the 35-in. bladed broadsword with steel basket guard of 'ladder' design, crimson and gold sword knot and steel scabbard as ordered for Heavy Cavalry officers. For other occasions they had a lighter, 32-in. bladed sword, with gilt knucklebow and boatshell guard, carried in a black leather scabbard with gilt mounts and suspended from a frog worn under the waistcoat.

Royal Horse Guards (Blue)

The dress of the Blues now closely followed that of the Life Guards, except for the reversed coat colours and the buff of turn-backs, breeches and belts. At the beginning of this period the coat was unlaced but by 1807 the lace had been restored, though the loops on collar and lapels were narrower than those of the Life Guards. A trooper at this date, based on a watercolour by Hamilton Smith, is shown in Fig. 31, Plate 12. The two buttons on the collar and the eight on the lapels conflict with the evidence of a surviving officer's coat of this period, which has only one button on the collar and seven on each lapel, the bottom six being in pairs. The coats of officers drawn by Robert Dighton the younger also have only one button on the collar, so it is curious that troopers should have had two, unless Hamilton Smith made an error. Officers' hats each had a scale loop like the Life Guards and were bound with gold lace. Their epaulettes were scarlet, embroidered with a gold knot pattern and a garter star at the base with a gold cord fringe. Their pouch belts had the same flask cord worn by the men, and their swords were the same as carried by the Life Guards.

Heavy Cavalry

The headdress for Dragoon Guards and Dragoons was described in the 1796 warrant as 'a plain cocked hat (i.e. without lace) with a scale loop and white feather.' By 1799 the latter had changed to white-over-red; according to standing orders of the 3rd Dragoons in 1804, the proportions were 7 and 5 in. respectively. The same orders stated that the hats were 'to be worn forward so as to rest upon the eyebrow, and square across the head'. Contemporary illustrations show the hats so worn when on duty but in the watercolours of the two Robert Dightons made between 1800–1808 Heavy Cavalry officers are mostly wearing them

fore-and-aft. The 2nd Dragoons continued to wear both hats and bearskin caps, the latter having a brass plate in front, a white plaited-cord festoon across the middle with tassels at the right side, and a feather at the left. Hamilton Smith shows the latter as all white in 1800 but white-over-red in 1807.

In 1800 the Infantry abandoned the hat on assuming the shako or cap (except for officers) and from the same date there is reference to caps for Heavy Cavalry, although the hat remained the regulation full dress headgear. Some drawings made by Hamilton Smith in 1800 show all the Dragoon Guards regiments in hats, but the Dragoons, less the 2nd, have black cylindrical caps without peaks, a curling feather at the left side and some sort of bag or 'fly' at the right. This was originally an undress, or watering cap, some patterns of which later acquired a folding peak and a smaller feather set in front, but in some regiments it began to replace the hat entirely, perhaps as being more convenient for active service, upon which many were by then engaged (see Fig. 32, Plate 12). In 1804 the officers and men of the 1st Dragoon Guards were noted as wearing caps 'on all occasions', and in the same year the same was observed of the 1st Royal Dragoons. In 1811 the latter regiment, having not had 'any new hats for three years', were issued with a fresh supply. In the painting of an officer of the 6th Dragoons, on which Fig. 32, Plate 12 is based, some mounted dragoons in the background have similar caps.

The 1796 alteration to the coats involved the shortening of the skirts so that they cleared the seat when mounted, the fastening of the front down to the waist with hooks and eyes, and the replacement of the epaulettes by shoulder straps in the facing colour, with red wings edged white, which were to be laced and interlined with iron or brass plates of sufficient strength to resist a sword cut. The lace loops on collar, cuffs and lapels were as before (see Fig. 26, Plate 10). In 1797 the lapels in the facing colour worn by Dragoon Guards were abolished. The coat fronts of both Dragoon Guards and Dragoons were henceforth to be single-breasted, fastening with a single row of buttons with lace loops either side, tapering towards the waist. The facing colour now showed only on the collar, cuffs and turnbacks of the shortened skirts. The cuffs of Dragoons Guards were indented; those of Dragoons were round, but this difference was hardly visible when gauntlet gloves were worn. This new arrangement appears to have taken some time to effect, for in Hamilton Smith's 1800 drawings all the Dragoon Guards still have lapels in the facing colour. Once the new coats were taken into use, Dragoon Guards could still be distinguished from Dragoons by a vertical strip of lace down the centre front under and just to the right of the buttons.

Worn with the white 'plush' breeches (buff for the 6th Dragoons) were knee-high boots which, from 1796, were to have the seam in front instead of behind. The stiff tops were henceforth to be hollowed out behind the knee. On active service it increasingly became the practice to wear overalls (usually grey), sometimes reinforced with leather and with a coloured stripe or buttons or both down the sides, the bottoms being held down by a strap or chain under the instep, as shown in Fig. 32, Plate 12.

The accoutrements for a heavy dragoon consisted of two belts: one, 3 in. wide, over the left shoulder, with a swivel for the firearm, and a curved black cartouch box containing 30 rounds; the other, $2\frac{1}{2}$ in. wide, round the waist, with a bayonet frog and sword slings, and fastening with a rectangular brass clasp. In all except buff-faced regiments, the leather was to be whitened. A painting dated 1802 shows a private of the 4th Dragoons in service marching order with the above, plus camp equipage of white haversack and blue-painted wooden water bottle (see Fig. 30, Plate 11). In 1796 the cloth housings and holster caps were discontinued but the holsters were still covered by bearskin flounces. A regulation pattern saddle was sealed in the same year, for all regiments, to ensure a uniformity which had not hitherto existed. Its leather was brown but all associated straps, and the bridle, were black. The red cloak with sleeves was rolled to a length of 22 in. with the lining outwards and strapped to the back of the saddle, but in marching order, according to the standing orders of the 3rd Dragoon Guards in 1803, the cloaks were to be rolled 3 ft 4 in. long and carried over the holsters. When carried in this way the red was outwards, as can be seen in a Hamilton Smith watercolour of the 2nd Dragoons in 1807. In the latter a brown case or valise occupies the position at the rear of the saddle.

New weapons were introduced at the same time as the 1796 warrant. The sword had a straight 35-in. blade, the guard being an iron knucklebow broadening into a pear-shaped, pierced disc with buff leather knot, and an iron scabbard with two loose rings. The long cumbersome firelock was replaced by a carbine with 26-in. musket-bore barrel and a side bar and ring for attachment to the swivel. The regulations stated that the carbine was to be carried on the horse with the butt downwards but illustrations show that by 1805 this was reversed. The bayonet blade was reduced to 15 in. and only one pistol was to be carried.

Two uniforms were authorised for officers: their field dress, which was 'to be shaped and laced in the same manner as those of the men, with gold or silver, according to regimental regulation' and, when not under arms, on parade or duty, their former uniform with cut-away coat. Their hats conformed to the men's in both cases. The 1796 board of officers had recommended that the various commissioned ranks should be visibly differenced but no action followed and officers' field coats had wings and shoulder straps like the men's, though with gold or silver lace and nothing to distinguish the individual rank. A surviving field dress coat of a 6th Dragoon Guards officer has two lace loops, each $4\frac{1}{2}$ in. long, on the white collar but with buttons only on the right. The

---

PLATE 10: 1796–1811

26. Private, 3rd (Prince of Wales's) Dragoon Guards, 1796.
27. Officer, 10th Prince of Wales's Own Light Dragoons, 1805.
28. Private, 8th (King's Royal Irish) Light Dragoons, 1808 (India).

Figure 26 shows how the Heavy Cavalry hat, now shorn of lace, had acquired a bicorne shape. The coat, fastened to the waist from 1796, lost its lapels from the following year, becoming almost identical to the Dragoon style (see Plate 11), with only the cuff shape distinguishing Dragoon Guards from Dragoons. From 1796 the tops of all cavalry boots were hollowed out behind. The sword belt had returned to the waist, its slings supporting the 1796 sword illustrated here, and with a frog for the bayonet. Figure 27, based on a watercolour by R Dighton the younger, shows how the Light Dragoon uniform was influenced by Continental hussar fashions: such as the 'mirleton' or 'flügel' cap, the pelisse, barrel sash, pantaloons, Hessian boots and sabretache. The Mameluke-hilted sabre was a popular legacy of the 1801 Egyptian campaign. Figure 28 has the jacket which replaced the former shell and under-jacket from 1796, but in French-grey, the colour prescribed for India and the Cape. The helmet is the special lightweight pattern for hot climates with the harp badge of the 8th. The private is armed with the 1796 Light Cavalry sword.

26. Pte, 3rd Dragoon Guards, 1796.

28. Pte, 8th Light Dragoons, 1808.

27. Offr, 10th Light Dragoons, 1805.

loops in front are in pairs, tapering from $4\frac{1}{2}$ in. at the top to 3 in. at the bottom; the vertical lace down the front continuing all the way round the bottom edge to outline the turnbacks which have a star ornament in wire and sequins where they meet. Two buttons at the back of the waist have lace around them in a bastion shape which descends along the seams under the turnbacks. The four buttons and chevron loops on the lower forearm are in pairs, the lowest being on the white indented cuff. The silver scales on the shoulder straps and wings are mounted on black cloth with white cloth and silver braid edging all round. The lace on this surviving field dress coat has a black stripe; whether such stripes were universal — and were also on the men's white lace — is uncertain.

Officers and quartermasters were ordered to have a blue greatcoat which was to be carried on the horse in a round cloth case behind the saddle. The 1804 standing orders of the 4th Dragoons mention that this case was blue and was to be carried in field day order; in marching order, however, a black leather valise took its place behind the saddle, and the coat was folded in front. The sash and sword belt were worn round the waist and when mounted on duty a shoulder belt suspending a small black pouch containing 12 pistol rounds was to be worn. The dress and undress swords were as already described for the Household Cavalry. The abolition of housings and holster caps did not at first apply to officers and quartermasters whose 'furniture was to remain as at present'. In the 1799 plates for the *British Military Library*, officers of the 1st and 5th Dragoon Guards merely have bearskin flounces like the men, while the figure for the 2nd Dragoons has both the latter and a housing of white goatskin. However, in the Reinagle 1808 painting of a 4th Dragoons officer, housings and holster caps are again in evidence (see Fig. 29, Plate 11) but they were doubtless discarded on active service.

In 1809 the rank of troop quartermaster was abolished and his duties were henceforth undertaken by a troop-sergeant-major. Chevrons, worn on the right upper arm, had been instituted in 1803 to denote the rank of NCOs. Each bar was edged with a narrow strip of the facing colour, sergeant-majors and quartermaster-sergeants having four bars, sergeants three and corporals two. Each regiment had been ordered to have a sergeant-major from 1800 and when chevrons were introduced he was to have a crown above the four bars to denote his status as the senior NCO of the regiment.

There was nothing in the 1796 warrant that altered the dress of either trumpeters or farriers, which presumably continued as before, though with the same basic changes to their coats as the men. A farrier's blue coat appears in a painting of the 4th Dragoons in 1802, in this case with that regiment's green facings and worn with a round fur cap bearing a horseshoe badge. However, the traditional negro trumpeter of this regiment wears a white coat faced red and trimmed with Royal lace, which is at odds with both the customary Royal livery and reversed colours. His turban is white, bound with a dark cord or chain, with a green and red plume on the left side, the colours divided vertically. As usual for trumpeters, he rides a grey horse. Following a shortage of the traditional black horses, it was ordered in 1796 that this regiment, together with the 3rd Dragoon Guards and 6th Dragoons, were in future to have brown, bay and chestnut horses throughout each regiment, an order that had previously also been applied to the 5th and 6th Dragoon Guards. Since the 2nd Dragoon Guards had long had bays, and the 2nd Dragoons their greys, less than half the regiments of Heavy Cavalry now retained the once-universal blacks.

Light Dragoons

The 1796 warrant made no change in the Tarleton helmets of the Light Dragoons, although from 1800 the turbans of all were to be black, but it also mentioned a 'leather watering cap'. It is probably these caps which appear in watercolours of the 17th Light Dragoons, c 1800, by an officer of the regiment, Thomas Ellis, who shows the caps as tall and cylindrical, tapering slightly towards the top with square-cut, possibly folding peaks and white cap lines, each with a curling white feather on the left side and the regimental crest on the front.

The skulls of the helmets were found unsuitable for hot climates such as India and the Cape of Good Hope, so a board of officers recommended in 1796 that a helmet made of tin and lined with white linen should be provided for such places. These were the same basic shape as the Tarleton,

Officer, 12th (Prince of Wales's) Light Dragoons, 1801. From 1796 the shell and underjacket were replaced by a single jacket buttoned to the waist. Compare with Page 57. Watercolour by Robert Dighton.

with peak and turban, but instead of the bearskin crest, the crown was fitted with a metal comb to which a horsehair mane was attached. For the 8th Light Dragoons, serving at the Cape, in Egypt and India during this period, the mane was red and the front bore the crown over the harp above a metal strip showing the regimental title as worn on the home service helmet (see Fig. 28, Plate 10). A similar helmet was worn by the 20th Light Dragoons in the West Indies, their front plate bearing 'XX LD' above an alligator.

From 1796 the blue shell and the under-jacket of the 1784 pattern were replaced by a single jacket, similar to the under-jacket but with the front buttons, and the narrow, flat white braid linking them, set on closer together. The jackets of the 10th had a frame of white lace sewn round the outside of the outer row of buttons. The collar and cuffs were as before. The jacket was shortened slightly in the waist some time around 1800.

There was considerable discussion in 1796 as to the colour of jackets to be worn by Light Dragoons in hot climates. Eventually it was agreed that the colour first proposed, French grey, should be adopted, and it was ordered in August of that year for the 8th, 19th, 25th, 27th and 28th Light Dragoons, as well as for any others that might in future serve in India or at the Cape. Regiments in the West Indies were to wear blue.

The netherwear for soldiers was unaltered but their accoutrements and horse furniture underwent the same changes as the Heavy Cavalry, though with narrower belts: the shoulder belt, with swivel and pouch, was $2\frac{1}{2}$ in., the waistbelt, for sword and bayonet, was $2\frac{1}{4}$ in. The Ellis watercolours of the 17th show a black valise with square ends, each end with an oval brass plate in the centre, fastened to the rear of the saddle. The new carbine and bayonet also applied to the Light Dragoons, as did the carriage of only one pistol. They received a new sabre, wih curved $32\frac{1}{2}$–33 in. blade, wrought-iron stirrup guard, and scabbard of the same metal with two loose rings.

The 1796 warrant required that officers' uniforms be 'shaped and laced in the same manner as those of the men'; the lace, of course, was silver, except for the 13th who had gold, and its arrangement more intricate, with regimental variations. The white collar and cuffs of the 7th, for example, were edged with blue, on which two narrow silver braids showed the blue between. Elaboration of braid patterns increased as the period progressed. The warrant also stated that the jackets were to have 'scale epaulets and wings', but in the several

portraits of Light Dragoon officers in this period by the two Robert Dightons and others, there is no evidence of these being worn. The influence on Light Dragoon officers of the emigré Hussar regiments in British service during the French Revolutionary War became increasingly evident in their appearance. One example was the adoption, as an alternative to the Tarleton helmet, of the 'mirleton' and 'flügel' cap, seen in many of the Dighton portraits. It was a tall, conical cap (usually in cloth of the facing colour), with a gold lace circle at the bottom, silver lace round the top, a white-over-red feather, cap-lines and flounders, and a pointed 'fly'—black on one side, regimental colour on the other—which could be twisted round the cap to show the black side or left hanging (see Fig. 27, Plate 10). Some officers are shown with black watering caps, and while off-duty a cocked hat with a white-over-red feather was worn, usually fore-and-aft. Although the Dighton pictures, painted in the first few years of the new century, show flügel caps worn by several regiments (not merely those soon to become Hussars), the helmet was not abolished, and a

PLATE 11: 1796–1811

29. Officer, 4th Queen's Own Dragoons, 1808.
30. Private, 4th Queen's Own Dragoons, 1802.

This plate, based on paintings by Reinagle and R Dighton for the officer, and by Scott for the private, shows the dress differences between ranks in one regiment of Heavy Cavalry after the 1796 dress changes. The private wears his hat athwart in the regulation way, but towards the end of this period it was being worn, by officers at least, fore-and-aft. The single-breasted jacket with lace loops has the round cuff of the Dragoons, as opposed to the indented style of Dragoon Guards, but the private's green wings are contrary to the 1796 regulations which ordered red wings and shoulder straps in the facing colour. The same ruling applied to officers' jackets, and tailors' pattern books for the 4th adhere to it, but in the source paintings for Figure 29 only a narrow silver shoulder cord is shown. The private is equipped for marching order, with haversack and water bottle, and the bayonet still forms part of his armament. His hair is dressed in the queue, 10 in. overall before being shortened in 1804; while the officer's hair is cut short in accordance with the 1808 regulation. Although the officer still has the housings and holster-caps embroidered with the Queen's cypher, such furniture had been abolished for soldiers in 1796. The officer's cuff, concealed by the gauntlet, is shown in detail.

29. Offr, 4th Dragoons, 1808.

30. Pte, 4th Dragoons, 1802.

Sir Bellingham Graham, 10th Prince of Wales's Own Hussars, c 1810. The facings are yellow, lace silver, the cap and pelisse-fur grey. The sabretache is scarlet with silver embroidery. At this date Hussars were chiefly distinguished from Light Dragoons by the headdress and pelisse. Painting by Sir William Beechey.

portrait by Hoppner of Lord Paget when Paget was commanding the 7th shows him with this headdress, although his uniform is as worn when off-duty.

Another item of hussar origin, the fur-trimmed pelisse (or slung jacket) was also adopted unofficially by many Light Dragoon officers when the old shell was abolished, seemingly in prefer-

ence to a blue greatcoat, like the Heavy Cavalry's ordered in the 1796 warrant. Another novelty, much affected by Light Dragoon officers, was the use of close-fitting pantaloons, in white, blue or grey if the jackets were that colour, the two latter with gold or silver embroidery on the thighs and lace up the seams and round the seat, worn with tasselled Hessian boots.

The hussar influence was also manifested in the officers' accoutrements with the adoption of the sabretache, suspended by slings from the sword waistbelt. Originally a useful sack hung from the belt by the Magyar horsemen from whom the hussars originated, it had developed into a flat pouch with a plain black flap for undress, but in dress with a flap usually in the facing colour, laced all round and embroidered with regimental devices. Those of the 26th Light Dragoons were covered in leopardskin with the numeral in the centre. Sabres were similar to the men's but from 1800 many officers adopted decorative weapons of the Mameluke type. The same shoulder belt with pouch for pistol ammunition that had been ordered for Heavy Cavalry officers was to be worn when mounted and on duty by Light Dragoons. However the Dighton pictures show these also worn off-duty when in hats. All in all, Light Cavalry officers in the early years of the new century had an exotic, un-British air about their uniforms which contrasted strangely with the sober and more familiar appearance of the heavies.

NCOs' dress conformed with the men's and acquired the rank badges already described. No mention of trumpeters is made in the warrant, which suggests the earlier rulings were still effective. There is little pictorial evidence of their dress in this period, but the Ellis watercolours of the 17th show two trumpeters dressed, rather surprisingly for a non-Royal regiment, in red jackets with white facings and the same watering caps as the men.

Hussars

The disbandment in 1802 of the emigré York Hussars left the Army without any troops dressed in this fashion. This was soon rectified by the Prince Regent and the Duke of Cumberland turning out one troop each of their regiments, the 10th and 15th Light Dragoons, in hussar costume. In 1805 the two regiments were officially authorised to be clothed entirely as Hussars, a concession also extended to the 7th and, two years later, to the 18th. The change-over to the new dress was completed in the 7th by September

1806, the 10th and 15th by about the end of 1807, and the 18th by the autumn of 1808. Since the Light Dragoon jacket was by then already in the hussar style, the new dress required little more than a change of headdress and the issue of pelisses.

The hussar cap, popularly known as a 'busby' after the London hatter who supplied them, was a tall fur cylinder open at both ends; inside it was a cloth bag which was drawn up through the cylinder to fall at one side. As the caps were worn tilted to the right, the bag usually hung on that side. At the top in front was a white feather with red base and the cap was encircled with white cap-lines terminating in braided flounders and tassels. Oilskin covers were issued for bad weather. The colour of the fur and bag for each regiment is given in Appendix 5, note a.

In addition, presumably to preserve the fur cap, each man had another headdress, possibly of the flügel or watering type mentioned earlier—documents of the 7th mentioned 'leather caps'—and a stable cap; the latter was a pointed bag with a tasselled end and the base turned up.

Each man had a dress and undress jacket and a flannel stable jacket. The two former were similar and in the style described for the Light Dragoons, but the undress version had less braid and seems to have been of inferior cloth. A description of the buttons for the dress jacket quotes balls and half-balls, but for the undress they are listed simply as 'buttons'. The facing colours of collars and cuffs are in Appendix 5. From 1811 the 7th were granted yellow lace instead of white.

The pelisse followed the lines of the jacket but with fur at the collar and cuffs. The 10th's had the same outer frame of lace round the front braiding as appeared on their jackets. In summer review order the pelisse was slung over the left shoulder by means of neck-lines connected by a toggle and terminating in flounders and tassels. In winter the pelisse was worn instead of the jacket.

White leather pantaloons were worn in review order with plain Hessian boots; white trousers in stable dress; and in marching order, field days and drills, blue (later grey) overalls, the latter usually buttoning down the outside of the leg and furnished with leather strapping.

Around the waist was worn the hussar or 'barrelled' sash which was, in effect, a number of thin cords slotted through woven cylinders or barrels, terminating at one end with a toggle, at the other in a loop formed between two slides and gathered into two tassels at the extremities. This

Private, 10th Prince of Wales's Own Hussars, 1808. The soldier's uniform differed from the officer's in the previous black and white illustration in the brown fur of the cap with its short plume, the white pelisse fur, the frame round the lace loopings on both jacket and pelisse, and the plain sabretache. Also, the lace was white and less ornate. Watercolour by Robert Dighton the younger.

was wrapped two or three times round the waist, secured at the back by the toggle and loop, and the tasselled ends brought round the right side to be tied about the sash in front and hang loose. The sash worn by the 15th had crimson ends and yellow barrels, slides and tassels, the other regiments having blue and white.

The hussar's accoutrements were the same as for a light dragoon but with the addition of a plain black leather sabretache suspended from the sword belt by two slings. An entirely new saddle and bridle were issued to the Hussar regiments. With this were provided a white sheepskin saddle cloth and a dark blue shabraque with 'vandyked' (zig-zag) border, scarlet for the 15th and white for the others. At the back of the saddle was fastened a dark blue cylindrical valise, piped at the ends in the same colour as the shabraque border, with the abbreviated title of the regiment.

The arms for a hussar were: the 1796 light cavalry sabre, one pistol and a carbine. The 7th were issued with an even shorter firearm than the 1796 carbine, with 16-in. barrel and a ramrod attached to the barrel by a swivel. Paget, the Colonel of the 7th , was credited with the design of this carbine, which became known by his name and subsequently was adopted as the regulation pattern by all Light Cavalry.

The officers' uniforms were of the same style as the men's, though naturally of superior material and much more richly and extensively embroidered and laced. The cap-lines and the barrelled sash were crimson and gold, and the lace and braiding on both dress and undress jackets, as well as on the pelisse, were of silver. The dress garments had additional lace loopings between those loops linking the buttons, so that very little blue showed on the breast. During 1810–1811 two more rows of buttons were added to the dress jacket and pelisse. The arrangement of lace and braiding on collar, cuffs, button loopings and back seams varied between regiments, each having its distinctive pattern. For example, the 10th used a design resembling the Prince of Wales's feathers on the cuffs, while the 15th made much use of the Austrian knot and their button loops terminated in trefoil knots below the collar. The fur trimming on the pelisse also varied, not only between regiments, but in the 7th and 10th between ranks (see Appendix 5). White pantaloons, cotton in summer, leather in winter, were the regulation nether garment, but the blue type with lace embroidery which had been worn as Light Dragoons continued in use for some time. The tassels and binding on the Hessian boots were black for the 7th, silver for the 10th and 15th, while the 18th had silver tassels only. For the evenings, special dress pantaloons, probably red, were worn with yellow boots from 1810–1811. Grey overalls are shown by Richard Dighton as having a double silver lace stripe with buttons and

black leather strapping for the 7th, a single silver stripe and brown strapping for the 10th, and double scarlet stripes, silver buttons and brown strapping for the 15th. The overalls were fastened under the boots by silver chains, which in the case of the 10th were secured on the outside of the strapping, the latter extending to mid-calf. Spurs were ordinarily steel, but in 'dress' the 7th's officers had gilt.

The officers' accoutrements—of pouch-belt, waistbelt for sword and sabretache, the latter requiring three slings—were different for dress and undress. In the latter the pouch and sabretache were plain black leather, the belts being white or occasionally black for the waistbelt. The dress set was more decorative and varied between regiments. Red russia leather was the favoured material but either covered or embroidered with gold or silver lace, while the flaps of pouch and sabretache were covered in laced, coloured cloth—white for the 7th, scarlet for the 10th and 15th, and blue for the 18th—which was embroidered with regimental devices: for the 7th, the Queen's cypher, reversed and interlaced, and the crown in gold; for the 10th, 15th and 18th,

---

PLATE 12: 1796–1811

31. **Private, Royal Horse Guards (Blue), 1807.**
32. **Officer, 6th (Inniskilling) Dragoons, 1811.**
33. **Sergeant, 15th (King's) Light Dragoons (Hussars), 1808.**

A comparison of Figure 31, from a Hamilton Smith watercolour, with Figure 23 shows the effect of the 1796 regulations on this regiment's dress, notably the hat, the stand-up collar, and coat fastened to the waist. Unlike the Dragoon Guards, the Blues retained their lapelled coats, though the cross-belts reduced in width. Figure 32, after a Dighton watercolour, shows an officer in field dress, with the single-breasted laced jacket with shortened skirts, like the men's. Instead of the hat, white breeches and long boots of full dress, he wears a shako (or cap) and grey, strapped overalls with ankle boots. This figure shows how the Heavy Cavalry uniform had acquired a different style in the closing years of the eighteenth century. Figure 33, also after a Dighton watercolour, is typical of the first British hussar dress, as adopted by the 7th, 10th, 15th and 18th Light Dragoons. In the 15th the brown pelisse fur was peculiar to sergeants; officers and men having black. Officers' caps were also black. The Hanoverian crown above the chevrons was a regimental badge, not part of the rank insignia. The drooping moustaches worn by all hussars were a novelty in a hitherto clean-shaven Army.

31. Pte, Royal Horse Guards, 1807.

32. Offr, 6th Dragoons, 1811.

33. Sgt, 15th Hussars, 1808.

Private, 7th Queen's Own Light Dragoons (Hussars), 1808. Facings and lace white, cap fur brown, pelisse fur white, sash black and white. Watercolour by Robert Dighton the younger.

Officer, 15th (the King's) Light Dragoons (Hussars), 1809, without pelisse. Cap fur black; facings, sabretache and shabraque all scarlet; lace and embroidery all silver. Watercolour by Robert Dighton the younger.

the Royal cypher and crown similarly but in silver with, respectively, the Prince of Wales's feathers above, 'EMSDORF' above, and a laurel wreath below. The colours and lace of the sabretaches were repeated in the shabraques, and the saddle cloths were, for the 7th, black sheepskin with scarlet scalloped edging, for the 10th, leopardskin with sheepskin edging and for the 15th and 18th, black bearskin, the former having a scarlet scalloped edge. In undress a plain, dark blue shabraque seems to have been used by all regiments. Black bridles of plain leather were customary in undress, but the dress pattern was studded with cowrie shells and decorated with scarlet and shell bosses. Ordinarily, officers carried the 1796 pattern sabre in a steel scabbard but their dress weapon had a Mameluke hilt and a black leather scabbard with gilt mounts. The latter had a crimson and gold knot, the former white buff like the men.

The NCOs wore the chevrons ordered in 1803 with, in the 15th, a crown above. The clothing of sergeants appears to have differed from the rank and file's since it was always listed separately in clothing documents. There may have been other, more visible differences, such as silver braid, instead of white, superior fur trimming on the pelisse and, in the 15th at least, a light brown fur cap instead of the black of officers and privates (see Fig. 33, Plate 12). According to clothing bills for the 7th, the sergeant-major was to have 'better lace than the Serjts—superfine cloth which he will pay for'.

It is clear from the latter documents that the 7th's band and trumpeters had scarlet or red pelisses, lined white, edged with 'black Cremer Fur', changed in 1806 to 'Raccoon fur', and trimmed with Royal cord or braid. The 'Master of the Band' was to have 'silver lace and fringe', the trumpet-major 'silver and blue fringe'.

During the Corunna campaign of 1808–1809, in which all four Hussar regiments were engaged, the tall fur cap proved unsuitable for active service. On the regiments' return to England it was reserved for parade wear by the 7th, 10th and 15th, who received an alternative headdress; the castor cap, a cylindrical felt shako, widening slightly at the top where it was bound with lace, with the same tuft or feather as the fur cap, cap-lines and brass chin-scales. Some versions were without a peak, others had a peak which could be turned up. The 18th, however, retained their fur caps for all occasions.

Dress 1812–1819

General

Following the accession of the Prince of Wales as Prince Regent and the re-appointment of his brother, the Duke of York, as Commander-in-Chief in 1811, a board of officers was ordered to recommend changes in the clothing of the Cavalry, much of which had been unsatisfactory in the Peninsular campaign. The resulting new dress was authorised by a Royal warrant dated 12 March 1812 and revised on 17 August of the same year, but the changes were not completed by some regiments until 1814.

The Hussars' expensive dress suffered least from these changes, but the appearance of the Household and Heavy Cavalry was altered significantly, while the Light Dragoon uniform changed entirely, losing in the process most of the hussar features of the former dress and gaining instead something very akin to their enemy counterparts, the French *chasseurs à cheval*. Emulation of foreign fashions, which had begun with the Hussars and resulted in the Austrian-inspired new dress of the Heavies, was however characteristic of the time and culminated, in 1816, with the adoption of a Polish costume for the regiments newly converted to Lancers.

Two changes were applicable to all regiments in this period. First, an order was issued in July 1812 that henceforth, to avoid the dangers incurred on service by trumpeters from their distinctive clothing, they were to be dressed as privates but with special lace. Second, a general order dated 14 September 1815 discontinued the wearing of breeches and pantaloons with the relevant boots, in favour of dark grey or blue-grey cloth overalls and ankle boots, an order amended in October 1816 to dark grey kersey overalls.

Household Cavalry

In this period the Household Cavalry's dress, or portions of it, underwent three changes, in 1812,

in 1814 and in 1817. Although the Blues did not attain to the full honours and privileges of Household troops until 1820, they were brigaded with the two regiments of Life Guards on active service, and since their uniform, save for the reversed colours, closely paralleled the latter from 1814, they will henceforth be considered under this heading.

For the first dress, worn by the service squadrons of the Life Guards that sailed to the Peninsula in late 1812, there is very little evidence for officers and practically none for the men. The old cocked hat was replaced by a crested helmet with flowing horsehair mane of the type shortly to be described for the Heavy Cavalry. Instead of the lapelled coat there was worn, at least by officers, a short-tailed jacket, apparently double-breasted since it had two rows of buttons down the front, the buttons connected horizontally by gold looping. The collar and round cuffs had square-ended gold loops and an aiguillette was attached to the right shoulder. Details of the men's jackets are unknown but they had blue and yellow woven waist sashes in contrast to the crimson and gold for officers. Grey overalls, or 'pantaloon trousers',

Private, 1st Life Guards, in the dress uniform adopted from 1814, and trumpeter in state dress. The scarlet, single-breasted jacket was laced down the front, fastening with hooks and eyes. Housings blue, laced gold. Sheepskin white with scarlet scalloped border. Engraving after C Hamilton Smith.

were worn with short boots on service, but the white breeches and jack-boots were retained for 'the King's Life Guard, royal escorts, guards of honour and State occasions'. The muskets, bayonets and large horse-pistols formerly carried were replaced by carbines and smaller calibre pistols.

While the Life Guards seem to have been equipped with new clothing for the Peninsular campaign, it would appear that the Blues fought in Spain in their old dress with cocked hats, although, for officers at least, there is evidence of their having the more serviceable overalls. However, when the 1812 uniform was revised after the return of the Household Cavalry to England in mid-1814, the Blues were kitted out before the Life Guards with the altered dress that was to be worn by all the Household Cavalry in the Waterloo campaign the following year.

The helmet taken into use in 1814, essentially the same for all three regiments, had a black leather skull with metal peak and fittings (gilt for officers, brass for the men), which consisted of three rows of scales round the base of the skull, with chin-scales attached by rosettes, a front plate with double foliated border bearing the Royal cypher, reversed and interlaced, with the crown above and an oval plaque below displaying the regimental title, and a fluted crest holding a silken or worsted 'chenille' of blue sandwiched between crimson. At the left side was a white-over-red plume in a metal socket. Whereas the peak of the helmet for the Life Guards was metal, that of the Blues was apparently of leather bound with brass, though this may have only applied to the men.

All ranks had two uniforms, dress and undress (or frock), the helmet being worn with both. The latter was worn during the Waterloo campaign. The chief components of both were the same for all ranks, the officers' clothing being distinguished by superior materials and embellishments. Officers' gold lace, for example, was of the type known as 'diamond and vellum', whereas the men's was of a cheap tinselly quality and, in the Blues, may only have been of yellow worsted. The upper garment was a single-breasted jacket (or 'collett'), having short tails at the back with turnbacks. The dress version, which fastened down the front with hooks and eyes, had gauntlet cuffs and was laced round the top and front of the collar, down each side of the front opening and on the turnbacks and cuffs. The cuffs and turnbacks were in the facing colour (velvet for Life Guards officers), as was the collar in the Blues, which in

their case also had a gold loop and button. The Life Guards collar appears to have differed between the two regiments, the 1st having scarlet with a blue patch at the front, the 2nd having all blue. Officers' shoulder straps were of twisted gold cord, the men's of lace-covered cloth. With the dress jacket the men wore leather breeches— white in the Life Guards, buff in the Blues—and jack-boots. Officers wore the same for the special occasions mentioned earlier but, for 'duties not immediately connected with the Royal Person', grey overalls with a single gold lace stripe and ankle boots were ordered. Around the waist the men wore a girdle of yellow webbing with two scarlet stripes; the officers having a similar girdle in gold with three crimson stripes, or a waist sash with tasselled ends in the same colours, tying on the left side and, in the case of the Blues, with the tie covered by a large trefoil knot. Leather gauntlet gloves matching the breeches completed the dress uniform.

The undress jacket was the same shape as the dress collett but fastened in front with ten but-

---

PLATE 13: 1812–1819

34. Corporal (sergeant), 1st Life Guards, 1815.
35. Private, 10th (Prince of Wales's Own Royal) Light Dragoons (Hussars), 1815.
36. Private, 2nd Royal North British Dragoons, 1815.

This plate and the first two figures of the next are representative of the service dress worn in the Waterloo campaign and the changes that followed 1812. Figure 34 wears the 1814 Household Cavalry helmet and the undress uniform of frock collett and overalls with ankle boots, instead of the dress jacket, leather breeches and jacked boots. The pouch flap had a brass oval plate bearing the Royal arms. Figure 35, based on paintings by Denis Dighton and sketches by Norblin, wears a shako, introduced as an alternative to the fur cap, whose unsuitability for service had been proved in the Peninsula. The 15th Hussars also had scarlet shakos, the 7th blue, but by Waterloo these had worn out and both regiments wore their fur caps, as did the 18th. The jacket and pelisse now had five rows of buttons, the frame around them being a peculiarity of the 10th only. Not shown is the private's carbine, based on the Baker rifle with 20-in. barrel. The 1812 pattern jacket of Figure 36 has the pointed Dragoon cuff; Dragoon Guards having a gauntlet type. The bearskin caps may have had the feathers removed at Waterloo and Dighton shows some in oilskin covers. This was the only regiment permitted moustaches, other than Hussars.

34. Cpl (sgt), 1st Life Guards, 1815.

35. Pte, 10th Hussars, 1815.

36. Pte, 2nd Dragoons, 1815.

Officers and men, Royal Horse Guards (Blue), 1814, in dress jackets. The undress overalls are bright blue with gold stripes, though elsewhere they are shown as dark grey with red stripes. Sabretache and horse furniture scarlet, laced gold. Watercolour by Denis Dighton.

tons and had small round cuffs. The facing colour showed on the turnbacks (Life Guards only), cuffs, the men's shoulder straps, and patches at the front of the collar. Each patch and cuff had two gold lace loops and buttons. Officers' shoulder straps were the same as on the dress jacket. The Blues had buff turnbacks and buff piping all round the edges of the jacket. Corporals of the

Life Guards wore a sergeant's three-bar chevron on the right upper arm of this jacket and gold lace edging to the shoulder straps (see Fig. 34, Plate 13). All ranks of all three regiments wore dark grey overalls with a scarlet stripe, except Blues' officers who had a double stripe. The girdles were the same as in dress and short white or buff leather gloves replaced the gauntlets.

Accoutrements consisted of a pouch-belt, with carbine swivel for the men, and a waistbelt with slings for the sword and sabretache. Since December 1811, the waistbelt had been ordered for all ranks of all cavalry. In the Household and Heavy Cavalry the sabretache was suspended higher than in the Light Cavalry, the officers' dress pattern having three slings, their undress and the men's only two. The men's accoutrements were the same for dress and undress, the belts and slings being of whitened leather, or buff for the Blues, the pouch and sabretache of black leather with, for the Life Guards, a brass oval plate bearing the Royal arms, and the crowned Royal cypher on an eight-pointed brass star. The waistbelt had a snake clasp. The pouch-belts of the Blues retained the crimson flask cord. In undress the officers' belts, pouches and sabretaches were of the same plain materials, but the waistbelt clasp was gilt, rectangular and with a silver garter star; and the pouch and sabretache of the Life Guards bore a gilt Royal crest. Their dress belts and slings were covered with gold lace and had the same waistbelt clasp. The flap and outer face of the pouch and sabretache were covered in blue velvet for the Life Guards, scarlet or crimson velvet for the Blues; edged with gold lace and embroidered with a silver garter star upon a gold trophy of flags, arms and trumpets beneath the crown.

The sheepskin saddle cloth was black for officers and white for the men, the latter's having a red scalloped border in the 1st Life Guards, a blue border in the 2nd. The dress shabraques and holster covers for Life Guards and Blues were in the facing colour, edged with gold or yellow worsted lace with a central stripe matching the jacket, and embroidered with the crown and cypher. When the valise, of which details are unknown, was secured to the back of the saddle, the cloak was rolled across the holsters.

Arms carried by men included the 1796 Heavy Cavalry troopers' sword, the 1802 New Land pattern pistol with swivel ramrod, and the 1796 Heavy Cavalry carbine with 25-in. barrel. On service, officers used the 1796 Heavy Cavalry officers' sword, but from 1814, they had a weapon

Troop-sergeant-major and officer, 1st (Royal) Dragoons in the 1812 helmet, dress jacket and blue-grey overalls with red stripe worn on service. Note the pointed Dragoon cuffs as distinct from the Dragoon Guards' gauntlet cuffs. Watercolour by A Sauerweid.

based on the Continental cuirassiers' *pallasch* for parade wear. This was a straight, heavy sword with a gilt, half-basket guard in which was set an escutcheon bearing the crown and Royal crest. It had a brass scabbard.

The peace that followed Waterloo gave the Prince Regent the opportunity to inflict an even more magnificent and expensive dress upon his Household Cavalry. In 1817 a new 'Roman' helmet of polished steel, with brass ornaments and huge bearskin crest curling forwards over the top, was ordered for both regiments of Life Guards and the Blues. These were to be followed by grenadier caps, double-breasted coatees with long tails, claret-coloured overalls and the return of the cuirass. However, as this finery would continue throughout George IV's reign, it will be considered more fully under the next period.

Heavy Cavalry

The first pattern helmet ordered for Dragoon Guards and Dragoons in January 1812 was similar to the 1814 pattern, already mentioned for the Household Cavalry, with a chenille upon a fluted metal comb, but with a leather peak bound in gilt or brass. However, the chenille was pronounced 'in every way objectionable' and was replaced the following August by a black horsehair mane, similar to that worn by French dragoons. The leather skull, with rows of scales round the base, chin-scales and a front plate with cypher and oval plaque was like the Household Cavalry helmet but there was no plume or feather at the side (see Fig. 38, Plate 14).

The 2nd Dragoons were unaffected by the helmet changes and retained their bearskin caps. At the back, near the top was the badge of the white horse of Hanover on a circular piece of scarlet cloth. Below the brass front plate bearing the Royal arms was a leather peak, at the corners of which were brass chin-scales. The plume was all-white and the cap-lines were now gold or yellow to conform with the 1811 change from white to yellow lace. Denis Dighton's famous painting of the Greys at Waterloo shows the plumes removed and some men wearing oilskin covers over the whole cap.

The 1812 changes introduced a single-breasted collett similar in cut to the Household Cavalry's dress jacket, once again differing as far as officers and men were concerned in the quality of materials used: officers had gold or silver lace, the men had yellow or white. The Dragoon Guards had gauntlet cuffs (velvet for officers, as were their collars and turnbacks), whereas Dragoons' cuffs were pointed. Double lace with a coloured stripe in between was sewn down the front edges of the collar, on either side of the front opening, around the bottom, the turnbacks and the cuffs. Soldiers had laced shoulder straps in the facing colour, officers twisted gold or silver shoulder cords. The facings and lace of each regiment are given in Appendix 6. For parades all ranks wore white leather breeches with jack-boots, but grey overalls and ankle boots on other occasions; the

overalls were usually strapped round the bottoms and up the inside leg with leather, officers having a single scarlet, gold or silver stripe, the men generally having two scarlet stripes, or, in the case of the 2nd Dragoons, two blue stripes with buttons in between. Officers' dress girdles were the same as for the Household Cavalry, but in marching order a plain crimson waist sash was worn. Soldiers' girdles were of yellow webbing with stripes in the facing colour, or scarlet stripes if the facings were yellow. All ranks had very full scarlet cloaks, without sleeves, collars in the facing colour and a cape over the shoulders. When rolled up this was strapped to the back of the saddle, or over the holsters when the valise was carried. The wearing of gloves followed the system in the Household Cavalry.

In addition to their dress uniform, the men had a forage cap and a stable jacket. The former was a plain blue, round or 'muffin' cap with a coloured band. Those of the Greys, according to a Waterloo painting by Howe, had a red band with a yellow vandyke and a red tourie on top; while a

---

PLATE 14: 1812–1819

37. Private, 11th Light Dragoons, 1817.
38. Officer, 1st (King's) Dragoon Guards, 1815.
39. Private, 9th Light Dragoons (Lancers), 1817.

The central figure, based on an officer's portrait, illustrates the second version of the 1812 Heavy Cavalry helmet and the Dragoon Guards jacket or collett, with the undress sash, pantaloons, belts and sabretache as worn during the Waterloo campaign. The sword has the so-called 'honeysuckle' hilt. Figure 37 wears the entirely new dress ordered for Light Dragoons from 1812. The lapelled jacket has very short tails at the rear with turnbacks, a white fringe or 'waterfall' at the waist and slash pockets, each with three buttons. The shako's central device with Roman numeral was adopted instead of the cartwheel design after Waterloo. The cap-lines were gold or yellow regardless of the lace colour. This and Figure 39 are based on drawings by Denis Dighton who shows single trouser stripes but some authorities indicate double stripes. The first British lancer uniform, in Figure 39, has a jacket very similar to that of the Light Dragoons except for the collar lace and shoulder scales. Dighton's drawing shows round cuffs and a single trouser stripe, but in a watercolour of officers done at the same date the cuffs are pointed and the stripes double. The same differences between officers and men appear in a print of the 19th Lancers at this date. The pouch-belt for lancers had no carbine swivel.

1812-1819

37. Pte, 11th Light Dragoons, 1817.

38. Offr, 1st Dragoon Guards, 1815.

39. Pte, 9th Lancers, 1817.

*Private, 3rd (King's Own) Dragoons in the 1812
uniform with dress breeches and jacked boots, showing
the rear view of the heavy cavalry jacket. Note the
carbine and pouch-belt and the sword belt worn under
the girdle. Facings, horse furniture blue, lace yellow.
Engraving after C Hamilton Smith.*

painting of the 4th Dragoon Guards dated slightly
later, 1824, shows the same cap with a white
band, presumably to match the regimental lace
which was white. The stable jacket is shown in a
watercolour by Hamilton Smith as a plain, waist
length red garment with collar and cuffs in the
facing colour, but in the Howe painting the Greys
have all-white jackets. Officers also had a round
forage cap, but theirs was made of fur with gold or
silver band and a tassel hanging from the crown;
this was worn with a heavily braided, double-
breasted long blue coat, confusingly called a
pelisse-coat, and if on duty, with a crimson waist
sash, black leather sword belt and pouch-belt.

Heavy Cavalry accoutrements were of the same
type as the Household Cavalry's including the
sabretache. Those worn by officers in dress had
laced belts and slings, and cloth-covered, lace-
edged sabretaches and pouches bearing appropri-
ate regimental insignia. The waistbelt clasps for
all ranks were usually rectangular, gilt or brass
with the Royal cypher or special device, although
the officers' undress belts of the King's Dragoon
Guards are shown in two paintings with snake
clasps. Notwithstanding the 1811 order that
Heavy Cavalry should buckle their sabretaches
high, several illustrations c 1815 show them hanging at about calf-level, as affected by the Light
Cavalry. Weapons were as described for the
Household regiments and the horse furniture also
followed the same principles of shabraques and
holster covers in the facing colour, laced all round
and with regimental devices, but not, apparently,
with sheepskins. The valise, which formerly had
been rectangular, was now cylindrical and of red
cloth, with the abbreviated title at the ends: the
Greys, for example, as 2nd Royal North British
Dragoons had $N_D^R B$ in blue letters, the 1st King's
Dragoon Guards KGD.

The equipment carried on man and horse on
service is well illustrated in Denis Dighton's
painting of the Greys at Waterloo. On the man
went a pouch-belt with its carbine swivel, waistbelt with sword and sabretache, and, over his
right shoulder, a haversack and water bottle (see
Fig. 36, Plate 13). On his mount, apart from the
bridle, horse-blanket, saddle with holsters, carbine bucket and horseshoe wallet attached to it,
there was the rolled red cloak over the holsters
with the horse's nosebag strapped to it, the red
valise with canvas waterdeck wrapped round it to
which the mess-tin in its black cover was attached, and the twin cornsacks tied between the
man and the valise.

The chief alteration in the post-Waterloo
period, until the next dress change, was the
aforementioned adoption of overalls for all purposes. In addition, battle honours awarded for the
Napoleonic War were placed on helmets and
appointments (pouches and sabretaches); an example occurs in a painting by Denis Dighton of
the Greys in 1816 with a 'WATERLOO' scroll added
to their bearskin caps above the front plate.

Light Dragoons
The Tarleton helmets and braided jackets of the
Light Dragoons, so favoured by George III, were
swept away by his son who preferred an entirely
new costume, the chief characteristic of which

Officer, 9th Light Dragoons in review order, showing the new uniform of 1812 which replaced the helmet and looped jacket. Facings crimson, lace gold, horse furniture dark blue, black sheepskin with crimson scalloped border. Engraving after C Hamilton Smith.

the top was a band of gold/yellow or silver/white lace, with a gold or yellow cockade in front below a white-over-red plume in a metal socket. From the cockade a braid loop of the same material descended to a regimental button set in the centre of a braid cartwheel. The metal chin-scales matched the lace but the cap-lines were gold or yellow for all regiments. A black oilskin cover was provided for marching order.

The jacket's cut was the same for officers and men, differing only in the quality of the cloth and lace. Of blue cloth, it was double-breasted, with small, short skirts at the rear; and unlaced collar, lapels, pointed cuffs and turnbacks in the facing colour. The latter and the lace/button colour for each regiment are given in Appendix 5. When the lapels were buttoned back to form a plastron in the facing colour, the front was fastened by hooks and eyes (see Fig. 37, Plate 14), but in marching order they were buttoned across so that only the blue showed. Each skirt had a slashed pocket flap with three vertical buttons, connected at waist level by a fringe, or 'waterfall' in the lace colour. The piping on the back seams of the coat and sleeves, and on the pockets, matched the facings. There were two buttons at the cuff, ten on each lapel, and one on each shoulder for the epaulette which was laced and fringed.

Epaulettes for officers were alike, but in accordance with an order of December 1811, field officers were to be distinguished by embroidered badges in reverse metal to the lace. A colonel was to have a crown and star, a lieutenant-colonel a crown, and a major a star. Captains and subalterns were indistinguishable, being without badges. This order applied only to Light Dragoons who alone of the Cavalry at this date wore epaulettes.

In addition to their dress jackets, officers had for service wear what was called a pelisse but which was really a garment similar to the jacket, but with the tops of the lapels cut square, and lined and faced in the facing colour with a rough material known as 'shag'. For undress they had a pelisse-coat of the type already described for the Heavies.

On parades all ranks wore white leather breeches, or buff for regiments so faced, with hussar boots, which for officers were bound and tasselled in regimental lace. For all other purposes ankle boots and grey overalls were customary; the latter had double or single stripes of lace for officers, in the facing colour for soldiers. Around the waist went a girdle, striped in crimson

was the dislike it inspired in its wearers on account of its French aspect. The customary delays between approval and issue followed, particularly for regiments fighting in Spain, so that, although the 9th and 13th had the new clothing, or most of it, by the end of 1812, other regiments overseas did not receive it until returning home in 1814. There were also instances of mixed dress, old and new, being worn in the Peninsula. Regiments in India may have kept the old dress even longer, as suggested by a watercolour of an officer of the 17th of this period still wearing the braided French grey jacket.

The new headdress was a black felt 'chaco cap', widening at the top, with a flattish peak in front and a false, turned-up peak at the back. Round and gold for officers, in blue and the facing colour for the men. The cloaks were blue, with a standing collar in the facing colour.

Accoutrements were as described for the Heavies. Officers' dress belts were laced, with a central stripe matching the facings, and their pouch-belts were fitted with silver pickers and chains. The dress sabretache was blue, edged with lace and embroidered with a crowned double cypher and small spray of laurel leaves. Shabraques were blue, lace-edged, with rounded corners and a crowned cypher over the regimental initials in the corners. Over it went a sheepskin, white for soldiers, black with red edging for officers. The cylindrical blue valise was piped and lettered in the facing colour. Weapons consisted of the 1796 Light Cavalry sabre, a pistol and, for the men, the 16-in. barrelled Paget carbine. When mounted, the latter was always strapped on butt uppermost.

Hussars

Although there were numerous regimental changes of detail in this period, the basic features of hussar dress and accoutrements underwent little change. The men's jackets acquired the five rows of buttons worn by officers (except in the 18th), and the facings of the 7th were altered to blue in 1812, the same affecting the 10th in 1814, three years after they had changed from yellow to scarlet on being designated a Royal regiment once the Prince of Wales became Regent. Therefore, the jackets of these two regiments had no contrasting facing colour and their lace and loopings became gold or yellow. Their men's sashes also changed to crimson and yellow. Apart from head-dress and insignia, their most obvious distinguishing features were now the colour of the pelisse fur (see Appendix 5) and the dark blue nether garments assumed by the 7th, in contrast to the white breeches or grey overalls of other regiments.

The main difference between this period and the last is one already touched on in the previous section—the increasing use of a shako instead of the fur cap. The hussar shako was similar to the Light Dragoons type but covered in cloth: blue for the 7th, scarlet for the 10th and 15th. These coloured shakos were worn by the 7th and 15th when the Hussar regiments returned to the Peninsula in 1813, but the 10th had to make do with black shakos. However, by 1815 the 10th were re-equipped with the scarlet shako (see Fig. 35, Plate 13), whereas the 7th and 15th, whose shakos were by then worn out, reverted to the fur cap for the Waterloo campaign. The 18th,

whose dress apparently was always below the standard of the other three regiments, never seem to have had shakos at all and adhered to their fur caps. By 1815 the practice of indicating officers' rank by rows of interlinked circles round the top of the shako had come into use, as can be seen in the figures of Lord Paget and an officer of the 10th in Denis Dighton's painting of the Light Cavalry charging at Waterloo.

In the post-war years the shako was resumed by all regiments except the 18th, but by 1819, while the 7th and 15th had them in blue and scarlet respectively, the 10th had reverted to black, with a drooping plume in the same colour, the other two having an upright white-over-red feather.

Accoutrements generally were unchanged but the facing cloth of the dress sabretaches and pouches for officers of the 7th was altered from white to scarlet, a colour shared with the 10th and 15th, although the latter's pouch flap was silver; the 18th retaining blue. These articles became more richly embellished, particularly after the peace when battle honours were added to them. Officers' horse furniture, too, underwent some changes: dress saddle-cloths for the 7th and 10th were to be of leopardskin, undress of black sheepskin; their dress shabraques were, respectively, blue bordered with a red vandyke, and scarlet, both edged with gold lace and embellished with regimental devices. The 15th and 18th contented themselves with black sheepskin saddle-cloths and lace-edged blue shabraques, the 15th also having a red vandyke border.

Left: Light Dragoons in India. Privates of the (from left) 24th, 8th and 22nd in hot-weather white shakos. The French-grey looped jackets, formerly worn in hot climates, were discontinued after the introduction of the 1812 uniform. Facings (from left) grey, scarlet, pink. Engraving after C Hamilton Smith.

Right: Private, 7th (Queen's Own) Light Dragoons (Hussars) in service dress. By 1815 this regiment's white facings and lace had changed to blue and yellow, and the blue-grey overalls to dark blue. Engraving after C Hamilton Smith.

Below: The 10th (Prince of Wales's Own Royal) Light Dragoons (Hussars) on service in Spain, 1813. Except for the two central figures in forage caps, the others wear the peakless black shakos or castor caps. These were worn in the field instead of the fur cap until the issue of the scarlet shako before Waterloo. The jackets have the red facings worn between 1811–1814. Note the booted overalls, blue-grey with red stripes.

Hussars' weapons followed those of the Light Dragoons, except for the Mameluke sabre carried by officers at levées and in review order, and the use by the 7th and 10th of a carbine-bore Baker rifle with 20-in. barrel during the Waterloo campaign. Camp equipage for active service was similar to that described for the Heavies, as can be noted from the recorded issue to the 7th, just before the Waterloo campaign, of one canteen (water bottle) and strap, one haversack and one blanket per man, with one camp kettle and one billhook for every five men.

Lancers

The decision in 1816 to convert the 9th, 12th, 16th and 23rd Light Dragoons to Lancers afforded opportunity for yet another ostentatious cavalry dress, with little consideration for its wearers' comfort or the expense involved in the conversion. At first the latter was taken into some account, as the jacket remained as it had been for Light Dragoons, worn with the same girdle and the regiments concerned retaining their facings, except for the 12th, who changed from yellow with silver lace to scarlet with gold. The novelty of the costume lay in the adoption of the lancer cap, based on the square-topped Polish 'schapska', worn by all foreign lancers, and the replacement of overalls by generously cut 'Cossack' trousers. Thus the regiments chosen for conversion, having lost in 1812 a headdress of wholly English character in favour of a French-style cap, were now to be tricked out in a costume which originated in eastern Europe. A private of the 9th in 1817 appears in Fig. 39, Plate 14 but it is not proposed to discuss the dress in any detail here, since it had exaggerated elements more typical of, and hence more suitably considered under the next and more flamboyant period. It might, however, be mentioned that the ordinary lancer, now burdened with lance and sabre, was at least relieved of his carbine.

Dress 1820–1828

General

The accession of the Prince Regent as George IV heralded a period in which, with peace in Europe and overseas, the dress of the Army reached heights of costliness and impracticability never seen before or since. Headgear increased in height and weight, garments were padded and tightened to accentuate, even exaggerate, the natural figure, and embellishments such as lace, plumes, elaborate cap-lines and aiguillettes proliferated. Nowhere was this more evident than in the Cavalry, particularly in the Hussars and Lancers.

This period also saw the issue, in 1822, of the first dress regulations for officers, which incorporated changes that had been taking place since the end of the Napoleonic War. Such regulations listed three orders of dress for officers: *full dress*, worn only at Court, levées and attendance at the King's Drawing Room, *dress*, for reviews and ceremonial occasions, and *undress*, for field days and ordinary occasions. Soldiers merely had dress and undress.

Accoutrements for cavalrymen of all types continued to consist of the pouch-belt, with carbine swivel for the men, except Lancers, and the waistbelt for sword and sabretache, both suspended by slings; the waistbelt was broader in the Heavy Cavalry and had a rectangular clasp, the Light Cavalry usually having a snake clasp. Officers' dress belts were laced and, in the Heavies, edged with the facing colour, while the Light Cavalry had a central stripe of the same. The cloth fronts of sabretaches and the flaps of pouches became more richly decorated with cyphers, regimental insignia and battle honours, all bordered with lace. The men's belts were now all of whitened leather, their pouches and sabretaches of black.

New pattern swords were approved in this period but the firearms remained as before until 1828 when a report recommended a universal carbine and the abolition of the single pistol carried by the men.

Household Cavalry

The uniform of the Blues was now closely assimilated to that of the 1st and 2nd Life Guards, though of course in reversed colours and with one important and some minor exceptions. In 1817 all three regiments had adopted new helmets as described above. In 1820 a grenadier bearskin cap was approved for the Life Guards and their helmets were to be preserved in store. However, in the following year the helmets were resumed for guards and ordinary duties, the fur cap being reserved for ceremonial occasions. These two headdresses were the prerogative of the Life Guards only, the Blues having the helmet for all occasions. The grenadier cap was some 20 in. high, and was furnished with a short peak and gilt plate with the Royal arms in front, gold plaited cap-lines with flounders and tassels, a gilt grenade

at the back near the top, and a white feather issuing from a socket at the left side and passing over the top of the cap; gilt chin-scales secured it on the head.

The two regiments of Life Guards were virtually indistinguishable from a distance but nevertheless there were a number of minor differences, such as insignia, officers' lace patterns and horse furniture. The short-tailed jacket of the former period was replaced by a long-tailed coatee, with gold-embroidered Prussian collar, gauntlet cuffs and turnbacks in the facing colour (white in the Blues). Officers were distinguished by epaulettes with gold-embroidered strap, crescent and bullion fringe, and a gold aiguillette at the right shoulder. The men had brass shoulder scales and crescent, NCOs having an aiguillette at the left shoulder. The cuffs and front of the coatee were concealed by white leather gauntlet gloves and the re-introduction of the cuirass, steel back-and-breast, with edgings in the facing colour and, for Life Guards only, until about 1825, a large brass

Officers, 2nd Life Guards. Watercolour by Denis Dighton dated 1817 which, since the cuirass was not worn until 1821, probably shows the projected new uniform of this regiment. The 1817 pattern helmet is worn with the new double-breasted coatee. The officer at left with the cocked hat is in full (or court) dress.

sunburst ornament on the front. The cuirass also hid most of the officers' waist sashes (see Fig. 41, Plate 15).

Nether garments were of two types: either white breeches with jack-boots, or, for the Life Guards, claret overalls with broad scarlet stripe (gold for officers in dress). Contemporary pictures show both worn with the grenadier cap and the helmet. A painting of the Blues by Denis Dighton dated 1821 shows the same breeches and boots but the overalls are bright blue with a scarlet stripe (see Fig 40, Plate 15).

The Blues' belts, for so long buff, were now changed to white. Officers' dress sabretaches acquired honours for the late war and the 2nd Life

Guards received a new badge, a grenade, which also appeared on the pouch flap. Shabraques of the two Life Guards regiments were embroidered with the same badges as the sabretaches with the numerals 1 and 2 respectively, being further distinguished by the 1st Regiment having pointed corners, the 2nd rounded. The Blues' shabraque was scarlet, bordered with two gold laces showing a blue light and scarlet outer edging, with a re-versed Royal cypher surmounted by a scroll 'PENINSULA' and a crown, and RHG on the hind corners.

In the 1822 dress regulations three swords were prescribed for Life Guards officers: in full dress, a small sword with boatshell guard; in dress, the heavy 'pallasch' already mentioned; and in un-dress, a slightly curved sword with open shell guard. Blues officers had the same dress sword but the full dress type also served them for undress. In 1820 a new sword with brass-studded steel guard was approved for men of the 1st Life Guards, but the 2nd appear to have had a four-bar brass-hilted sword. The Blues weapon is uncer-tain, but the aforementioned Dighton painting shows a trooper with what seems to be the Heavy Cavalry 1796 pattern.

Other uniform items appear in contemporary pictures: for officers, a peaked, broad-crowned forage cap, either all black or with an oilskin cover, and a single-breasted blue frock coat; for men of the Life Guards, a claret forage cap (with gold band for NCOs, scarlet for troopers, without a peak) and a scarlet stable jacket with plain blue collar and cuffs and nine buttons in front; for the Blues, a blue forage cap with yellow band and blue stable jacket faced scarlet.

Heavy Cavalry

The date of introduction for the Heavy Cavalry's new helmet is uncertain, but it was between 1818–1820. The shape and curling bearskin crest of the new helmet resembled that of the House-hold Cavalry, but the skull and comb were painted black, with a gilt or brass fluted plate in front, binding to the peak, chin-scales and laurel leaf ornamentation on either side. The 2nd Dra-goons received a new bearskin cap, rather larger than before, and resembling that of the Life Guards but quite plain at the back without the grenade (see Fig. 43, Plate 16).

The short jacket gave way to a coatee with long skirts at the rear. In some respects it resembled the pre-1812 garment, being single-breasted with eight buttons and graduated lace loops down the front. It had chevron loops with buttons—four for Dragoon Guards, three for Dragoons—above the cuffs and on the skirts. The Prussian collar, which also had a loop and button, was laced all round, as were the turnbacks. The collar, cuffs and turn-backs were in the facing colour and the lace was gold or silver for officers, yellow or white for the men with a stripe in the facing colour. Details are given in Appendix 6. Officers had twisted gold cord shoulder straps with an aiguillette at the right shoulder. From 1824 brass shoulder scales were ordered for all Heavy Dragoons.

Although officers still had cocked hats, breeches and stockings for wear in full dress, the normal netherwear for all ranks was blue-grey overalls, of cossack cut, with $1\frac{3}{4}$-in. laced stripe. From 1822 the stripe changed to the facing colour for the men but reverted to lace in 1827. A waist girdle was worn, as in the previous period, but

---

PLATE 15: 1820–1828

40. Private, Royal Horse Guards (The Blues), 1821.

41. Officer, 2nd Life Guards, 1822.

42. Private, 7th (Queen's Own) Light Dragoons (Hussars), 1825.

This and the following plate are representative of the extravagant George IV period. Figure 40, based on a Denis Dighton watercolour, has the 'Roman' helmet introduced for the Household Cavalry in 1817; the two regiments of Life Guards also having the grenadier cap in Figure 41 for certain ceremonial occasions. Over the double-breasted coatee is worn the re-introduced cuirass, officers in the Life Guards having theirs embellished with a sunburst. For certain duties white leather breeches and jacked boots were worn instead of the overalls shown here. The buff accoutrements, so long worn by the Blues, were now white, the pouch-belt having the crimson flask-cord. The waistbelt with slings for sword and sabretache is concealed by the cuirass. The sword in Figure 41 is the 'pallasch' type worn in dress. His aiguillette, signifying rank, is worn at the right shoulder, NCOs having theirs at the left. His cap had a gilt grenade embroidered on the back near the top. This figure is from a watercolour by W Heath. The cuffs of both uniforms are shown in detail. All of these uniforms have the Prussian collar assumed in this period, so that the stock only showed above the upper edge. Figure 42, also based on D Dighton, shows the shako, now worn by all Hussars, in an oilskin cover as required for marching order. The dark blue overalls were only worn by the 7th Hussars. This private's carbine is not illustrated.

40. Pte, Royal Horse Guards, 1821.

41. Offr, 2nd Life Guards, 1822.

42. Pte, 7th Hussars, 1825.

this was largely obscured by the waistbelt and was discontinued in 1827.

Pictorial evidence as to the Heavies' horse furniture is slight but a letter dated 1823 stated that 'housings and holster caps have not been generally supplied to the Heavy Cavalry' and indicated that they might be re-introduced.

Dress and undress swords were ordered for officers under the 1822 regulations: the former was the light, boatshell-hilted pattern of 1796; the latter had a slightly curved blade, steel scroll-pattern guard and steel scabbard. The dress sword also served for full dress. For the men a new pattern was approved in 1821: slightly curved blade, steel bowl guard and steel scabbard. However, so extensive were stocks of the 1796 sword, that the new weapon was not actually issued until 1832–1836.

For undress, officers had a single-breasted, scarlet shell or stable jacket fastening with hooks and eyes, laced all round the edges, with Prussian collar and pointed cuffs in the facing colour also laced round, and gold 'gimp' shoulder straps. As an alternative they had a blue frock coat with braided loops. The forage cap was blue, with lace band and patent leather peak. The men's blue caps had yellow or white bands and no peaks and their stable jackets were as described for the Life Guards. All ranks wore the blue-grey overalls with stripe in winter, but white in summer. In undress, officers' accoutrements were of plain white and black leather like the men's. Cloaks were scarlet, lined white with collars in the facing colour.

Light Dragoons

After Waterloo the 1812 shako acquired various embellishments, such as regimental numerals in Roman figures, or insignia and battle honours; the 17th, for example, before becoming Lancers in 1822 dispensed entirely with the cartwheel and braid loops in favour of their death's head. This pattern was superseded by another, broadly similar, which had a more drooping peak and was more bell-topped in shape, being 8 in. (and from 1826 9 in.) deep and 11 in. across the top. It had broad lace round the top, chin-scales, gold or yellow cap-lines, and, on the front, a double Royal cypher within the garter, decorated with rose, thistle and shamrock, connected by a chain loop with the rosette or boss on the band above. The upright plume gave way to a falling one in the same colours.

The uniform was basically as before, but with

Officer, 5th (Princess Charlotte of Wales's) Dragoon Guards in the new, black-painted Heavy Cavalry helmet, single-breasted coatee laced across the front, and 'cossack' trousers of the 1822 regulations. Facings green, lace gold, buttons in pairs. Lithograph after William Heath.

the jacket lapels cut to give a more waisted effect, a Prussian collar, and with richer embroidery for officers. Facings and lace are given in Appendix 5. Overalls were described in the 1822 regulations as 'sky-blue', but blue-grey from 1826, with a double stripe (each $\frac{3}{4}$-in. wide), in the same materials as for the Heavies. The girdles were unchanged.

Unlike the Heavies, Light Dragoons continued with the blue shabraques, which, with the officers' sabretaches, became more decorative with honours added. The waistbelts were worn so that, in front they were either concealed by the girdle or showed just below it, and behind passed underneath the jacket's small skirts. The 1822 regulations prescribed a new sword for all Light Cavalry officers with three-bar steel hilt and scabbard. A similar sword had been introduced in the previous year for all Light Cavalry soldiers but several years elapsed before issue. Sword knots for officers were of crimson and gold cord with gold bullion tassel, for men buff leather.

Undress uniforms for all ranks were in the same style as the Heavies but in blue and piped on the seams in the facing colour. The men's jackets fastened with buttons, the officers' with hooks and eyes but with a row of studs showing between the laced edges. Winter overalls were the same as in dress but with stripes of the facing colour for officers; in summer white was worn. Cloaks were blue, lined red with collars in the facing colour.

It will be remembered that from 1812 trumpeters were dressed similarly to the rank and file, but a painting of the 4th Light Dragoons in 1822 by Pardon shows a negro trumpeter with red shako, white jacket faced and lapelled red, and red trousers (see Fig. 45, Plate 16).

Hussars

With the disbandment of the 18th Hussars in 1821 the fur cap ceased to be worn and shakos became the regulation headdress. The shako for Hussars was similar in construction to the Light Dragoon pattern but with a falling black plume (of cock's feathers for officers). Soldiers' caps had a lace band round the top but officers' caps had rows of interlinked circles. In the 15th the body of the shako was covered with scarlet cloth. In an 1822 painting by Denis Dighton the plumes are shown as upright, white-over-red; but an officer's portrait of 1826 shows the black cock's feathers, his rank, lieutenant-colonel, indicated by three bands of gold lace instead of the rings. Cap-lines, which encircled the shako three times,

were gold or yellow regardless of a regiment's lace, although the 8th, converted to Hussars in 1823, briefly had silver lines. Officers' peaks were edged with lace, as were the turned-up ones at the back, but the men's were plain. The fronts bore a braided cartwheel, connected to the rosette at the top by a chain loop. Oilskin covers were worn in marching order (see Fig. 42, Plate 15).

Except for a Prussian collar, the jackets remained the same, with five rows of buttons in front; although officers' lace became more elaborate (its intricacies on the cuff almost reaching to the elbow), and the dull gold or silver loopings on the front were arranged to give the popular waisted effect, and highlighted by bright braid between them, the whole set on so closely that little of the blue showed through. The fur trimming of the pelisse was ordered to be grey for all

Officer's charger, groom and horse furniture of the 4th (Queen's Own) Light Dragoons, 1822, with officers, a trumpeter (see Plate 16) and the regiment in the background. Shabraque and sabretache dark blue, silver embroidery. Painting, possibly by J Pardon.

regiments but from 1823 the 10th were permitted white for all ranks and the 15th were allowed to retain black. Denis Dighton's painting of the 7th, c 1825, also shows black fur. The same artist does, however, portray the 8th in its first hussar dress with grey fur, also with crimson linings to the officers' pelisses. Some regimental orders of the 15th, dated 1827, stated that, when the men had their pelisses slung, the whole of the jacket collar was to be revealed and the left edge of the pelisse was to hang between the middle and left rows of buttons on the jackets.

Officers in full dress wore scarlet pantaloons richly embroidered on the thighs, with Hessian boots; in dress, scarlet cossack trousers with regimental lace up the seams were worn; in undress, blue-grey cossacks with the same lace. In the 7th, dark blue replaced scarlet. The men's overalls were of the general cavalry pattern already described. The barrel sash was as before.

Officers' sabretaches for all four regiments were faced scarlet, with lace and embroidery, gold for the 7th and 10th, silver for the 8th and 15th. According to orders for the 15th, the sabretache was to hang so that a man at attention could touch the top with his middle finger. Officers' belts were generally lace-covered with scarlet central stripe or edging, but the 10th's pouch-belt was black patent leather covered with gilt chain. Shabraque corners for the Hussars were pointed, in contrast to the Light Dragoons' which were rounded; and were blue for the 7th and 8th, scarlet for the 10th and 15th, all with lace and embroidery in the regimental colour. In marching order the hind corners were looped up. All officers had leopardskin saddle-cloths, the men white sheepskin. Hussar swords were as for the Light Dragoons but in levée dress officers carried a Mameluke-hilted sabre.

Hussar undress was similar to that of Light Dragoons. Dighton's painting of the 7th has an officer in the blue frock with braiding, probably black, across the chest, white overalls and plain blue forage cap, apparently without a peak. The 15th's regimental orders of 1827 state that, whereas the shako was to be worn straight, the forage cap was to be set obliquely over the right eye.

The same orders provide interesting information as to what was to be worn in different orders of dress in summer and winter; the latter lasting from 1st November to 14th April. In 'review order all year round', all ranks were to wear the shako with dress jacket and sash, slung pelisse; officers scarlet cossacks, men best overalls. Re-

view marching order was identical but with the valise carried on the horse. Officers at levées or attending H.M. drawing room, wore full dress (pantaloons and Hessians), but at balls they wore scarlet cossacks. Marching order required the covered shako with plume, men otherwise in dress, officers in undress jackets with sash and pelisse; valise on the horse. In light marching order the pelisse was dispensed with in summer, but in winter it was worn buttoned up; no plumes on the shako. Field day order was the same but with plumes and no shabraques. Forage caps and undress uniform, with minor variations such as white trousers in summer, were the rule for routine duties like field exercise, riding school, watering parades and stable duties. The white trousers were also worn in summer for full dress parades on foot, with the dress jacket and sash, but without pelisse.

Lancers
The lancer cap described in the 1822 regulations had a trencher top 10 in. square in the facing

---

PLATE 16: 1820–1828

43. **Sergeant-Major, 2nd Royal North British Dragoons, 1821.**
44. **Officer, 17th Light Dragoons (Lancers), 1825.**
45. **Trumpeter, 4th (Queen's Own) Light Dragoons, 1822.**

Figure 43, from an anonymous painting, shows the Heavy Cavalry coatee with Prussian collar and lace loopings which superseded the 1812 jacket. The bearskin cap is larger than previously; other Heavy Cavalry having the helmet in Figure 46. The gold coatee lace befits the regiment's senior NCO but lower ranks had yellow. Figure 44 is based on a Denis Dighton watercolour and three officers' portraits and is generally in accord with the 1822 Dress Regulations. The latter required the aiguillette to be worn at the right shoulder but the sources mentioned all show the 17th's officers wearing it at the left; in each case the aiguillette is arranged slightly differently. Figure 44 wears the full dress trousers and sword scabbard as opposed to the blue-grey type and steel scabbard of dress. The cap plume changed in 1826 from cock's to swan's feathers. The white lapels could be buttoned over blue for marching order or in bad weather. Figure 45, from a painting by Pardon, shows the cut of the Light Dragoon uniform in this period, but in the exotic colours used for trumpeters of this regiment, which continued the earlier tradition of enlisting negroes for this duty.

43. Sgt-Major, 2nd Dragoons, 1821.

44. Offr, 17th Lancers, 1825.

45. Tptr, 4th Light Dragoons, 1822.

colour (see Appendix 5), the fluted sides of which tapered down to a slender waist encircled in regimental lace, from where cords in the lace colour ascended the four angles to run transversely across the top. The black leather skull had a peak in front and another turned up behind. For officers the peaks were edged with broad and narrow braiding in the lace colour. Above the front peak was a gilt or silver fluted metal plate with the Royal arms and regimental insignia; chin-scales were secured by lion's heads and were worn either round the chin or looped up above the plate. On an officer's cap the space between the plate and the back peak was filled by lace. Caplines, fitted with olivets, flounders and tassels, were gold or yellow (regardless of the regimental lace colour) and descended from a ring on the right corner, to be fastened round the body in a number of different ways. At the left front of the top was a boss or rosette, from behind which sprang a drooping white and crimson or red plume: of horsehair for men, from 1822 of

cock's feathers for officers: swan's feathers from 1826.

The jackets were basically the same as the Light Dragoon pattern, including epaulettes, but the Prussian collar had two loops of regimental lace and the pointed cuffs were also laced round. Officers had a gold or silver aiguillette which, according to the regulations, was attached at the right shoulder, but there exist paintings of the 17th in which it is sometimes shown on the right, in others on the left (see Fig. 44, Plate 16). Yellow or white aiguillettes also appear to have been worn by men of the 12th and 17th respectively. The jacket could be worn with the facing colour showing on the lapels, giving the impression of a plastron, or buttoned across to show only blue as was the practice in marching order. Officers' girdles were striped crimson and gold, the men's blue and the facing colour.

All ranks wore cossack trousers, in blue-grey, with a double stripe in the facings for the men and officers' undress, in lace for officers' dress. For full dress, officers had cossacks in the facing colour with single $1\frac{3}{4}$-in. lace stripe, although from 1825 the 17th adopted dark blue cossacks instead of white.

Accoutrements followed the Light Cavalry pattern, the officers' dress belts being laced and striped as described above. Their pouch-belts were fitted with a silver plate, picker and chains, and their pouch flaps were silver with a crowned cypher in gilt. Their dress sabretaches were faced with blue cloth, edged and embroidered with regimental lace. Although the men had no need of a carbine swivel, the pouch was retained for pistol ammunition.

The shabraques were initially of Light Dragoon pattern but these gave way, at least for the 12th and 17th, to the hussar type with pointed ends. The sheepskin saddle-cloths were black for officers and white for men in the 9th, black for all in the 12th, white for all in the 17th; the 16th's at this time are uncertain.

The men were armed with the 1821 Light

Cavalry sword, a pistol and the lance, which was fitted with a red and white pennon, or flag. At first the lance was a 16-ft spear with ash shaft, but was soon reduced to 9 ft. Officers had three swords: for full dress, a Mameluke-hilted sabre in a crimson velvet (blue for the 17th), gilt-mounted scabbard; for dress, a similar weapon but in a steel scabbard; for undress the 1822 Light Cavalry officers' pattern. Sword knots for all three were crimson and gold cord, with gold acorn.

Undress followed the patterns described except that Lancer officers had a cap similiar to the dress cap but lower, and with no front plate or back peak, the skull being entirely laced round. Cloaks were as for Light Dragoons.

Although little is known of trumpeters' dress in this period, it is known that in the 17th they had all-red plumes, their girdles, cap lace and trumpet cords were red and yellow, and a mixed blue and white lace went all round the collar and cuffs.

Dress 1829–1839

General

The rising costs of uniform, particularly for officers, in the preceding period led to a complete review of it in 1827. The ensuing simplification began to take effect from 1828 and this, followed by William IV's desire to have the whole Army in red, resulted in major dress changes which notably affected the Light Cavalry, hitherto dressed in blue. The changes were promulgated in the 1831 officers' dress regulations, and were slightly revised in those of 1834. Three features common to all Line Cavalry were the abolition of grey overalls in favour of dark blue; the reduction of officers' uniforms to dress and undress; and the substitution of all silver lace and embroidery for gold. Fixed breadths of lace were established for all Line Cavalry.

Moustaches were forbidden for all regiments except Household Cavalry and Hussars, although this order was rescinded in 1839. The hair of NCOs and men was 'to be cut close at the sides and back of the head, instead of being worn in that bushy and unbecoming fashion adopted by some regiments'. Since this order was still being repeated in 1837 it would seem not to have been always obeyed.

The new dress of the men followed that of the officers in most respects, with the usual differences of inferior materials and the use of yellow lace, braid and cord instead of gold, and brass instead of gilt. Equipment continued without any

significant changes in its design, although the width of the belts varied between the different branches. In 1834 certain economies were ordered for the men: sabretaches were to be universal in the Light Dragoons and Hussars but confined to NCOs in the Heavies and Lancers; the swords of Heavy Cavalry only were to have a hilt lining; cloaks were to be without sleeves; and while all Light Cavalry were to have sheepskins and shabraques, the Heavies were to have only a leather flounce.

Except for Household Cavalry officers, swords remained unchanged. Indeed, the 1821 officers' undress swords (both types) would continue virtually unaltered until 1896, though the blades would receive some modifications. Nevertheless in 1831 the boat-hilted dress sword of the Heavies and the Mameluke sabres of Lancers and Hussars were officially discontinued but did not disappear entirely in practice. In 1828 a board of officers recommended the adoption of a universal carbine

PLATE 17: 1829–1839

46. Sergeant, 6th (Inniskilling) Dragoons, 1832.
47. Officer, 8th King's Royal Irish Light Dragoons (Hussars), 1832.
48. Private, 2nd Life Guards, 1833.

This and the next plate illustrate the 'scarlet' period instituted by William IV. In the Hussars this colour was confined to their pelisses, the blue jackets being retained as shown in Figure 47, based on Dubois Drahonet and Heath. This officer has the new, lower shako introduced for Light Cavalry from 1828, although the 7th Hussars kept the former, tall pattern. Regiments like the 8th, which hitherto had had silver lace, changed to gold from 1830. Figures 46 and 48, both based on Dubois Drahonet, have the helmet introduced in the former period, the Household Cavalry's being of polished steel. From 1834 the Heavies had a new brass helmet (see Figure 52) with the same, but removeable, bearskin crest. The Heavy Dragoon coatee is now plainer, following the removal of the chest lace after 1827. The tails at the rear had turnbacks in the facing colour edged with lace. The plain buckle of the waistbelt was only worn by the Inniskillings, other regiments having a rectangular plate. All three Household Cavalry regiments now had the bearskin cap, though plainer than before, for ceremonial, the helmet being reserved for guards and field days. The 2nd Life Guards was most obviously distinguished from the 1st by their blue flask-cords. All Cavalry trousers or overalls were now dark blue. The cuff detail of Figure 48 is shown separately.

46. Sgt, 6th Dragoons, 1832.

47. Offr, 8th Hussars, 1832.

48. Pte, 2nd Life Guards, 1833.

Cavalry officers, 1831, in the uniform favoured by William IV, of scarlet jackets for all Heavies, Light Dragoons and Lancers, scarlet pelisses for Hussars. From left: 12th (Prince of Wales's Royal) Lancers, 17th Light Dragoons (Lancers), unknown Dragoon Guards, 15th (King's) Light Dragoons (Hussars), 2nd Royal North British Dragoons, 14th (the King's) Light Dragoons, 4th Dragoon Guards, 10th (Prince of Wales's Own Royal) Light Dragoons (Hussars), 1st Life Guards, 2nd Life Guards, Royal Horse Guards (The Blues). Lithograph after E Hull.

for both Heavy and Light Cavalry. To this end the 1833 pattern Manton carbine with 20-in. barrel was approved, but by the time the first batch was ready for issue, further production was halted because of experiments with the percussion system, and the Manton was issued only to the 9th Lancers, in 1836, and the 7th Dragoon Guards, in 1837. This issue to a Lancer regiment was unusual but was at the express wish of William IV.

In 1836 good conduct chevrons were authorised for the rank and file; in the Cavalry they were to be worn high on the forearm under the elbow with the point uppermost.

In 1829 a system of distinguishing the respective ranks of Infantry officers was introduced, based on devices for field officers and the length of the epaulette fringe for others. From the same date all Cavalry officers except Hussars had epaulettes but their only rank distinctions were those authorised for field officers of Light Dragoons in 1811, and since there were no gradations in their fringes, captains and subalterns remained indistinguishable.

Household Cavalry

The Life Guards bearskin cap seems to have fallen into abeyance from 1827, only the crested steel helmet being worn, but from 1833 a new cap was approved, both for the Life Guards and the Blues. Though still of black bearskin, it was reduced to 14 in. in height, with gold tassels on the right side, a gilt grenade in front, gilt chin-scales and a feather plume which was white for Life Guards, red for the Blues, passing from the left side over the top. This cap was to be worn by all three regiments for ceremonial occasions but the helmet was retained for lesser duties, guards, field days and so on. In the ten paintings of the Household Cavalry commissioned from A J Dubois Drahonet by William IV, only two, of a corporal and a private, show the bearskin caps and neither of these appear to have the grenade.

The dress coatee was now single-breasted, with Prussian collar and gauntlet cuffs, both with embroidered loops, one on each side of the collar and two on the cuffs. The rear skirts had turn-backs in the facing colour. The coatees of the Blues, who were unaffected by William IV's desire for a red-coated Army, had scarlet edging down the front and around the waist. Officers had gold-embroidered epaulettes with crescent and fringe, the men brass shoulder scales and crescent. Rank was indicated by a gold aiguillette—at the right shoulder for officers, at the left for NCOs—a practice which has continued to the present day.

Much of the coatee was obscured by the white gauntlets and the cuirass. The latter were much as before, though without the Life Guards' sunburst. Officers had more ornate shoulder-pieces and waist straps and there were small variations between each of the three regiments. The aiguillette was worn over the cuirass.

The white leather breeches and jack-boots re-mained, but the Life Guards' claret overalls changed in 1833 to dark blue as worn by the Blues. The overall stripes were, for the Life Guards, two $1\frac{1}{2}$-in., of scarlet with a scarlet welt showing between, for the Blues, a single $2\frac{1}{2}$-in., scarlet (see Fig. 48, Plate 17).

The flask cords on the pouch-belts, so long worn by the Blues, were adopted by the Life Guards for all ranks from 1829; the 1st Regiment having them in red, the 2nd in blue. Officers' belts in all three regiments were gold-laced, but whereas the Blues had a black leather pouch with the Royal arms, the Life Guards had the flaps of theirs covered in blue velvet with gold wire embroidery, the 1st having the garter star, the 2nd a grenade. In undress all officers had white belts and black pouches like the men. The 1st Life Guards officers suspended their swords from gold-laced waistbelts; the 2nd Regiment and the Blues favoured white silk belts under the coatee—the former over the shoulder, the latter round the waist—and both had gold-laced slings, the Blues with a crimson stripe. When the cuirass was worn it not only hid the sword belt, except for the slings, but also hid most of the crimson and gold waist sash, with only the tasselled ends showing on the left side. Sabretaches had been discarded in the previous period.

Officers' shabraques in the Life Guards were blue, laced gold, but with variations between the

1st Life Guards, c 1832. From left: Trumpeter Jagger, Private Roberts, Corporal Winterbottom. The overalls have now changed from claret to dark blue. Note the aiguillette showing the corporal's rank. The trumpeter has a distinctive blue vandyke on the gold collar lace and on the cuffs, and a scarlet crest to the helmet. Painting by A J Dubois Drahonet.

two regiments in the width of the lace; in the embroidered insignia (both having a grenade and their numeral but with the garter star additionally for the 1st Regiment) and in the shape (the 1st having rounded corners in front but pointed behind, the 2nd having corners rounded throughout). Both had black lambskin saddle-cloths. Their men had white sheepskins, blue housings edged gold with a red stripe, an embroidered garter star for the 1st Regiment, and a grenade over '2' for the 2nd. The Blues officers' shabraques were shaped as the 1st Life Guards but were scarlet, laced gold, with the crown, garter star and a double scroll, 'WATERLOO PENINSULA'. Their men's were similar but possibly with yellow lace and all ranks had black sheepskins.

Life Guards officers' swords were reduced to two: the old boatshell-hilt type for full dress, and a new pattern, for dress and undress, which varied between the two regiments. The 1st had a half-basket, pierced steel hilt edged with brass studs; the 2nd had a gilt, four-bar hilt, ornamented with grenades, and a grip bent forward to meet the guard; both had steel scabbards, the 2nd's having a brass shoe. The Blues full dress and dress swords resembled the 2nd Life Guards patterns, though with rose and crown ornaments on the dress weapon. In contrast to the Life Guards, they had a third weapon for undress, boatshell-hilted like the full dress type but with longer blade. Their dress sword's scabbard was the same as the 2nd Life Guards, the other patterns having a black leather scabbard with gilt mounts.

Dubois Drahonet's paintings show Life Guards trumpeters: the 2nd Regiment's in the gold-laced, blue-faced crimson coat of state dress (first developed in the 17th Century and still worn today); the 1st Regiment's in coatee with special lace of a blue zigzag on gold on collar and cuffs and fringed epaulettes, cuirass, pouch-belt and overalls. Both wear the helmet but with a red crest. The kettle-drummer of the Blues is shown with a similar helmet, a regimental coatee with gold-laced scarlet wings, and pantaloons, with jack-boots, pouch-belt and waistbelt.

Farriers of the 1st and 2nd Life Guards are shown in pictures dated 1830 and 1840 respectively. Both have blue coatees with red, gold-laced collars and shoulder scales, but the former has a bearskin cap with peak and plate of the preceding period, while the latter has a perfectly plain bearskin with a red feather over the top. Neither wear cuirasses and the earlier figure has

claret overalls and a white apron, while the other is in pantaloons and jack-boots. Both have sword waistbelts and a shoulder belt suspending an axe at the right side.

The cloaks of the 1st Life Guards were scarlet, with blue collar and cape, those of the Blues were in reversed colours and those of the 2nd Life Guards were as for the 1st but with a scarlet cape.

Heavy Cavalry

The helmet of the last period continued until 1834 when a new pattern was approved for Dragoon Guards and Dragoons. (The Dubois Drahonet paintings, executed between 1832–1833, all show the former helmet.) The new type was of gilt metal or polished brass, with a pointed, fluted plate in front bearing the Royal arms and battle honours. Encircling the base, above the front and rear peaks, was a metal band with the regimental designation on the forepart. The skull was surmounted by a metal comb on which was set either

---

PLATE 18: 1829–1839

49. **Private, 3rd (King's Own) Light Dragoons, 1839 (Afghanistan).**
50. **Officer, 16th (The Queen's) Light Dragoons (Lancers), 1839 (Afghanistan).**
51. **Sergeant, 7th (Queen's Own) Light Dragoons (Hussars), 1839 (Canada).**

This plate shows cavalrymen in the same 'scarlet' period on active service, all based on eyewitness sketches or descriptions. In the First Afghan War the only concession to the climate was the white cover over the normal headdress, the rest of the uniform being as worn at home. The double-breasted jacket in Figure 49, which replaced the lapelled garment, was broadly similar for Light Dragoons and Lancers, though the latter had lace loops on the collar and slash cuffs. Besides his normal belt, Figure 49 is accoutred with haversack and water bottle of local manufacture. This regiment did not receive the blue jackets of the next period until 1843. The officer in Figure 50 wears his undress stable jacket, though his men wore their dress uniforms, a costume also displayed by this regiment in the Sikh Wars, by which time the 16th alone of Lancers retained the scarlet jacket. Although he has the undress waistbelt, the pouch-belt is the dress pattern. Figure 51, from a sketch made during the Canadian Rebellion, wears his pelisse for extra warmth, while the fur cap, gloves and 'wader' boots were acquired locally as protective garments. After returning from Canada in 1842, the 7th received the busby in place of their shakos and their pelisses reverted to blue.

49. Pte, 3rd Light Dragoons, 1839.

50. Offr, 16th Lancers, 1839.

51. Sgt, 7th Hussars, 1839.

7th (The Princess Royal's) Dragoon Guards. Left, dismounted: sergeant, 1831. Right, mounted: sergeant-major, 1838. The sergeant-major has the brass helmet which replaced the black-painted type of the sergeant from 1834. Facings black, overalls dark blue with yellow stripe. Paintings by A J Dubois Drahonet and J Dalby.

the fur crest of the obsolete pattern or a metal lion's head and shoulders. The chin-scales were secured by rosettes. Figure 46, Plate 17 shows the dress of this period but with the old helmet; the new helmet can be seen in Figure 52, Plate 19.

The 2nd Dragoons bearskin cap had a white feather curling over the top, a gold tassel at the right side, and a fluted plate in front bearing the Royal arms above a lozenge containing St Andrew with a scroll 'WATERLOO' below it, and a thistle wreath around. Their officers had an undress bearskin with no plate, tassels or feather but with gold cap-lines.

The lace loops were removed from the front of the coatee in 1827, but two remained on each side of the collar, with four (Dragoon Guards) or three (Dragoons) on the cuffs. Officers of the former had these in gold embroidery, officers of the latter in gold lace. The cuff loops were in chevrons but were largely concealed by white gauntlet gloves, introduced in 1828. The turnbacks were laced all round. The men's coatees, formerly red, were now scarlet. Shoulder straps were gilt (or brass)

scales terminating in a crescent, with a bullion fringe for officers but no aiguillettes. The crimson and gold sash for officers was largely obscured by the waistbelt except for the pendant tassels on the left side. The gold or yellow stripes on the new blue overalls were $1\frac{3}{4}$-in. wide.

The width of pouch and waistbelts was $2\frac{1}{2}$-in., of sword and sabretache slings $1\frac{1}{4}$ and $\frac{3}{4}$ in. respectively. Officers dress belts were edged and their pouch flaps and sabretaches covered with either velvet (Dragoon Guards) or cloth (Dragoons) of the facing colour. The body of the pouch and the sabretache were in Morocco leather matching the facings.

Officers in dress continued to have blue housings with square corners, trimmed with double gold lace for Dragoon Guards (single for Dragoons), and embroidered with the Royal cypher and the regimental device. Sheepskins were black, edged scarlet, and the flounces were black bearskin; only the two latter were used in undress. The cylindrical, scarlet valises had gold or yellow circles at the ends and the abbreviated title within in the same colouring; the Greys, for instance, now had a simple '2 D' instead of the former 'R NB D'.

In the sections of the 1831 and 1834 dress regulations dealing with undress there is no mention of the stable jacket formerly worn by officers. Only a single-breasted blue frock-coat with Prussian collar and scale shoulder straps is listed;

from 1834 the shoulder straps changed to gilt-edged blue cloth with gilt crescent. Forage caps were blue, encircled with a lace band and, from 1834, had a gold-braided figure on top, the black peak also embroidered.

Some watercolours by M A Hayes show trumpeters and bandsmen of the 2nd Dragoons wearing red feathers over their bearskins, gold aiguillettes at the right shoulder, no pouch-belts, and swords with Mameluke hilts. Their horses have white sheepskin saddle-cloths with red van-dyke edging.

Light Dragoons

The dress of the Light Dragoons underwent a complete transformation in this period. A new bell-top shako approved in 1828 was 6 in. high, 11 in. in diameter across the top, and had a band of gold or yellow lace round the top, in the centre of which was a crown, with below it a gilt or brass Maltese cross on which was displayed regimental insignia and honours. It was furnished with chin-scales and cap-lines attached by a ring to the right side of the top, from where they hung down the back, passing under the left armpit to be secured to the jacket buttons; from the ring, the other ends were plaited into a festoon which hung across the front of the cap before being caught up on the left side. Above the crown a socket held a drooping plume, of cock's feathers for officers, horsehair for the men. The plume was supposed to be all white but the Dubois Drahonet paintings of men of the 3rd and 14th show a portion of red at the base. A black oilskin cover was issued.

The new jacket, still blue when first approved in 1829, was double-breasted with two rows of eight buttons, $2\frac{1}{2}$ in. apart at the top and $1\frac{1}{2}$ in. at the bottom. There were very short tails at the back with three buttons on each flap and a 'waterfall' at waist level. The change from blue to scarlet in August 1830 necessitated alteration to the facings (see Appendix 7) on the Prussian collar, pointed cuffs and turnbacks. Officers' collars and cuffs were edged with gold lace and ornamented with gold braid tracery; the men's were edged all round with yellow braid. Laced and fringed epaulettes were the shoulder ornaments for officers; scales and crescent for the men. The waist girdles were crimson and gold, or red and yellow. The overall stripes were double, each $\frac{3}{4}$-in. wide, in gold or scarlet. The cossack style of trousers disappeared and those shown by Dubois Drahonet are cut straight, though quite wide in marked contrast to the tightness of the jacket. This clothing is shown in Fig. 49, Plate 18.

The waistbelts for Light Dragoons were narrower than for the Heavies, being $1\frac{1}{2}$ in. wide, and were worn below the girdle, less tightly buckled, so that the left side was pulled down slightly by the weight of sword and sabretache; the pouch-belts were 2 in. wide. Officers' dress belts and slings had a central stripe in the facings, their pouch-belts having silver plates, pickers, chains

2nd Royal North British Dragoons, 1832. From left: Private Wallace, Lieutenant-Colonel Lord AWM Hill, Sergeant Reid. Note the private's white summer trousers worn in dismounted order. The blue overalls have gold or yellow stripes. Painting by A J Dubois Drahonet.

14th (The King's) Light Dragoons, 1832. From left:
private, Captain J M Dawson, Sergeant Brookfield.
Scarlet jackets, faced blue, dark blue trousers with gold
or scarlet stripes. Painting by A J Dubois Drahonet.

and fittings; the black leather pouches having a
silver flap. Their sabretaches were of purple
leather, faced in blue cloth, edged and embroidered in gold; the men's were plain black with
only two slings. Shabraques had rounded corners
and were blue, edged with lace and embroidered
with the cypher and regimental devices; such
embroidery only appearing on the hind corners
for the men. Although a board of officers in 1833
recommended that the men's white sheepskins
should conform to the officers' black, this change
was not followed by all regiments.

Unlike the Heavies, Light Dragoon officers
retained their stable jackets in the same style as
before but in the new colours. They were also
permitted a blue 'greatcoat' with six loops in front
and four rows of olivets; the stand-up collar and
pointed cuffs being embellished with figured patterns. The forage caps were similar to those for
the Heavies and the trouser stripes were scarlet.
The undress waistbelts were of black leather, the
pouch-belt white.

Hussars

The new Light Dragoon shako was authorised for
Hussars with the same lines and festoon, but the
falling plumes were black and the ornaments on
the front were similar to the previous pattern. For
officers the ornaments were interlocking rings
round the top, with the cartwheel connected by
loops to a boss above; for the men, a circle of
yellow lace with a red stripe and a band of the
same round the top. Exceptions were found in the
15th, whose shakos continued to be covered with
scarlet cloth and whose cap-lines were mixed red
and yellow, and the 7th, who retained the former,
taller shako.

The most important change to the upper garments was the adoption, in deference to the
King's wishes, of scarlet pelisses, which for all
regiments were now trimmed with black fur. The
8th and 15th changed their silver/white lace and
loopings to gold/yellow in conformity with the
1830 order, and the jackets and pelisses of the
15th had only three rows of buttons instead of
the customary five. All Hussar sergeants had gold
lace, rather than the rank and file's yellow.

The dark blue overalls, formerly worn only by
the 7th, were now common to all, with a $1\frac{1}{2}$-in.
lace stripe. In 1846 the 10th were authorised to
have double stripes, but two paintings of an
officer and a private, c 1832, show that the practice had already been adopted by this regiment
several years previously. The new dress is shown
in Fig. 47, Plate 17.

Equipment generally followed the Light Dragoon patterns, though the cloth facings of officers'
dress sabretaches were scarlet in all four regiments, and their dress belts had scarlet edging,
except for the 10th whose officers had a chain-
covered black belt (only the latter appears to have
had pickers and chains at this period). The 1831

Hussars, 1832, with the scarlet pelisse of this period.
From left: 8th (Royal Irish), private, in foul weather
shako, and Captain Lyon; 15th (The King's), Sergeant
Toms. Pelisse fur black for the 8th, brown for the 15th.
The 15th's scarlet shako was of the former pattern and
their jackets and pelisses had only three rows of buttons.
Shako plumes black, trouser stripes gold or yellow.
Painting by A J Dubois Drahonet.

other regiments (together with the custom of
mounting trumpeters on greys).

The Hussars saw no active service in this
period, except for the 7th who were in Canada
during the rebellion of 1838–1839. Figure 51,
Plate 18 shows a sergeant with his elaborate home
service uniform adapted for the climate by the
addition of a fur cap, gauntlets and wader boots.
A portrait of an officer of the same regiment shows
similar boots but in black leather.

Lancers
Since scarlet jackets were ordered for all Lancers
in 1830, this required a change of facings to blue
for all except the 17th. This, in turn affected the
lance-cap, of which a new pattern was approved.
Essentially this was the same design as before,
with 10-in. square trencher top in the facing
colour, but was supposedly a little lower and was
fractionally less waisted, with a shorter peak and a
chin-chain. A lace band with central red stripe
went round the waist, and the front and turned-
up back peaks of officers' caps were also laced.
The drooping plumes were black cock's feathers

Lancers, 1832. From left: 17th, private, in white summer trousers for dismounted duties, and Lieutenant-Colonel Lord Bingham; 9th (Queen's Royal), Sergeant Reece. Scarlet jackets, faced white for 17th, blue for 9th; all plumes black, all trouser stripes scarlet. The 9th had a special all-black cap and did not wear the girdle. Painting by A J Dubois Drahonet.

for officers, horsehair for the men, and the cap-lines terminated in two flounders and tassels. From 1832 the 9th were permitted a special cap, of similar shape but covered with black patent leather, and with the lace waist band in a rope design.

The scarlet jackets were of the same cut as the Light Dragoons' jackets but with certain differences. Two lace loops were set on the forepart of the collar, the cuffs were round with a scarlet flap or slash, fastened by five buttons for officers, three for the men, and there was no waterfall at the back of the waist. However, in 1834 the waterfall was restored and the slashed cuff replaced by a pointed one, except in the 16th. This cuff change was not always visible because, in the previous year, gauntlet gloves were ordered for all Lancers. Undress was similar to that of the Light Dragoons, but officers' stable jackets had the same cuffs as their dress jackets.

Overalls, girdles, accoutrements, horse furniture and swords all followed the Light Dragoon patterns, though with minor and, of course, inter-regimental differences. Girdles were not worn by the 9th, who instead wore a waistbelt of the same width as the Heavies. Sabretaches were

discontinued from 1833, except for officers and NCOs, and since no carbines were carried, the pouch-belts were without a swivel. The same delays over issue of the 1821 pattern sword also seem to have affected Lancer regiments, except for the 17th, who received the new sword after their conversion to Lancers in 1822. A new, lighter lance, with ash shaft and triangular point, was approved in 1829, being 9 ft 1 in. in length; the red and white pennon being 2 ft 3 in. long and 1 ft 4 in. wide. An experimental bamboo lance was issued to the 12th in 1835 but was not generally adopted for over 30 years.

A watercolour by M A Hayes shows the 17th in review order in 1839, headed by the band, who are distinguished by having red plumes, no pouch-belts, white sheepskins and grey horses.

An officer of the 16th in the dress worn during the First Afghan War appears in Fig. 50, Plate 18, but as this campaign continued into the next period, it will be considered below.

Dress 1840–1854

General

In this period, the last before the complete re-fashioning and overdue modernisation of the Army's dress in 1855, the various uniforms remained unchanged in their cut and design except for minor economies. There were, however, major changes of headdress in the Household and Heavy Cavalry, the Light Dragoons and Hussars and a minor change in the Lancers. It is also noteworthy for the reversion to blue as the major uniform colour of the Light Cavalry. These alterations were promulgated in the 1846 officers dress regulations, the men's clothing following the same patterns as for the officers, with the usual differences of lace and plain accoutrements. The design of the latter was as before, except that the introduction of percussion firearms required the addition of a small leather pouch for the percussion caps, usually attached to the right front of the waistbelt.

Heavy and Light Cavalry officers continued to use their respective 1822 pattern swords, but in 1853 a new universal sword was approved for all cavalry soldiers, with slightly curved blade and iron three-bar hilt and scabbard. According to eyewitness sketches, neither the Heavy nor Light Brigade in the Crimea had this sword. The new percussion carbine, also universal for Heavy and Light regiments except Lancers, was the Victoria pattern of 1841 with 26-in. barrel. For Lancers, and sergeant-majors and trumpeters of all other regiments, a percussion pistol with 9-in. barrel was approved.

Although one or two regiments of Light Dragoons, and the 16th Lancers, had seen active service in India, the bulk of the Cavalry had not been engaged since Waterloo. From 1840 onwards, however, both Heavy and Light regiments were to be involved in operations in Canada, the Cape and India, culminating in the first European conflict since 1815 in the Crimea. Since the Army's uniforms at this date were designed primarily for display, and since the concept of a special dress for campaigning was undreamed of, officers and men had to fight in the clothing they wore for parades at home, regardless of climate or terrain, or else adjust it accordingly as best they could. In the event, this came down to either using their undress uniform or dispensing with as many articles of no practical use as possible. There were no general orders or regulations on the subject. As far as the Army authorities was concerned, their regiments embarked on a cam-

Officer and men of the Royal Horse Guards (The Blues) c 1845, with the new helmet introduced from 1843. Note the trumpeter at left wears no cuirass. The officer's shabraque is scarlet with gold embroidery, the sheepskin black. The men only have sheepskins.

paign in the dress laid down for marching order plus the necessary items of camp equipage. Any alleviation of, or improvement to the impractical and uncomfortable uniform when on service was left to the discretion of a regiment's commanding officer.

Special badges on officers' epaulettes to distinguish rank continued to apply only to field officers; captains and subalterns remaining indistinguishable. Since Hussars wore no epaulettes, their field officers had a larger figure embroidered on the sleeves of both jacket and pelisse. In 1850 a Horse Guards circular confirmed the rank chevrons of NCOs as: for all Line Cavalry, less Hussars, four bars with crown above for the regimental sergeant-major; three and a crown for troop-sergeant-majors; sergeants and corporals to have three and two respectively. Hussar regimental and troop sergeant-majors all had four below a regimental badge; sergeants three and a badge, but without the latter in undress; corporals two. The badges are given in the Hussar section. All chevrons were worn on the right arm only, and on both jacket and pelisse by Hussars. Specialists like farriers, roughriders and trumpeters had special yellow worsted badges denoting their trade on the right upper arm.

Household Cavalry

Apart from the necessary insignia changes resulting from Queen Victoria's accession, the dress of the Household Cavalry remained as before except for the headdress. The bearskin caps continued in use until 1843, but in the previous year an entirely new helmet had been approved which superseded both the caps and the old 'Roman' helmet. This, commonly known as the 'Albert' helmet from the Prince Consort's interest, was inspired by then current German and Russian designs. Apart from its ornamentation and a leaf-shaped socket for the falling plume on top, this helmet was of the shape still in use in full dress today. The metal was described as German silver, with the following gilt ornamentation: scroll work on the peak and an oak and laurel wreath around a silver garter star with crown above. The same helmet was worn by all three regiments, with a white plume for the Life Guards and red for the Blues, the latter colour also being worn by trumpeters of the Life Guards. This helmet would remain in service until 1871.

The shabraques of the 2nd Life Guards lost their grenade, both regiments now having the garter star; in the 1st, only on the rear corners

below a double cypher 'LG', a scroll and a crown, with a crown and '1 LG' on the front corners; in the 2nd, the star had the Queen's crest above, the numeral '2' below, and a laurel branch on either side with 'PENINSULA' and 'WATERLOO', the numeral being omitted on the front corners. The Blues had a crown and star in both corners. The men's housings were dispensed with in this period, only the white or black sheepskins being used.

The troopers' swords for the 1st Life Guards remained of the 1820 pattern, but the 2nd Regiment and the Blues received a new sword in 1848 with steel basket guard in scroll pattern. These swords would continue in service until 1882. The Victoria carbine was also issued.

PLATE 19: 1840–1854

52. Corporal, 7th (The Princess Royal's) Dragoon Guards, 1845 (South Africa).
53. Officer, 14th (The King's) Light Dragoons, 1849 (India).
54. Private, 12th (Prince of Wales's) Lancers, 1852 (South Africa).

This plate illustrates the increasing use of the stable jacket on service overseas and the reversion to blue uniforms of the Light Cavalry. The undress jacket worn with the 1834 helmet, less its bearskin crest, is shown in an eyewitness sketch of the 7th Dragoon Guards in action against the Boers in 1845, but the yellow-banded blue forage caps were adopted in the subsequent Seventh Kaffir War. Their trousers were reinforced with untanned leather under local arrangements. Against the Boers, the regiment was issued with a non-cavalry weapon, the Brunswick rifle, but reverted to carbines in the Kaffir War. In the Basuto expedition and Eighth Kaffir War the 12th Lancers wore undress with covered forage caps as more suitable for bush fighting, as illustrated in Figure 54, after paintings by Barker and Goodrich. Owing to an issue of double-barrelled carbines, the pouch-belts had to be fitted with a cap pouch and carbine swivel, not normally required by Lancers. Figures 52 and 54 have the 1821 pattern Heavy and Light Cavalry swords. During the Sikh Wars most regiments adhered to the practice mentioned for Plate 18 of undress for officers, dress jackets for men with dress headgear and protective covers. Figure 53, after a painting by Wheeler, has the 1845 Light Dragoon shako. His undress overalls have scarlet stripes instead of gold. The black pouch-belt is contrary to the 1846 regulations which prescribed white for undress. Officers' stable jackets in the Heavies and Lancers were similar to that shown, but with variations in colour and depth of collar and cuffs.

52. Cpl, 7th Dragoon Guards, 1845.

53. Offr, 14th Light Dragoons, 1849.

54. Pte, 12th Lancers, 1852.

Officers in dress (mounted) and summer undress, 1st (Royal) Dragoons, with trumpeter and men, showing the Heavy Cavalry helmet of the 1843–1847 pattern, in which the brush and mane replaced the bearskin crest. The gold-banded forage cap and frock coat are dark blue, the latter with gilt shoulder scales. Officers' dress belts are laced gold, undress plain white. Only the officers have shabraques. Watercolour by Henry Martens.

Heavy Cavalry

In 1847 the coatee skirts of all ranks were shortened and squared but otherwise the clothing of Dragoon Guards and Dragoons was unaltered. The headdress, on the other hand, changed twice. In 1843 the existing brass helmet was re-fashioned by the replacement of the bearskin crest with a flowing horsehair mane, which terminated in front in a thistle-shaped brush, more or less identical to that which had adorned the 1812 helmet. Four years later a helmet of the same shape as the Household Cavalry's 1843 pattern was approved but in gilt or brass, ornamented on the peaks, and with a black plume. The front plate had 'VR' within a garter inscribed with the regimental title, mounted on an eight-pointed

star, set on a rococo shield all within an oak and laurel spray. Except for a change of plumes in the next period, this helmet served until 1871, but not all regiments received it until 1850.

By 1842 the front plate of the 2nd Dragoons' bearskin cap had been dispensed with and in the following year the white feather was discontinued. The size of the cap was also reduced but in 1845 the feather was resumed, though now 9 in. long and upright, and a metal grenade and white horse of Hanover were permitted on the front and back of the cap respectively; the two latter were, in fact, largely concealed by the fur.

Officers' epaulettes were described in the 1846 regulations as 'gold bullion, boxed, with strap and crescent embroidered in gold, on velvet for Dragoon Guards, on cloth for Dragoons, of the colour of the regimental facings. The badge of each regiment embroidered in silver within the crescent.'

The same regulations listed the officers' dark blue shabraques but in 1847 these were discontinued entirely; all ranks to have only the black sheepskin saddle-cloth.

From 1853 the forage caps of all ranks were

Captain Clements (facing left), NCOs and men of the 3rd (Prince of Wales's) Dragoon Guards, in the black-plumed helmet worn from 1847. The troop-sergeant-major (centre) has fringed epaulettes, the coporal (left) shoulder scales. Facings and trouser stripes are yellow. Sheepskins black, edged scarlet. At extreme right is a trumpeter with aiguillette, no pouch-belt and a grey horse. Painting by J E Ferneley Sen.

reduced in the width of the crown to assume a pillbox shape. Officers again had scarlet stable jackets, which were to be worn at drills and when the men paraded in undress; these were laced round the outer edge of the collar, round the pointed cuffs and all round the body, with a row of studs in front and twisted gold shoulder cords. The single-breasted blue frock-coat with loops and olivets was to be worn as 'a common morning riding dress in quarters and duties off parade'. The undress trousers had a $1\frac{3}{4}$-in. scarlet stripe but this was changed in 1851 to yellow in conformity with the men, except for the 6th Dragoon Guards who had white.

In the same year this regiment underwent a major dress change when, prior to sailing for India, it was ordered to convert to a regiment of Light Cavalry, adopting the blue Light Dragoon uniform but retaining the plumed helmet and title of Dragoon Guards, thus acquiring a unique appearance in the Line Cavalry.

A painting by Crozier of the Royal Dragoons in 1843 shows a trumpeter in the 1834 helmet with a red crest, a coatee, with scarlet turnbacks piped blue, two vertical lace loops on the cuffs and an

aiguillette at the right shoulder. The trumpeter's overalls have a double red stripe with a red light in between. He wears neither gauntlets, nor pouch-belt and has an all-brass Mameluke-hilted sabre. The trumpet cords are red and blue. He rides a grey horse with white sheepskin, edged with red vandykes. Another trumpeter of the same regiment, in a 1848 picture by Ferneley also has a red plume to the 1847 helmet, the aiguillette and no pouch-belt, but the coatee collar is laced all round without loops, and the laced cuffs are pointed. His overalls have a yellow stripe. The horse is again grey but carries a black sheepskin. In a painting by Quinton of the 4th Dragoon Guards departing for the Crimea, a trumpeter is dressed as for the

113

rank and file, except for the red plume and his horse is a light chestnut. A sketch by the French General Vanson of a Greys trumpeter in the Crimea gives him a dark-shaded plume, presumably red, of the old type curling over the bearskin. That the red plumes were not universal for musicians can be seen in a painting by Hayes of the 3rd Dragoon Guards, c 1852, in which the trumpeters and band all have white plumes, aiguillettes on the left shoulder and no pouch-belts; all appear to be mounted on piebald or skewbald horses. It is known that a few years previously red plumes had been worn by this regiment's musicians.

Turning to what was worn on campaign, a novel winter dress was adopted by the King's Dragoon Guards when serving during the Canadian rebellion. This consisted of a fur cap with a red bag (something like a hussar busby but wedge-shaped), a dark blue, double-breasted frock-coat or pea jacket with the shoulder scales from the coatee, and long boots and gloves lined with sheepskin. Protecting the face was a form of Balaclava helmet, though whether this was part of the cap, attached to the coat, or separate from both is uncertain. 'Very good and sensible', an officer described it, 'but most assuredly not according to regulations.'

Between 1845–1847 the 7th Dragoon Guards saw service at the Cape. Some eyewitness drawings of the regiment in action against the Boers in 1845 show all ranks dressed in stable jackets and overalls but with the 1843 helmet fitted with the brass lion's head instead of the horsehair mane (see Fig. 52, Plate 19). The helmets proved quite unsuitable for such warfare and in the Seventh Kaffir War a year later all ranks wore forage caps. The blue overalls were reinforced with leather strapping. The regiment was issued with rifled muskets taken over from the 60th Rifles for fighting against the Boers, but so difficult were these to load when mounted that carbines were resumed against the Kaffirs.

The regiments forming the Heavy Brigade in the Crimea—the 4th and 5th Dragoon Guards, and 1st, 2nd and 6th Dragoons—wore full dress headgear without plumes, coatees without shoulder scales, and gauntlets and overalls (see Fig. 55, Plate 20). A sketch by Vanson of privates of each regiment at Varna before the landing in the Crimea shows booted overalls in each case, (i.e. strapped with leather) except the Greys who do not seem to have followed this practice until later in the war. The same drawing reveals that the 5th Dragoon Guards and the Royal Dragoons had

their cap pouches sewn into the lower right front of their coatees, the other regiments having them on their waistbelts. In addition to pouch and waistbelts, both haversacks and water bottles were carried over the right shoulder. Officers wore their undress belts. The Vanson sketch attempts to show the different waist-plate badges and, though none too clear, these appear to be: the 4th Dragoon Guards, a harp; the 5th Dragoon Guards, a crown and star; the Royals, a crown; and the Greys, a thistle; the 6th Inniskillings have a plain square buckle, not a plate like the others. What is very clear is the 1821 pattern sword with bowl guard carried by each regiment.

Light Dragoons

In 1840 the Light Dragoon jackets, though remaining of the same design, reverted from scarlet to blue, with consequent change of facings, from blue back to scarlet for the 3rd, 4th and 14th: the 13th, being faced buff, were unaffected. The latter were also unique in having a double buff stripe on officers' undress and on the men's overalls.

PLATE 20: 1840–1854

55. Private, 5th (Princess Charlotte of Wales's) Dragoon Guards, 1854 (Crimea).
56. Sergeant, 11th (Prince Albert's Own) Hussars, 1854 (Crimea).

This plate, based on various photographs, paintings and drawings, is representative of the Heavy and Light Cavalry brigades of the Crimean War. In contrast to the service uniforms of the previous plate, both men wear the home service marching order of full dress with certain modifications—no headdress plumes or shoulder scales on the dragoon jacket, the reinforced or 'booted' overalls of the dragoon and the absence of the hussar's pelisse, which had been left on board the transports and was not resumed until after Balaclava. The men of both brigades were armed with their respective 1821 pattern swords and Victoria percussion carbines. The cap pouch for the latter can be seen on the hussar's sword belt, a practice followed by some of the Heavies, though Figure 55 and the Royal Dragoons carried theirs in slit pockets on the lower right front of the jacket. Only Hussars wore the sabretache in the Crimea. The crown above the sergeant's chevrons is a regimental arm badge, not part of the rank insignia. The splendour of the uniforms depicted here quickly deteriorated under active service conditions. According to one eyewitness picture, the 5th Dragoon Guards and Greys had their valises (as in Figure 55) at Balaclava but other regiments did not.

55. Pte, 5th Dragoon Guards, 1854.

56. Sgt, 11th Hussars, 1854.

6th (Inniskilling) Dragoons, c 1850. The mounted private is in marching order with haversack and water bottle. To his left, an officer with epaulettes, sash, sabretache, undress belts and booted overalls. The indented cuff worn by Dragoons is visible on the man in the forage cap. At left rear is a trumpeter with red plume and aiguillette. Facings yellow, plumes black. Painting by M A Hayes.

The major change was a new shako, which had the same lace band round the top and the same Maltese cross plate as the bell-topped type, but was more or less cylindrical, being 7 in. high in front, 8 in. at the back and 8 in. in diameter across the top. The cap-lines were simplified, without the festoon and terminating in two acorns. The falling plume was white; of swan's feathers for officers, horsehair for the men (officers in India had the latter). As with previous shakos, oilskin covers were issued to protect the cap on active service or in bad weather, when the plumes were also removed. Officers had a special 'foul weather' shako of the same shape but made of oilskin stretched across a cane frame.

In 1849 the double red stripes on officers' undress and soldiers' overalls were changed to yellow except as mentioned above for the 13th. In 1854 the latter regiment received grey overalls, which were issued to certain regiments for trials.

The only change in accoutrements was the abolition of the sabretache for all ranks of Light Dragoons in 1854. Shabraques were normally dispensed with on service, only the sheepskins being carried.

Apart from their worsted arm badges, trumpeters were distinguished from the men by piping in the facing colour on the back seams and by red plumes. Trumpeters are usually portrayed in contemporary pictures without pouch-belts, though on service they were probably required for trumpeters' pistol ammunition.

All four Light Dragoon regiments saw service in this period, either in Afghanistan, India or the Crimea. Despite the 1840 change to blue uniforms, the 3rd fought in the First Afghan War in their scarlet dress jackets and bell-topped shakos. The only concession to the climate was a white quilted cover and neck curtain for the shako (see Fig. 49, Plate 18). The water bottles issued as camp equipage were of local manufacture, the

Top: *Officers and men, 14th (The King's) Light Dragoons, c 1846, after the reversion to the blue jacket and the introduction of the 1846 shako. The mounted officer and men to the left rear are in dress. The three dismounted officers in the foreground are in undress of frock coat (left) – worn off parade – and stable jackets with foul-weather shako (centre) and forage caps with black leather belts. Extreme right is a private in undress. Facings scarlet. Shabraques and dress sabretache dark blue. Lithograph after Henry Martens.*

Sergeant and privates, 4th (Queen's Own) Light Dragoons in dress. Facings scarlet, plume white. A photograph taken in 1855 but showing the uniform of the 1846–1854 period.

117

Officer, trumpeter and private, 8th The King's Royal Irish Light Dragoons (Hussars), in review order, c 1850. Plumes white over scarlet, busby-bag scarlet, shabraque blue. Watercolour by Henry Martens.

blue-painted circular home pattern never being used by troops in India. The 3rd received its blue uniforms in 1843 and fought in this during both Sikh Wars. Although the men wore their dress jackets in the field, officers wore stable jackets and undress overalls and accoutrements. In the First Sikh War all ranks appear to have worn forage caps with white covers but at Chillianwallah, in 1849, the dress was covered shakos. An officer who was present recalled that all ranks wore gauntlet gloves despite these not being regulation for Light Dragoons. The 14th were engaged in the Second Sikh War and dressed similarly to the 3rd (see Fig. 53, Plate 19); a member of the regiment noted that most of the men managed to 'lose' their shakos early on and wore a towel soaked in water round their heads like a turban.

Both the 4th and 13th served in the Crimean Light Brigade, wearing 'foul-weather' shakos with cap-lines but without plumes, dress jackets without epaulettes or shoulder scales, and girdles and overalls; the 13th wearing their grey ones. Officers seem to have had booted overalls from the beginning of the war, with the seam stripes sewn down over the leather, but the men did not receive these until after the early battles. Both regiments had the 1821 Light Cavalry sword and Victoria carbine.

Hussars

Apart from some simplification of the uniform, the chief changes for Hussars were the resumption of the blue pelisse and the return of the fur cap (or busby) in place of the shako. The second followed the conversion to Hussars of the 11th Light Dragoons in 1840. As this was the first regiment to become Hussars outright (the others still officially being Light Dragoons), it adopted the busby as its new headdress and soon the other regiments asked to follow suit: the 10th receiving approval in 1841, the 7th taking the busby on its return from Canada in 1842, and the 8th in 1844. The new busby was of brown fur, 9 in. high, with scarlet bag, gold or yellow cap-lines and gilt or brass chin-chain; the upright feather was white

*The Hussars, 1846. The central figures are, from left:
officer, 8th (Royal Irish), marching order; two officers,
11th (Prince Albert's Own), undress and review order;
10th (Prince of Wales's Own Royal), an officer and*

*private, review order, private, marching order. The fur
cap was now regulation for all Hussars, except the 15th
who retained their scarlet shako. Lithograph by Walker
after M A Hayes.*

10th (Prince of Wales's Own Royal) Light Dragoons (Hussars) 1854, showing the special regimental pattern shako adopted in India as more suitable than the fur cap. From left: orderly troop-sergeant-major, in undress; officer, in review order; orderly officer, in undress with covered shako; officer, in evening stable dress. The 10th continued to wear this cap on proceeding to the Crimea in 1855. Lithograph by Walker after Lieutenant Fairlie, 10th Hussars.

with a scarlet base. In the 11th the bag and feather base were crimson.

The shako, however, did not disappear entirely for the 15th eschewed the busby in favour of the new Light Dragoon shako, covered in their traditional scarlet cloth and with a falling black plume. Furthermore, the 10th, though authorised the busby, went to India in 1846, where a shako of regimental design was adopted. This was ornamented in a fashion similar to the previous shako but was cylindrical in shape, with a broad peak and falling black horsehair plume; in the hot weather it was furnished with a white cover and detachable curtain.

In 1842 the rows of buttons on the men's jackets and pelisses were reduced from five to three and the sergeants' lace and loopings were downgraded from gold to yellow. The distinctive crimson or cherry overalls worn by all ranks of the 11th in all orders of dress had double gold or yellow stripes, as already worn by the 10th. Apart from these trouser distinctions and the 15th's shakos, there was now little to distinguish one regiment from another at a glance, except for the numerals on the men's valises, when carried, and the regimental differences in officers' belts, pouches, sabretaches and shabraques. The 11th's

crimson colour was also permitted for officers, instead of scarlet or blue, on the edging of belts and on the leather and facing of the sabretache and the shabraque. Their dress pouches were of gilt metal with silver ornaments. Their saddle-cloths were of black lambskin.

Whereas officers' stable jackets in the Heavy Cavalry and Light Dragoons were similar except for the colour, for Hussars they were described as 'single-breasted, with olivets and gold lace according to regimental pattern'. Their frock coats had loops, olivets and braiding, and in the 7th, 10th and 15th a rolling collar; in the 8th and 11th, a stand-up collar. All ranks of the 11th and 15th were permitted crimson and scarlet forage caps respectively, which had the same lace bands as on the other regiments' blue caps.

The regimental arm badges worn above the chevrons from 1850 by NCOs were as follows: 7th, 11th and 15th, a crown; the 8th, a harp and crown; the 10th, a crown and Prince of Wales's feathers. Trumpeters may have had mixed red and yellow loopings, crimson and yellow for the 11th. A painting by Hayes dated 1844 includes a trumpeter of the 11th with an all-crimson plume in a busby of light grey or fawn, this same fur trimming the pelisse.

On landing in the Crimea the 8th and 11th wore busbies without plumes, dress jackets, barrel sashes and overalls. The pelisses were left on board ship and were not received until the winter (see Fig. 56, Plate 20). Officers had booted overalls and apparently wore their dress belts and slings but undress sabretaches. Shabraques and valises were also left on the transports, with only the sheepskins being taken ashore. The men had haversacks and water bottles and both regiments had the 1821 sword and Victoria carbine.

The 10th went direct from India to the Crimea but did not arrive until April 1855. They retained their 'Indian' shakos, with oilskin covers and without plumes, and appear to have worn the pelisse either over (or instead of) the jacket. According to the regimental history they had knee boots of untanned leather, made rather wide to be pulled on over their overalls.

Lancers

In 1840 Lancer regiments changed the colour of their jackets back to blue, except for the 16th who kept to scarlet and continued to do so thereafter. The 9th and 12th, therefore, reverted to scarlet facings, the latter changing the tops of their caps accordingly while the 9th continued with their

all-black caps. The 1846 regulations described the cap as being $8\frac{3}{4}$ in. deep in front, $9\frac{1}{2}$ in. at back, with a top $9\frac{1}{2} \times 9\frac{1}{2}$ in. square; a little later the dimensions were reduced to 8 in. deep with a $8\frac{1}{2} \times 8\frac{1}{2}$ in. square top. The central stripe on the lace band round the waist of the cap changed to blue. The plumes continued black, horsehair being used by all ranks in India. Like the Light Dragoons the men had oilskin covers, officers having a special foul-weather cap. The cap-lines were simplified, with acorn ends instead of the former tassels and flounders.

The 16th's scarlet jackets retained the old round cuff with slash and had no waterfall at the back of the waist. The lace loops on the collars and the braiding on the cuffs continued until abolished in 1853, leaving all ranks with plain collars and cuffs. The 1853 order to Light Dragoons changing the overall stripes to double yellow also applied to Lancers, except the 17th who kept the double white stripes they had had for some years. This regiment was one of those to receive the experimental grey overalls in 1854.

17th Light Dragoons (Lancers) c 1850 in foul weather caps. A lancer's firearm was the pistol, as shown here, instead of the carbine of other cavalry. Facings and trouser stripes white. The rear corners of the shabraques are hooked up as for marching order. An officer (without lance) is at left. Watercolour by M A Hayes.

The girdles remained as before except for soldiers of the 9th who did not wear them.

The 1846 regulations observed that the 17th's officers did not wear the sabretache and in 1854 this article was abolished in all Lancers.

Stable jackets and officers' frock coats followed the pattern of the Light Dragoons. Officers' forage caps had braided quarter welts crossing the top, symbolising the lance-cap's square top, an embellishment which would later be applied to the men's forage caps, but not, apparently at this date. In the 17th the men's forage caps had a white band, their trumpeters having white caps with a red band.

This red band matched the plumes worn by the

17th's trumpeters on their lance-caps, a practice probably common to the other regiments, certainly to the 12th, whose musicians' lance-caps were entirely scarlet (except for the front and turned-up back peaks), as were their forage caps. A sketch dated 1854 by Ebsworth shows the 17th's kettle-drummer mounted on a grey, his dress as for a private except for the red plume, and very plain drum banners in dark blue or black, laced gold all round, bearing only the silver death's head and motto 'Or Glory'. The 12th's band were mounted on bays. On service, trumpeters of all types of Cavalry carried trumpet and bugle, the latter for sounding the field calls.

All four regiments saw active service in this period: the 9th and 16th in India and Afghanistan, the 12th in South Africa and the 17th in the Crimea. In the Sikh Wars the two former followed the practice of the 3rd and 14th Light Dragoons; officers in stable jackets, soldiers in dress jackets, but all wearing the lance-cap and cap-lines, with either a white quilted cover or the black oilskin without plume. At the Battle of Aliwal in 1846 the lance-flags of the 16th became so caked in blood that thereafter it became a regimental custom to crimp the flags. In the Eighth Kaffir War of 1850–1853 the 12th adopted a more relaxed costume of forage caps with white covers and curtains, stable jackets for all, girdles and overalls (see Fig. 54, Plate 19). For this campaign the regiment received an issue of double-barrelled carbines fitted with a side-bar and ring for which their pouch-belts had to be adapted to take a carbine swivel. In bush warfare it was the practice to arm part of the regiment only with these carbines while the remainder followed up with lance and pistol. Before sailing for the Cape the 12th's officers equipped themselves with the new Colt revolver, which had attracted much interest at the Great Exhibition of 1851. In the Crimea the 17th's fighting dress followed the lines already described for the Light Dragoons including, like the 13th Light Dragoons, the grey overalls.

Dress 1855–1870

General

The major uniform changes that emerged in 1855 were not, as is sometimes believed, a sudden reaction to the deficiencies of the existing dress as revealed by the rigours of the Crimean War, but rather the culmination of attempts to reform the Army's dress which had begun in the 1830s.

Influenced by such factors as colonial campaigning experience, the soldiers' health, the expense and, perhaps most significant of all, the new fashions adopted by Continental armies, the re-forming movement, at first led and voiced by individuals, began to engage the attention of the authorities from 1849 onwards. After considerable discussion and experiment, the first official announcement of the new dress was made in Horse Guards circular memorandum of 18th August 1854. Except for six Infantry regiments who were to receive the new clothing in 1855–1856, other regiments were not to adopt it until the clothing year 1856–1857. Details of the new dress for officers were first promulgated in the 1855 dress regulations, which were followed by those of 1857 and 1864, though the two latter only contained minor modifications where the Cavalry were concerned. Soldiers' dress followed the officers' general cut with the customary variations of lace and braid.

PLATE 21: 1855–1870

57. Trumpeter, 8th The King's Royal Irish Light Dragoons (Hussars), 1856.
58. Lieutenant, 4th (Queen's Own) Light Dragoons, 1857.
59. Private, 2nd Royal North British Dragoons, 1860.

This and Plate 22 illustrate the 1855 dress changes and the introduction of the tunic which, initially, was looser fitting than it later became. Overalls or trousers were unchanged, but for mounted duties were booted as in Figure 57, a practice not officially authorised until 1861. The Hussar and Light Dragoon (Figure 58) tunic differed chiefly in the number of loops on the front, and the latter's contrasting facing colours. Figure 57, from a watercolour by Hayes, has the pre-Crimean pattern busby, without plume as he is in marching order; and, as a trumpeter, he has no pouch-belt. Only Hussars now had the sabretache. Figure 58, from a print after Martens, shows the last of the Light Dragoon uniform, as from 1861 the remaining such regiments converted to Hussars. The newly introduced rank badges can be seen on the collar; rank also being indicated by variations of the embroidery around the cuff-knot. Figure 59, from a print after Thomas, shows the scarlet tunic of the Heavies, with the bearskin cap of the Greys instead of the 1847 helmet of the remainder. The Dragoon cuff is shown in detail. The accoutrements for the Heavies were as before, with the addition of a cap pouch on the front of the pouch-belt. Figures 57 and 59 have the universal 1853 sword.

57. Tptr, 8th Hussars, 1856.

58. Offr, 4th Light Dragoons, 1857.

59. Pte, 2nd Dragoons, 1860.

Dismounted private of the Royal Horse Guards (The Blues), 1855, without cuirass and wearing the old coatee which was replaced by the tunic in 1857.

The most important change of the new era was the replacement of the coatee and jacket (neither of which afforded adequate protection below the waist) by the tunic; a garment with skirts all round, inspired by the popular frock coats worn by officers in undress. At the same time the opportunity was taken to dispense with superfluous lace and braiding and the expensive epaulettes of officers.

With the abolition of epaulettes a universal system for distinguishing each commissioned rank was introduced. Displayed on the collar, one star was shared by majors and cornets, a crown by lieutenant-colonels and lieutenants, a crown and a star by colonels and captains; field officers were further distinguished from troop officers by additional lace on the collar and cuffs.

The headdress changes will be described under each type of cavalry, but the rest of the uniform continued much as before with only minor altera-

tions. The Crimean practice of having booted overalls, i.e. strapped with leather, now became universal for all mounted duties, though not officially authorised until 1861. All cavalry bands and trumpeters were to wear the same colour tunic as the rest of their regiment, unlike the Infantry whose musicians were distinguished by white tunics. Except for minor changes of detail (of cut and of footwear), this uniform would remain essentially the same until 1914, after which full dress ceased to be universal.

The main difference in the accoutrements was that, with the tunic, the sling waistbelt was worn under it by all ranks of Light Cavalry. The cap pouch was moved from the waistbelt to the pouch-belt or carried in a slit pocket on the front of the tunic. The men's pouch-belts lost the carbine swivel, from the mid-1860s, when the breech-loading Snider carbine was issued; this weapon no longer having the bar and sliding ring of previous carbines, but being fitted with a sling like an infantry rifle. In 1868 the old practice, when mounted, of carrying the carbine resting across the man's right thigh with the muzzle in a short bucket below the right holster or wallet was abolished in favour of placing the weapon muzzle down in a deep bucket buckled to the saddle behind the man's right leg. Sabretaches were now only carried by Hussars, although towards the end of this period an undress black leather type, with regimental device, was resumed by officers of the Heavies and Lancers. Shabraques having been re-introduced for the Heavy Cavalry in 1857, they continued in use for all ranks of all Line Cavalry, the Heavies having square corners, Light Dragoons and Lancers rounded, and Hussars pointed. In marching order the rear corners of rounded and pointed shabraques were to be looped up and secured together with a hook and eye under the valise.

Although the Snider became the regulation carbine for all cavalry in 1866, various other breech-loaders had been issued experimentally from 1857. For example, the 2nd Dragoon Guards and 8th Hussars used the American Sharps during the Indian Mutiny, and between 1864 and 1866 the 10th, 13th and 18th Hussars received the Westley-Richards, the latter regiment having formerly been equipped with the Terry. Apart from minor modifications, the swords of Line Cavalry officers remained as before, but the universal troopers' pattern of 1853 received a new guard in 1864, of sheet steel with a pierced Maltese cross device.

Household Cavalry

Other than the 1843 helmet which continued in use, the adoption of the tunic by the Household Cavalry during 1857 gave its three regiments an appearance which, except for minor details, still exists in their full dress today. The tunic was single-breasted with nine buttons in front, the collar, cuffs and edging down the front being in the facing colour. The foreparts of the collar were richly embroidered for officers, and laced round with a button for the men; the cuffs were similarly decorated, the men's lace being in a chevron. Officers and NCOs wore twisted gold shoulder cords and aiguillettes as before, the men having a plain shoulder strap in the facing colour laced all round: by 1871, a numeral '1' was being worn on the latter by the 1st Life Guards. Officers had three rectangles of lace set on vertically below each of the buttons at the back of the waist. The men's back skirts had two slashes with three points edged in the facing colour, each with three buttons.

The rest of the uniform and accoutrements underwent little change in their essential features.

Private, 1st Life Guards, 1857, in the 1843 helmet and the new tunic. Note the carbine strapped on the horse and the white sheepskin which, for this regiment, changed to black in the next period. Watercolour by Henry Martens.

The two regiments of Life Guards continued to be distinguished most obviously by their flask cords, the arrangement of the red striping on their undress blue overalls, the officers' shabraques and the initials on the men's valises, but also by a number of small details, some almost indiscernible.

A corporal of the 2nd Life Guards in the new dress is shown in Fig. 60, Plate 22.

Heavy Cavalry

The 1847 helmet was retained but with certain alterations. Dragoon Guards were still to have theirs of gilt brass, but the 1st Royal and 6th Inniskilling Dragoons were to have white metal with gilt ornaments, the Greys retaining bearskin caps. In addition, the helmets of each regiment were henceforth to be distinguished by different coloured plumes (see Appendix 6).

The cut of the tunic was as described for the Household Cavalry but the embellishments differed. All ranks had a lace chevron and central button on the cuffs though these were usually hidden by the gauntlet gloves. Field officers had their collars laced all round and further lace round the top of the cuff, troop officers having lace only round the top and front of the collar. Officers' badges of rank were stitched on lace loops 4½ in. long on either front of the collar, and instead of epaulettes their shoulder straps were of twisted gold cord. The men's shoulder straps were in the facing colour, laced all round, and with the regimental initials; their collars had a lace loop but no lace edging. From 1857 the collar loops were removed from the tunics of all ranks, the men's then being edged with braid. This change, as far as the men were concerned, may have taken some years to effect: a painting by Hayes of the 5th Dragoon Guards in 1863 shows braided collars, whereas in an Orlando Norie painting of 1867 the 7th Dragoon Guards appear still to have looped collars. The Hayes painting also shows three-buttoned slashes on the back skirts, although initially the men's tunics had lace rectangles like the officers. A private of the 2nd Dragoons is shown in Fig. 59, Plate 21.

Officers' stable jackets became plainer and more like the men's, with ten small buttons in front, two at the cuff, a plain collar and pointed cuffs in the facing colour, and a gold cord on each shoulder. In 1858 the Heavy Cavalry cloaks, so long scarlet, changed to blue in conformity with the other regiments. Apart from these changes and those mentioned in the General section, the rest of the uniform and accoutrements remained as before.

The 6th Dragoon Guards (Carabiniers) continued to wear the helmet but were otherwise dressed and accoutred as Light Dragoons (see Fig. 61, Plate 22). However, in 1864 their tunics lost the front loopings, thereby giving the regiment a uniform that was unique among the Line Cavalry (a tunic of Heavy Cavalry cut, but in blue). Following this change, the Heavies' practice of wearing the sling waistbelt outside the tunic was also resumed.

This regiment was in India when the Mutiny broke out. Although troops in the sub-continent were issued with white clothing for wear in the hot weather—which some regiments dyed to varying shades of khaki during the Mutiny—the

Carabiniers were observed at the Siege of Delhi as looking 'dreadfully heavy and oppressed in their blue clothing and overalls'. They also wore their brass helmets, but without the plumes, and with only a white cover or puggaree (turban) wrapped round to diminish the heat of the sun. The Heavy Cavalry had not hitherto served in India but such were the exigencies of the Mutiny that the 1st, 2nd and 3rd Dragoon Guards were all sent out as reinforcements. It was not always possible for new regiments to obtain suitable campaigning kit before going into action and the Bays (2 DG) were reported charging at Lucknow in March 1858 'in their bright scarlet uniform and brass helmets'.

The 1st or King's Dragoon Guards went on from India to take part in the Third China War of 1860. Here again no special service kit was issued and drawings made in China by Colonel H H Crealock show the regiment in their home service clothing, the only concession to campaigning being puggarees wrapped round the plumeless

---

PLATE 22: 1855–1870

60. **Corporal, 2nd Life Guards, 1860.**
61. **Private, 6th Dragoon Guards (Carabiniers), 1860.**
62. **Troop-Sergeant-Major, 12th (Prince of Wales's Royal) Lancers, 1860.**

In this period the Household Cavalry's full dress (Figure 60, from a print after Thomas) became, essentially, that which still exists today, except for the 1843 helmet and minor differences in the cut of the tunic and the accoutrements. This NCO's rank is indicated by his shoulder cords and aiguillette at the left shoulder; officers having theirs on the right. The sword is the 1848 pattern, carried by this regiment and the Blues, the 1st Life Guards having the 1820 pattern. Figure 61, also from a Thomas print, shows the Light Dragoon uniform with the 1847 Heavy Cavalry helmet, worn until 1864 only by the Carabiniers; thereafter, the regiment retained the blue uniform but with the loopings and yellow piping abolished, and the sword belt worn outside the tunic in the normal Heavy Cavalry way. Figure 62, from a photograph, wears the 1856 pattern lance-cap, the last type to be sealed, and the first lancer tunic with the lapels turned back at the top to form the 'butterfly' and pointed cuffs in the facing colour (see detail). Unlike the booted overalls of Figure 61, this NCO has the overalls worn for dismounted duties. Lancers wore their sword-belt under the tunic. Since they were not armed with carbines, their pouch-belts had neither cap-pouches nor carbine swivels. The two latter were abolished for all Cavalry in the mid-1860s.

60. Cpl, 2nd Life Guards, 1860.

61. Pte, 6th Dragoon Guards, 1860.

62. TSM, 12th Lancers, 1860.

helmets, and long boots adopted by some officers (see Fig. 65, Plate 23).

That the brass helmet was preferred is curious, for various species of tropical helmets were devised during and after the Mutiny, and by 1860 a regulation pattern made of cork with an air pipe had been issued in India and indeed worn by some troops involved in the China War. Judging by a photograph of the 3rd Dragoon Guards in India in 1860, this helmet was only an alternative, as while some men are wearing it, others, in full dress, have the home service brass helmet. It was, however, increasingly adopted for active service and was worn by this regiment in the Abyssinian campaign of 1868. A painting by Orlando Norie shows them so equipped but with home service tunics and overalls, and the same dress is mentioned in a description of a review held during the campaign. In the field, however, they were described as wearing loose blouses and overalls of Indian material dyed khaki. This outfit was useful for the heat but did not wear well and, before long, it was said, the men resembled 'gangs of ruffians'.

Light Dragoons

The first six years of this period witnessed the final phase of this, once the most numerous branch of the Cavalry, for in 1861 the remaining regiments, 3rd, 4th, 13th and 14th were converted to Hussars. Their last shako had a Maltese cross and lace band round the top as before, but the dimensions changed to $5\frac{1}{4}$ in. in front, $6\frac{3}{8}$ in. at the sides and $9\frac{1}{8}$ in. at the back, the top being $1\frac{1}{8}$ in. less in diameter than the bottom. The peak was nearly horizontal, edged gold for officers. The plumes were of horsehair, in different colours for each regiment (see Appendix 7). Chin-chains and cap-lines completed its fittings.

The single-breasted blue tunic had five gold (or yellow) cord loops on each side in front, the top being 8 in. long, the bottom 4 in., each fastening with an olivet. The whole tunic was edged all round with the same cord, which also decorated the back seams, with eyes at the top and a knot at the bottom. The collar and pointed cuffs were in the facing colour and the latter were ornamented with a knot. The 1857 dress regulations ordered that field officers' collars were to be laced all round within the edging cord, other officers only having lace round the top. A double gold cord was attached to the shoulders of officers' tunics by a small regimental button (see Fig. 58, Plate 21). In 1855, officers' stable jackets were as

Officer, 4th Royal Irish Dragoon Guards in the first tunic, 1856. Plume white, facings and shabraque dark blue, sheepskin black edged scarlet. The Dragoon Guards' helmet was henceforth brass, that for Dragoons white metal. The lace rectangles on the tunic skirts were later replaced by three-button slashes. Lithograph after Henry Martens.

described for the Heavies but in blue, though in the 1861 regulations the gold lace edging was resumed. The latter also omitted any reference to the peaks of officers' forage caps, thus emulating the Hussars.

Unlike some of the Heavy regiments engaged in the Mutiny, the only Light Dragoons that took part, the 14th, dispensed with their home service headgear, wearing turbans wrapped round their forage caps with one end hanging down to protect the neck. Their tunics were worn open at the neck without stocks, but these tunics were soon discarded in favour of either shirt-sleeves or of loose cotton blouses dyed with curry powder.

Hussars

In 1855 the headdress continued as in the previous period, including the 15th's scarlet shako, but in 1857 a new pattern busby was introduced, which was also assumed by the 15th. This was of black fur, sable for officers, and was $7\frac{3}{4}$ in. high in front, 9 in. at the back. The plumes were of different colours for each regiment (see Ap-

Sergeants' Mess, 2nd The Queen's Dragoon Guards in India, 1865. In the back row are four NCOs, in review order with brass helmets and the four standards, though these last had officially been reduced to one per regiment in 1858. In the centre row are two NCOs in tropical helmets and marching order (second left and extreme right). Most are in undress, the stable jackets of the senior NCOs following the officers' laced pattern. Note kettle-drums in front and cap pouches on the pouch-belts. Facings buff (from 1855), plumes black.

pendix 7) and the bags were now decorated with vertical lines of gold (or yellow) braid with a button where they joined at the base. Except for the 11th's crimson, the bags remained scarlet; but other colours came in with the new 18th (raised in 1858), the conversion of the remaining Light Dragoon regiments, and the addition of the East India Company's European Cavalry regiments as 19th, 20th and 21st Hussars.

The Hussar tunic was similar to that for the Light Dragoons, but with six loops across the front and without facing colour except, after their conversion, for the 3rd and 13th who had scarlet and buff collars respectively. Officers' collars were laced round the top with additional braiding within the lace, which was figured for field officers, in 'eyes' for captains, and plain for subalterns; the same braiding embellished the Austrian knot on the cuffs. The pelisse was now discontinued.

Hussar overalls continued to have a single, $1\frac{1}{2}$-in. gold or yellow stripe, except in the 10th and 11th who had double stripes, as did the 13th

but in buff for the men (though described as buff in the regulations, these stripes and the collar were in fact pipeclayed white). The new dress is shown in Fig. 57, Plate 21.

Despite the simplification of Hussar uniform it was never to be worn in its entirety on active service. An eyewitness drawing by H H Crealock shows the 7th during the Indian Mutiny wearing loose-fitting khaki jackets above their home service overalls, while their forage caps are swathed in large turbans (see Fig. 64, Plate 23). In contrast, the 8th appear in a sketch by J N Crealock wearing blue stable jackets, overalls booted almost to the knee, and forage caps fitted with peaks and white covers and curtains; in addition to their pouch-belts and sword belts, they have haversacks slung over the right shoulder. Secured to the saddle are the rolled cloak, valise (with what may be a blanket rolled on top), and a water container of native manufacture with a spout. The 8th's men have their sabretaches but in the other sketch the 7th appear to have discarded them.

Lancers

The new lance-cap authorised in 1856 was reduced in size, being $6\frac{1}{2}$ in. in front, $8\frac{1}{2}$ in. at the back and the top $7\frac{1}{4} \times 7\frac{1}{4}$ in. square. This reduction in height gave the waist of the cap a more indented effect. The front plate became more ornate with additional battle honours, the cap-lines were simplified to terminate in acorns or olives, and the plumes—now of horsehair for all ranks—were in different regimental colours (see Appendix 7). Apart from minor modifications this cap would remain in service for as long as full dress was worn. The 9th continued to wear their special caps, with black patent leather top and gilt or brass plaited band round the waist, but in the same dimensions as other regiments.

The lancer tunic was double-breasted with collar and pointed cuffs in the facing colour, all regiments wearing blue except the 16th who retained scarlet. Except in marching order or bad weather the lapels were buttoned back above the fourth button from the top to show a 'butterfly' in the facing colour on the chest. Welts in the facing colour appeared on the back and sleeve seams, down the edge of the front and round the skirt. On each shoulder were narrow gold or yellow cords fastened by a button. Officers wore their rank badges on the collar; this was laced all round for field officers, on the front and top only for troop officers. Field officers' cuffs had two chevrons of lace, other officers had one, but the cuffs of all ranks were largely concealed by gauntlet gloves.

A photograph of the 17th in 1856 in the new dress shows the sling waistbelt for the sword worn outside the tunic, but the usual practice was for this belt to be under the tunic, while the waist girdle—crimson and gold for officers, scarlet and yellow for men—went over it. The overalls had double gold or yellow stripes except for the 17th who had white for all ranks.

The new dress, as worn by the 12th, is shown in Fig. 62, Plate 22. A photograph of the same

regiment in 1860 illustrates the undress uniform. The dark blue 'pillbox' forage caps, for sergeants and above, are without peaks and have gold lace bands and the gold cord welts, peculiar to Lancers, across the top with a button in the centre where they meet. The bands varied in width, officers having the widest. Caps for the rank and file, though not in the photograph, were the same but with yellow embellishments, while the band's caps were scarlet.

Two of the officers are in stable jackets, which are laced all round as well as on the scarlet collar and cuffs. No badges of rank are worn but the field officer's lace is wider than that of the other. The stable jacket fastened in front, with gilt studs, hooks and eyes, and had scarlet piping on the back and sleeve seams. The other officers are in single-breasted frock-coats decorated with black cord, round the collar and forming an Austrian knot on the cuffs. The coat fastened with olivets and six rows of double cord loopings, at each end of which were further, purely decorative, olivets and a trefoil. No rank badges were

---

PLATE 23: 1855–1870

63. **Private, 9th (Queen's Royal) Light Dragoons (Lancers), 1857 (India).**
64. **Private, 7th (Queen's Own) Light Dragoons (Hussars), 1858 (India).**
65. **Captain, 1st (King's) Dragoon Guards, 1860 (China).**

This plate shows active service dress during this period, in the Indian Mutiny and Third China War. Figure 63, based on a sketch by Captain Upton of the regiment, is in the Indian summer stable dress as worn by the 9th at the siege of Delhi. According to eyewitness drawings by H H Crealock (on which Figures 64 and 65 are based) the 7th Hussars, one of the reinforcing regiments sent out to the Mutiny, wore the home service booted overalls with jackets, described by an officer as 'the colour of dust' and issued in India. Unlike Figure 63's covered forage cap, the 7th's caps were swathed in a puggaree with a loose end to protect the neck. The swords of both figures are the 1853 pattern. In China, the King's Dragoon Guards (Figure 65) wore their home service clothing and the 1847 helmet, with plume removed and puggaree folded round it. The non-regulation boots of this officer were either acquired locally or were a relic of Crimean or Mutiny service. The men wore the normal booted overalls. The officer's tunic is the dress pattern but his belts are undress; the pouch made from black patent leather. His sword is the Heavy Cavalry officers' 1821 undress type with scroll pattern guard.

63. Pte, 9th Lancers, 1857.

64. Pte, 7th Hussars, 1858.

65. Offr, 1st Dragoon Guards, 1860.

6th Dragoon Guards (Carabiniers), c 1870. The blue tunics of this regiment have lost their Light Dragoon loopings (see Plate 22), but the officers' pouch-belts and the shabraques are still of Light Cavalry pattern. Note the booted overalls and trumpeters' white plumes, a colour adopted by the whole regiment in 1873, instead of black. Watercolour by Orlando Norie.

Sergeant-Major Bailey, 1st (Royal) Dragoons, 1856. His blue collar has the lace loop discontinued from 1857. The cap pouch, later attached to the pouch-belt, is in a slit pocket just above the waistbelt. Plume black, trouser stripe yellow.

worn. Dress pouch-belts were worn with the stable jacket but not with the frock-coat.

The men's stable jackets were similar in cut but fastened with ten buttons and were without lace, except for sergeant-majors who had it on collars and cuffs. The jackets of all ranks had gold or yellow shoulder cords as on the tunic. NCOs' rank badges were worn on the right arm only, sergeant-majors and sergeants having a regimental arm badge of the Prince of Wales's feathers surmounted by the crown in silver above their chevrons.

In the photograph one officer wears booted overalls but all the others are in the type worn for dismounted duties without the leather strapping.

A painting of a 17th officer, c 1865, shows the lancer shabraque. This is blue with rounded corners and a double band of gold lace: the Royal cypher and crown is shown on the fore-corners, while a crown over the skull and cross bones on crossed lances, with a scroll 'Or Glory' below and the title '17 L' are on the hind-corners. Over the shabraque and the valise, which also bears the death's head badge, is a black lambskin edged white. The same badge, in silver, appears on the otherwise plain black leather sabretache.

In India, regiments had an all-white stable

Captain Barthorp's Troop, 10th (Prince of Wales's Own) Hussars c 1870 in varied dress. Two privates near the centre are in full dress, the troop-sergeant-major (centre standing), the sergeants and some men are in undress, the remainder in working dress or plain clothes. The cap bands and braid of the sergeants, being gold, show light, whereas the yellow of the rank and file appears dark.

The same troop's officer, Captain Arthur Barthorp, in full dress. Note the rank badges on the collar, the chain-covered pouch-belt peculiar to the 10th Hussars, and the knee-boots introduced in 1871. Cap plume white over black, bag scarlet.

dress for hot weather of the same cut as the blue one. The 9th had their white jackets piped in red and it is in this dress, with the addition of neck curtains to the white-covered but peakless forage caps, that they are shown at the siege of Delhi in a sketch by Captain Upton of the regiment (see Fig. 63, Plate 23). The same dress is also shown in one of Captain Atkinson's Mutiny drawings, which includes an officer wearing his dress pouch-belt and a peak to the forage cap. The Delhi operations occurred throughout the hot weather of 1857, but by the relief of Lucknow in November, the 9th were described as wearing 'their blue uniforms and white turbans twisted round their forage caps'. The blue may have been the home service stable dress, the new tunic, or even, since the regiment had been in India since 1842 and dress changes took time to reach the sub-continent, the old dress jacket.

The 17th, as one of the reinforcing regiments sent out to the Mutiny, had to make do with their home service clothing and were observed as late in the campaign as April 1859 so dressed, though by then their forage caps were covered by large puggarees and fitted with peaks.

The remarks above, under Heavy Cavalry, about the increasing use of tropical helmets in India apply equally to other regiments. By 1861 the 17th had leather helmets covered with white cloth, made up regimentally, and henceforth they wore these in hot and cold weather alike.

Experiments with bamboo lances led to the adoption of a regulation bamboo pattern in 1868, of the same length as the ash type and with steel point and butt. The red over white pennons remained as before.

Officer, 17th Lancers in undress, c 1870. The stable jacket is laced gold all round and on the pointed white cuffs. The laced pouch-belt and waistbelt were worn in full dress and undress. On the forage cap can be seen the quarter welts peculiar to Lancers.

Dress 1871–1901

General

Apart from a universal tightening-up and shortening of the skirts, together with some minor changes, the tunic from the last period continued as the full dress upper garment throughout the next three decades and beyond. Some alterations to headdress took place in the Heavy Cavalry and the Hussars. However, the chief change at the start of this period—which applied to all Line Cavalry, and to a lesser extent to the Household Cavalry—was the abolition for mounted duties of booted overalls in favour of knee-boots and panta-loons, with the same stripes as before. The former had a V-cut at the top in front, and were hollowed out behind the knee. Overalls continued as before for dismounted duties. From 1893 the officers' gold lace stripes on pantaloons were changed to cloth, except in levée dress.

PLATE 24: 1871–1901

66. **Corporal, 1st (Royal) Dragoons, 1895.**
67. **Regimental-Quartermaster-Sergeant, 11th (Prince Albert's Own) Hussars, 1898.**
68. **Captain, 17th (Duke of Cambridge's Own) Lancers, 1898.**

This plate, based on photographs, illustrates the essential features of the full dress of Dragoons, Hussars and Lancers in its final form, which persisted up to its discontinuance in 1914, except for minor details. A major change instituted in this period was the replacement of booted overalls by pantaloons and knee-boots, as in Figures 66 and 68, though overalls were still worn for dismounted duties, as in Figure 67. The helmet of Figure 66, of the 1871 pattern, was only worn by this regiment and by the 6th Dragoons; all Dragoon Guards having brass, and the 2nd Dragoons their bearskin caps (see Figure 75). The helmet plumes varied regimentally but there was no difference between tunics and panta-loons of Dragoon Guards and Dragoons, except for the facings. Note the cuff detail. This NCO is armed with the Martini-Henry carbine and 1885 pattern sword. The senior NCO, Figure 67, displaying the distinctive crimson busby-bag and overalls of his regiment, wears the 1888 pattern busby. Between the star and chevrons denoting his rank is the regimental arm badge of Prince Albert's crest. A comparison of this hussar tunic with that in Figure 57 reveals how much closer-fitting it had become. Since the 5th, 9th and 12th Lancers all had scarlet facings, Figure 68's uniform and the scarlet, faced blue of the 16th gave these two regiments a distinctive appearance. The square-topped boots were peculiar to officers of the 17th.

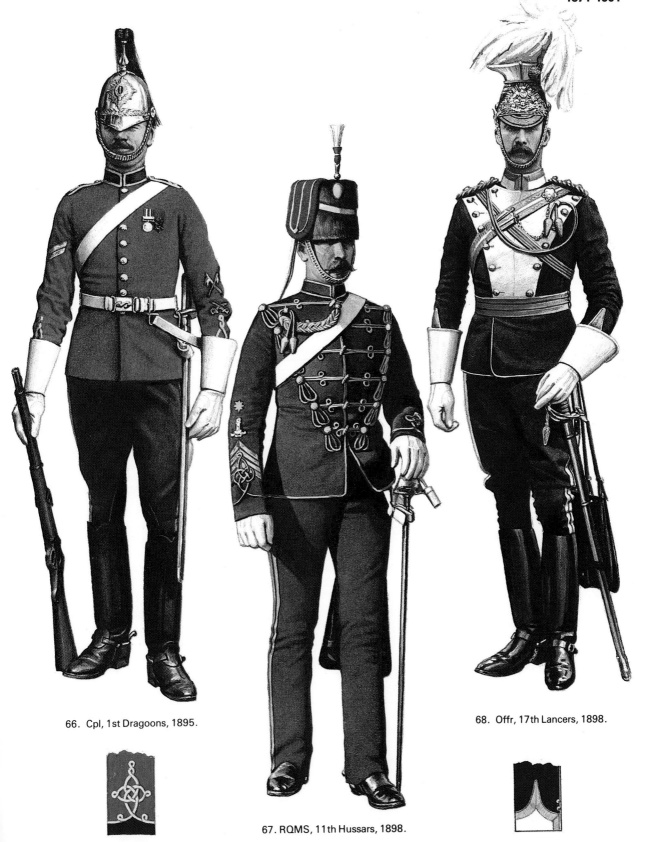

66. Cpl, 1st Dragoons, 1895.

67. RQMS, 11th Hussars, 1898.

68. Offr, 17th Lancers, 1898.

1st Life Guards in marching order on manoeuvres, 1871. The helmets are without plumes, and blue pantaloons with knee-boots are worn instead of breeches and jacked boots. On the horses are rolled cloaks, valises with mess-tins strapped on, forage bags and carbine buckets on the off-side. The man examining his helmet has the aiguillette of an NCO at his left shoulder. Behind the trumpeter are two officers with aiguillettes on the right. Watercolour by Orlando Norie.

In 1880 all officers' rank badges were removed from the collar and placed on gold plaited shoulder cords. The badges were in silver embroidery and the combination of stars and crowns changed as follows: colonels, crown and two stars; lieutenant-colonels, crown and star; majors, a crown; captain, two stars; lieutenants, one star; second-lieutenants, no badge. In the 1900 dress regulations, collar badges were authorised for wear on tunics and frocks by all Line Cavalry. A photograph of the Royal Dragoons officers in 1896 shows such badges being worn, but, generally, there is little evidence of them being worn until well into the following decade, and then by no means universally.

The shabraque ceased to be part of a soldier's horse furniture from the start of this period and in 1897 it was abolished for all officers except in the Household Cavalry. In the previous year sheepskins and the cloth-covered circular valises were also dispensed with. Another important change was the transfer of the sword from the man to the saddle where it was suspended in a frog on the near side, guard to the rear, behind the man's thigh. This practice began in India after it had been observed during the Second Afghan War how encumbered by his sword a cavalryman was when fighting dismounted with his carbine. A photograph of the 7th Hussars in India in 1890 shows this method in use, but it was not sanctioned for regiments at home until 1891. When parading dismounted the sword was still attached to the slings of the waistbelt; worn over the tunic by Heavies, under it by Hussars and Lancers; when mounted the slings were buckled together.

After the Valise pattern equipment was introduced for the Infantry from 1871, its barrel-shaped wooden water-bottle was adopted by the Cavalry to replace the old, circular keg-type and was worn over the right shoulder resting on the haversack in marching order or fastened to the rear near side of the saddle. In due course this gave way to the round, cloth-covered bottle of the Slade-Wallace equipment, except for regiments in India who had a more square-shaped bottle with brown leather strap. A circular mess-tin was also introduced for Cavalry instead of the D-shaped type used by the Infantry; this was carried, in marching order, buckled to the off-side shoe case which was attached to the saddle behind the carbine bucket. An expense ammunition pouch was introduced also in 1878, and was worn on the right front of the waistbelt by the Heavies, or of the girdle by Lancers when this branch received carbines instead of pistols from 1876 onwards. This waist pouch was additional to the pouch-belt

tions were the fixed rings on the 1882 scabbard and the re-positioning of the rings on either side and just below the mouth on the 1885 pattern. This change remained on succeeding scabbards.

The 1822 Heavy Cavalry officers' sword with steel scroll guard remained unchanged except for some alterations to the blade. In 1896, Light Cavalry officers were to adopt the same sword, instead of their 1821 pattern, so that henceforth there were standard swords for officers and men throughout the Line Cavalry. The unsuitability of steel scabbards and the sling method of suspension was proved in the colonial wars of this period and led to the use of leather scabbards and the Sam Browne belt. Unofficially adopted by officers during the Second Afghan War, it gained popularity in other overseas territories until its official authorisation for all active service and field use was promulgated in 1899. The early patterns had only one cross brace but the later type was furnished with two braces.

At the start of this period all Line Cavalry officers in undress wore the round, pillbox forage cap with either a stable jacket or a blue frock-coat, as had been the system from before the 1855 dress changes. At the turn of the century Line Cavalry officers wore either the forage cap or the folding field service cap, with a frock coat for the Heavies and a patrol jacket for Hussars and Lancers, or a serge frock (a simplified tunic-style garment) in scarlet or blue. The field service cap in regimental colours (of the type still worn and known today as a side hat) was introduced in about 1895, but had been preceded by another folding pattern, the 'Torin' cap, which came into use from 1883 'for active service and peace manoeuvres'. A fur-trimmed, braided patrol jacket was authorised as a substitute for the frock-coat in the 1883 dress regulations, but had already been in use for some years. Serge frocks with patch pockets were prescribed in the 1891 regulations but had also been worn in the previous decade; from 1897 a new pattern, matching the full dress tunic in colour, with collar in the facings and with pockets was approved and the braided patrol jacket was abolished. In the following year steel shoulder chains were added, a device worn for many years by the Indian Cavalry.

which continued to serve as an ammunition carrier, but towards the end of this period cavalry regiments in the 1898 Sudan campaign and the South African War were issued with 50-round brown leather bandoliers. Each group of ten cartridge loops on this carrier was covered by a flap fastening on to two studs; the bandolier first saw active service in the Gordon Relief Expedition of 1884 when it was issued to cavalry detachments forming the Heavy and Light Camel regiments.

From 1878 the Martini-Henry carbine replaced the Snider as the standard cavalry firearm for all regiments. In the 1890s the Martini carbine was converted by the substitution of, first, Metford, and later, Enfield barrels, until in 1894 the first bolt-action carbine, the magazine Lee-Metford, was introduced, followed in 1896 by the Lee Enfield. Attempts to improve the 1864 pattern troopers' sword resulted in new models, produced in 1882, 1885, 1890 and 1899, (exclusive of experimental weapons). All except the last had the 1864 guard with minor modifications (the 1899 guard not having the pierced cross) and all had a slightly curved blade, but differed in blade length, construction and weight. More obvious altera-

With the issue to the men of serge frocks and field caps from 1880 onwards, the stable jacket and forage cap became reserved for occasions that required a greater degree of smartness than was provided by the frock but less than was provided by the full dress tunic. From the mid-1890s the stable jackets and forage caps were only worn when walking out. They were formally abolished in 1897. Cloaks were blue for all Line Cavalry, but with regimental differences in the collars and lining. In India a white uniform had replaced the home service clothing in the hot season for many years, and in 1887 a white uniform was authorised for all hot climates. The officers' shoulder straps varied according to regiment: for Dragoon Guards and Dragoons, scarlet silk; for Hussars, scarlet edged white; for Lancers, light blue. These were abolished in 1896 and replaced by plain white. On overseas stations the white foreign service helmet with gilt spike was used all the year round; it was worn with a puggaree in India, Egypt and the Sudan but without at the Cape. During the Second Afghan War the helmets (with spikes removed) were fitted with khaki covers; and khaki jackets or frocks, usually worn with home service pantaloons and either knee boots or puttees, were taken into use. These frocks were initially the white garments dyed in a rudimentary fashion, but towards the end of the campaign a permanently dyed khaki cotton drill material was produced. From 1885 khaki became universal for all regiments in India, except on ceremonial occasions. In Africa home service clothing was usually worn but with the foreign service helmet, although, as will be seen, more practical costumes made their appearance in the campaigns of the mid-1880s. In 1896 the home authorities approved an all-khaki uniform of cotton drill frock, cord breeches and puttees for all foreign service outside Europe. First worn in action by the 21st Lancers in the 1898 Sudan campaign, it was issued a year later to all regiments going out to the South African War. During the course of the war khaki serge replaced the drill material, and the slouch hat, as worn by the Colonial troops, became a widely-used alternative to the helmet. A new pattern helmet with flatter brim, the Wolseley, was worn by officers of the 21st Lancers in the Sudan and by officers of several regiments in South Africa.

Household Cavalry

In this period the full dress of the three regiments remained essentially as before, apart from the introduction, from 1871, of a less ornate helmet with a ball and spike holder of the type still worn in full dress today (except for very minor differences). During the 1870s the tunics of the 2nd Life Guards differed in cut from the 1st Regiment, the skirts being cut away below the waist and the collars rounded in front. From 1881, however, the square cut of the senior regiment was adopted by the 2nd. Knee boots were introduced for wear in marching order with blue, red-striped pantaloons instead of the white leather breeches and jack-boots; in this order of dress the helmet plumes were removed. Overalls were worn for most dismounted duties and when walking out.

The aiguillettes worn at the left shoulder by NCOs were of two types: 1st Class, having four cord rings above the points, for ranks of troop-corporal-major and above; and 2nd Class, without

PLATE 25: 1871–1901

69. Sergeant, 9th (Queen's Royal) Lancers, 1880 (Afghanistan).
70. Private, 4th Royal Irish Dragoon Guards, 1882 (Egypt).
71. Officer, 10th (Prince of Wales's Own Royal) Hussars, 1884 (Sudan).

In contrast with the preceding plate, this and Plate 26 show examples of active service dress in this period. A variety of khaki clothing made up under regimental arrangement was used during the Second Afghan War, and Figure 69, based on a photograph, shows the double-breasted, quilted jackets, worn over blue serge frocks with home service pantaloons, adopted by the 9th Lancers in the winter of 1880. The white foreign service helmet had a khaki cover; and puttees, instead of knee-boots, were widely used for the first time in this campaign. The brown strap over the right shoulder suspends a buckram-covered water container of Indian manufacture. The force sent from England to Egypt in 1882 generally wore home service clothing, but with the undress serge frock instead of the tunic and the white helmet, complete with sungoggles and face veil. Figure 70's regiment retained knee-boots but the Household Cavalry and 7th Dragoon Guards adopted dark blue puttees. The Oliver pattern water bottle was slung over the left shoulder. For the Sudan, Figure 71 (from eye-witness pictures by Melton Prior and G D Giles), wears a regimental pattern khaki frock which had been made up in India and used in the Afghan War. The Sam Browne belt had been widely used in Afghanistan to carry sword and revolver, though some of the 10th's officers continued to use sling-belts for the sword, as shown here. The plain sabretache bore the Prince of Wales's feathers in silver.

69. Sgt, 9th Lancers, 1880.

70. Pte, 4th Dragoon Guards, 1882.

71. Offr, 10th Hussars, 1884.

Quarter-guard of the 2nd Dragoons (Royal Scots Greys) in dismounted full dress, 1886, with mounted orderly and supernumeraries in undress. Next to the orderly is a trumpeter with crimson feather curling over his bearskin cap, and yellow aiguillette at the left shoulder. As no swords are carried, the sword slings are buckled together. Expense ammunition pouches are attached to the right front of the waistbelt.

The same regiment on manoeuvres in 1893 in marching order with scarlet serge frocks. Haversacks are worn over the right shoulder, water bottles strapped to the rear nearside of the saddle. With backs to camera are (left) a sergeant-major and (right) an officer, with sabretache. Some of the men have lances, introduced for the front ranks of Heavy Cavalry at this time.

the rings, for corporals and corporals of horse[8]. Additionally troop-corporal-majors and above had gold lace edging all round the top of the collar and on the top and rear of the gauntlet cuffs. This edging was slightly wider for regimental-corporal-majors and quartermaster-corporal-majors, who were further distinguished by having lace rectangles on the back skirts instead of the slash flaps worn by junior ranks.

In undress, officers wore a peaked forage cap with scarlet band and welt and a blue frock-coat, braided, with olivets and broad, falling black loops. A short jacket similarly ornamented and known as a 'summer frock' was also worn, though unofficially. In the 1890s a plainer frock with patch pockets was authorised in addition to the frock-coat, and the field service cap became an alternative to the forage cap.

At the start of this period the men's undress was forage cap and stable jacket. NCOs had chevrons on the latter instead of aiguillettes: four-bar chevron for troop (later squadron)-corporal-majors; three-bar for corporals of horse; and two-bar for corporals (after 1878); all with a crown above. The regimental-corporal-major had an inverted four-bar chevron with crown above on the right forearm. Photographs of the 1st Life Guards in the 1870s show a loose serge jacket in use for stable duties, but in the next decade red serge frocks were issued, blue for the Royal Horse Guards. The field service cap was also used by the Household Cavalry.

From the start of this period officers of all three regiments had a standard sword for all occasions;

[8] Rank equivalent to sergeant, introduced in 1878.

this had a steel guard with brass ornaments and steel scabbard with brass mountings, each regiment having its own minute differences. A new pattern Household Cavalry troopers' sword with scroll basket guard was authorised in 1882. This was modified in 1888 and replaced in 1892 by another pattern, almost identical in appearance.

A major change to the horse furniture was the adoption of black sheepskins by the 1st Life Guards in the mid-1880s instead of white which continued for the 2nd Regiment. The Blues had black as before.

The Household Cavalry had seen no action since Waterloo but in 1882 a squadron from each of the three regiments formed a composite regiment for the Egyptian War. All ranks wore the foreign service helmet (stained khaki after arrival in Egypt), red or blue serge frocks and home service pantaloons. Smoked goggles and anti-fly face veils were specially issued. Officers wore knee-boots, but while some illustrations made before the departure show blue puttees for the men, photographs taken after the campaign show knee-boots also. If puttees were worn, they may have been too tattered for the later photographs. Evidence as to whether the serge frocks had collars in the facing colour also conflicts, though

The Prince of Wales as Colonel, the Commanding Officer (Valentine Baker) and a trumpeter, 10th Prince of Wales's Own Royal Hussars, 1871. The 1857 pattern cap is worn. Sabretache scarlet, shabraque dark blue with leopardskin cover. The latter only applicable to officers.

photographs suggest they did not. Frocks for officers and men both had five-button fastenings, the former having patch breast pockets. Officers were accoutred with Sam Browne belts for sword and pistol, and brown gauntlets, but once again there is conflicting evidence about the accoutrements of the men. The pre-departure illustrations show the white sling waistbelt with rectangular clasp and the full dress pouch-belt with flask cord, together with haversack, water bottle and white gauntlets. On the other hand, the post-campaign photographs and some illustrations of the fighting (possibly based on these photographs) show no gauntlets, but the same waistbelt, haversack and water bottle, with the pouch strapped to the back of the waistbelt and no shoulder belt, and an additional white expense pouch on the right front of the waistbelt. It is possible that the regiment went out to Egypt with the complete pouch-belt but discarded the belt in the field.

Whatever was actually worn in 1882, a different costume was issued for the eight officers and 129 men drawn from all three regiments who formed part of the Heavy Camel Regiment in the Gordon Relief Expedition of 1884. The men received a grey serge frock with five-button fastening and no pockets, Bedford cord breeches, blue puttees and brown ankle boots. Since the regiment was to act as mounted infantry, the equipment was part cavalry and part infantry: 50-round leather bandolier, brown leather waistbelt with snake clasp, bayonet frog (and possibly an expense pouch), haversack and water bottle. Weapons were the Martini-Henry rifle and sword bayonet. Although also grey, the officers' frocks reflected to some degree their own individual tastes, but generally seem to have been on the lines of a Norfolk jacket, with breast and skirt pockets. Cord breeches, brown butcher boots and brown gauntlets completed their clothing while the sword and revolver were supported by the Sam Browne belt (see Fig. 72, Plate 26). The white helmets of all ranks were stained a drab colour, the officers of the 2nd Life Guards distinguishing themselves by a red twist in their puggarees. The men of each detachment sewed their abbreviated regimental designations in red or blue on the upper right sleeve of the grey frock.

For the South African War another composite Household Regiment was formed, in which all ranks wore the universal khaki drill uniform approved in 1896. The officers had khaki helmets but the men's were white with khaki covers.

Photographs of the regiment parading before departure show the officers with Sam Browne belts with double braces and brown leather 'Stohwasser' leggings, the men with 50-round bandoliers, haversacks, no waistbelts and khaki puttees.

Heavy Cavalry

In 1871 a new helmet was approved. Though of the same basic shape and metal as before, it was much plainer and had a 12-pointed star plate and a four-sided fluted socket for the plume. The plumes remained unchanged, except for the 6th Dragoon Guards who adopted white instead of black in 1873. The officers' plates acquired distinctive regimental devices instead of the Royal cypher. From 1884 the brass helmets of men of the Dragoon Guards had a white metal numeral on black within a brass garter set upon a white metal star, while the white metal helmets of the 1st Royal and 6th Inniskilling Dragoons had the plate metals reversed. From 1874 the bearskin caps of the 2nd Dragoons were to be 10 in. high.

The scarlet tunics (blue for 6th Dragoon Guards) underwent some small modifications. The cuffs in the facing colour lost the lace chevron, becoming slightly pointed and surmounted by an Austrian knot. For officers the knot varied in size according to rank and was outlined in tracing braid. The collars were cut square in front, but with the same lace distinctions for the different ranks of officers, and braid all round for the men. Dragoon Guards, except for the 2nd, retained their traditional velvet facings. The back of the tunics continued to have two buttons at the waist with, below, the three-buttoned slash, edged with gold or yellow, which for officers was outlined with tracing braid. (See Fig. 66, Plate 24).

Alterations to nether garments and undress have already been covered under the General section. The field caps of the Heavies had blue flaps and a yellow body, except in the 2nd and 6th Dragoon Guards where the body was white.

The rectangular, crested waist plate of the men's sword belts changed to a simple brass snake fastening; a photograph, dated 1875, shows this in use but the precise date of change is uncertain. Officers' gold-laced, full dress sword belts and their undress white belts retained the rectangular plates, but the former became in effect a girdle, the sword and sabretache slings being attached to a web waistbelt worn under the tunic. The undress belts, when worn with the tunic as in field

day order, were buckled outside it as before.

From 1892 it was decided to increase the capacity of the Heavy Cavalry for shock action by equipping the front rank of each troop with lances in addition to sword and carbine.

The King's Dragoon Guards fought in the Zulu War in home service clothing and foreign service helmet but without a puggaree, as was the practice in South Africa; officers wore undress belts. The same dress prevailed in the Egyptian War for the 4th and 7th Dragoon Guards although the puggarees were retained and tunics replaced by scarlet serge frocks with collars and cuffs in the facing colour. The 4th appear to have kept to the knee-boots used at home but the 7th adopted blue puttees (see Fig. 70, Plate 25). Accoutrements in both these campaigns were of the normal home service pattern, to which haversacks and water bottles were added. The white gauntlets do not appear to have been worn in either case.

The 6th Dragoons were observed in South Africa at the time of the Transvaal War of 1881

PLATE 26: 1871–1901

72. Captain, 2nd Life Guards, Heavy Camel Regiment, 1885 (Sudan).
73. Private, 21st (Empress of India's) Lancers, 1898 (Sudan).
74. Corporal, 7th Queen's Own Hussars, 1901 (South Africa).

The Camel Corps for the Gordon Relief Expedition received a campaign kit of grey serge frock, Bedford cord pantaloons and, for the men, blue puttees. Officers' frocks varied slightly according to individual preference; Figure 72's (from a photograph) owed something to the Norfolk jacket. The red twist in the stained helmet's puggaree was a distinction of this regiment. Khaki drill had been worn in India since 1885 but not universally approved for foreign service until 1896. Figure 73 shows the Cavalry version as worn in the second Sudan campaign. The shoulder chains were copied by British Cavalry from their Indian counterparts. The large helmet sunshade was a peculiarity of the 21st. This uniform (without the shade) was widely worn in the opening months of the South African War but proved unserviceable and was replaced by a serge version (Figure 74). The slouch hat was a popular alternative to the helmet. The leather bandolier, replacing the pouch-belt, was first used by the Camel Corps in 1885. Figure 74's Infantry Lee-Metford rifle reflects the changing role of cavalry in South Africa. The water bottles of Figures 73 and 74 are from the Infantry's 1888 Slade-Wallace equipment.

72. Offr, 2nd Life Guards, 1885.

73. Pte, 21st Lancers, 1898.

74. Cpl, 7th Hussars, 1901.

4th (Queen's Own) Hussars in review order, 1894, with 1888 pattern cap. From left: corporal, regimental-sergeant-major, squadron-sergeant-major, private. The comparative quality of the gold or yellow braiding between ranks is clearly visible. Plumes scarlet, busby-bag yellow. The sword is now carried on the saddle.

Private, 3rd (King's Own) Hussars, 1899, in khaki marching order as worn in India. Note the shoulder chains. The slings of the sword belt, worn under the frock, are buckled together, the sword being carried on the saddle. Home-based regiments on foreign service at this date had the 50-round leather bandolier instead of the pouch-belt. The rectangular water bottle issued in India is just visible under the haversack.

looking 'as spick and span as could be', but for the Bechuanaland Field Force expedition of 1884 workmanlike brown corduroy jackets were served out. A photograph shows that the jackets worn by officers had two breast pockets and no shoulder straps, rank being indicated by a simple braid loop on the cuff. The breeches appear to have been of a paler shade than the jackets and, in one case, were worn with knee boots, in another, with puttees. Sam Browne belts supported the revolver, while the men's equipment was of the normal pattern. Slouch hats were adopted by elements of this force, including the mounted infantry company of the Royal Scots, but the two Inniskillings officers both have the foreign service helmet, stained and without puggaree.

Also in 1884, the 2nd, 4th and 5th Dragoon Guards plus the 1st and 2nd Dragoons provided detachments for the Heavy Camel Regiment. These were uniformed as described for the Household Cavalry.

Although the men's foreign service helmets were issued with khaki covers for the South African War, there were some exceptions. Photographs of the Greys, for example, show khaki helmets worn by the men with a strip of some darker colour, probably red, twisted through the puggaree. The 1st Royal Dragoons followed the Infantry practice of sewing the scarlet shoulder straps embroidered with '1 R D' from their serge frocks to the sides of the helmet. Officers of the 6th Dragoon Guards wore the new Wolseley helmet; while officers of the 6th Dragoons kept the old helmet, and a photograph shows them wearing bandoliers like the men.

At the end of this period, as a result of South African experience, the slouch hat was being adopted for manoeuvres at home, although khaki was not yet used for such training. Pictures of the 2nd Dragoon Guards exercising in 1901 show them in these hats, scarlet serge frocks, with white tabs on the forepart of the collar, and shoulder chains, blue pantaloons and knee-boots. A bandolier has replaced the pouch-belt while the haversack and water bottle hang from the right shoulder.

Hussars

Other than the general changes applicable to all Cavalry, the chief alteration during this period for Hussars was to the size of the busby. In 1888 a lower, lighter version, $6\frac{1}{4}$ in. high in front, $7\frac{3}{4}$ in. at the back, but with the same ornamentation as before, was approved. Three years later the officers' plume was lengthened to 13 in., and again in 1900 to 15 in. In the same year the bag was lengthened to reach the bottom edge of the busby. This pattern was unchanged thereafter.

The officers' collar and cuff lace and braiding was retained after the rank badges moved to the plaited gold shoulder cords. When knee-boots were introduced, Hussar officers had a removeable oval gold boss just below the V-cut at the top. In levée dress patent leather Hessian boots were ordered with a similar boss and lace round the top.

The field caps of all Hussars were entirely scarlet, except for the 11th who had crimson and the 13th who had blue flaps, white crown and body. The forage caps were blue (crimson and scarlet respectively for the 11th and 15th), with gold or yellow lace band. The braiding of the astrakhan-trimmed patrol jackets for officers varied between each regiment; all being illustrated in the 1900 dress regulations. That of the 13th was cut short at the waist like a stable jacket.

The cloth-faced, embroidered dress sabretache was now only carried by Hussar officers. The plain black type for Hussar NCOs was discontinued in 1888, and in 1901 all sabretaches were finally abolished throughout the Army. Unlike the Heavies and Lancers, whose officers' dress pouches were of a more or less uniform pattern, Hussar regiments had their own distinctive varieties, either in cloth or leather, with gilt or silver flaps; all of which were individually specified in the dress regulations. The last four regiments to be converted from Light Dragoons—the 3rd, 4th, 13th and 14th—all retained the Light Dragoon pouch of black leather with silver flap, as did the two junior regiments, 19th and 20th.

Until the introduction of the universal foreign service khaki, a variety of clothing was worn on active service. In the Second Afghan War, the 10th stained their white helmets and wore a khaki frock of a light brown shade over home service pantaloons, with blue puttees for the men and knee-boots for officers. In winter the home service tunic or a blue frock was worn under the khaki. The officers' khaki was of a special regimental pattern, the upper part—with cuffs gathered at the wrist and front buttons covered by a fly—having a blouse effect. On its return from India in 1884 the regiment was diverted to the campaign in the eastern Sudan where the same kit was worn, except that, according to eyewitness pictures, by G D Giles and Melton Prior of the regiment's charge at El Teb, the brass helmet spikes were not removed as had been done in Afghanistan (see Fig. 71, Plate 25).

The 19th Hussars seem to have fought in the Egyptian campaign dressed similarly to the two Dragoon Guards regiments though their home service frocks were, of course, blue and without facings. At some stage it would appear that they received Bedford cord breeches, though these, like the home service pantaloons, were worn with knee-boots. After the Egyptian campaign was completed, grey serge frocks were sent out, and the 19th, who remained to take part in the Sudan operations of 1884–1885, including the Gordon Relief Expedition, may have received these. Engravings in the illustrated papers show the regiment variously dressed in dark jackets with light breeches and vice versa, but with knee-boots in each case. The Light Camel Regiment formed from Hussar regiments in England was dressed in the fashion described for the Heavies.

In South Africa, in 1881, the 14th dyed their helmets and belts with red clay and took to the field in blue serge frocks, khaki pantaloons and puttees. Photographs of the same regiment

Above: *Home service marching order worn by the 16th (The Queen's) Lancers in 1878, the only regiment, other than the Heavies, to wear scarlet tunics. Carbines were issued to Lancers from 1876. The 17th fought in the Zulu War in this dress but with the foreign service helmet substituted. Watercolour by R Simkin.*

Left: *9th (Queen's Royal) Lancers in the same order of dress, 1890. The caps have foul-weather covers and the tunics are buttoned over to conceal the scarlet plastron. An expense pouch is attached to the girdle. Painting by T S Seccombe.*

the war in khaki serge uniforms and slouch hats (see Fig. 74, Plate 26).

Lancers

In this period the lance-cap was unaltered, although the 16th's plume colour changed in 1881 and the 17th underwent a temporary change of plumes between 1874–1883, while the 21st adopted a cap with French-grey top and white plume on being converted from Hussars in 1897 (see Appendix 7).

From 1873 the whole front above the waist of the double-breasted tunic was in the facing colour on one side; in blue (scarlet for the 16th) on the other. For review order the tunic was buttoned down the right side to display the facings in a contrasting plastron (see Fig. 68, Plate 24). In marching or field day order the tunic was buttoned down the left to show the tunic colour with only piping in the facings down the open side. The lacing on officers' tunics in the Lancers was

equipped for the second Boer War reveal that the officers had Wolseley helmets and Sam Browne belts with double braces, while the sergeants were accoutred with bandolier, haversack and sword belt (under the frock), with a brown leather waistbelt to support a revolver on the right side. No helmet insignia are visible in the photograph for the 14th, unlike the 13th who wore a blue and white flash on the left side. In common with other regiments that went direct to the war from India, the 19th appear to have had shoulder chains on their khaki frocks. Regiments from Britain did not have these. The 7th, who did not join the field army in South Africa until after 1900, went out to less elaborate than in the Hussars, appearing only on the outer edge of the collar and outlining the pointed cuffs; field officers were distinguished by additional lace round the base of the collar and a second line round the cuff.

Lancers' forage caps were blue (scarlet for the 12th), with gold or yellow band and piping crossing the crown at right angles in what were known as quarter welts. In the 9th and 17th the men's bands and piping were scarlet and white respectively. The field caps had blue flaps but a scarlet body except in the 17th and 21st where it was white and French grey respectively. When the Torin cap was in use, the 12th had all-scarlet, matching their forage cap. Unlike the Hussars, a universal pattern patrol jacket served for all Lancer officers, except the 5th who had special regimental braiding.

Officers' dress pouches were of scarlet leather, with metal flaps, except for blue leather in the 17th and black in the 21st. The 9th had no central stripe in the facing colour on their pouch-belts and sword slings.

During the Zulu War the 17th fought in home service marching order, with the tunics buttoned over blue, and the foreign service helmet without puggaree. Various photographs of the 9th during the Second Afghan War reveal that, in the field, khaki covers were worn over the white helmets and that, in addition to the dress tunic (kept for parades) and the blue serge frocks, a double-breasted garment in khaki, rather like a reefer jacket, was also used. The material of the latter appears to have been quilted, suggesting it was a winter jacket to be worn over the serge (see Fig. 69, Plate 25). Other NCOs have a single-breasted khaki jacket, apparently of drill material, with front pleats like a Norfolk jacket, which was probably for summer wear. Home service pantaloons, with knee boots or puttees, are worn in all cases.

The 5th and 16th provided detachments for the Heavy Camel Regiment in 1884. A photograph taken in Egypt before the expedition set out shows the 16th's detachment fully accoutred with bandolier, waistbelt, haversack and water bottle, and dressed as previously described, though the lighting conditions under which the photograph was taken makes it unclear whether grey serges are being worn or home service frocks, which all detachments had with them. In the photograph, the NCOs and men all have a crossed lances badge sewn on the right upper arm, one officer having the same on his right forearm. The officers

wear Sam Browne belts with double braces and butcher boots.

The whole of the 5th were employed in the eastern Sudan in 1885. Since the regiment went out from home where khaki was not available, they had grey frocks, cord breeches and blue puttees. The war artist C E Fripp's painting of the Battle of Tofrek includes a mounted trooper, who can only be a 5th Lancer (though without his lance), dressed thus and accoutred with the normal pouch-belt, haversack, water bottle and sling waistbelt worn over the frock.

For their famous charge at Omdurman in 1898, during the first all-khaki campaign outside India, the 21st wore covered helmets with large quilted neck curtains, the universal khaki drill frock with two breast pockets, cord breeches and khaki puttees. Since the regiment went to the Sudan from India the frocks of all ranks had shoulder chains. All NCOs and men had the 50-round bandolier, haversack and water bottle, to which was added a brown leather waistbelt supporting a revolver for sergeants and trumpeters. Some paintings of the charge show the men wearing buff sling waistbelts but these were not worn when mounted since the sword was carried on the saddle; when dismounted these belts were worn over the frock. Chevrons for NCOs were of gold lace on red backing, trumpeters' badges and good conduct stripes were of red cloth. Officers had the Wolseley helmet without curtain, khaki frocks with four pockets (under the collar of which was worn a white hunting stock), cord breeches and Stohwasser gaiters. All had Sam Browne belts, some with double braces, others with a cross brace. The rank and file were armed with sword, carbine and lance with pennon furled; officers, sergeants and trumpeters with sword and pistol (see Fig. 73, Plate 26).

The same dress with minor variations was worn by Lancer regiments in the South African War, though none had neck curtains. Until bandoliers, not in use in India, could be issued, regiments from India, such as the 9th and 16th, differed from those from Britain, such as the 12th and 17th, in the wearing of shoulder chains and of pouch-belts. Officers of the home regiments also had the Wolseley helmet. Helmet flashes do not appear to have been popular with Lancers, although the 17th wore their metal death's head badge on the left side. When the slouch hat was adopted, later in the war, the same badge was pinned to the turned-up left side on a circular blue patch with white edging.

The 20th Century

Background

The number of regiments, three of Household Cavalry and twenty-eight of Line Cavalry, remained unchanged until after World War 1. However, the lack of opportunities for mounted action and the vulnerability of horsed cavalry under the new conditions of warfare, in which artillery, machine-guns and eventually the tank predominated, coupled with post-war economies, resulted, between 1920–1922, in the reduction of the cavalry from 31 regiments to 22 by amalgamation, in pairs, of 18 regiments, as listed in Appendix 8. Only the Royal Horse Guards, the two senior regiments each of Dragoon Guards, Dragoons and Lancers[9], and the six senior regiments of Hussars remained unscathed. The gradual conversion from horsed to mechanised cavalry, which began when the 11th Hussars and 12th Lancers became armoured-car regiments in 1928–1929 and ended with the 1st and 2nd Dragoons in 1940–1941, led to the abolition of the old overall title of Cavalry of the Line, and the absorption of all its former regiments (though they retained their individual identities), into a new body, formed in 1939, and called the Royal Armoured Corps, which also embraced the Royal Tank Regiment (formerly Corps), which had started life in 1916 as the Heavy Section, Machine Gun Corps. The Household Cavalry remained—as they do today—outside the new organisation.

During World War 2, six new regiments were formed, the 22nd and 25th Dragoons, the 23rd and 26th Hussars, and the 24th and 27th Lancers, but all were disbanded at the end of the war.

The Army was maintained by conscription, later called National Service, from 1939 and the regiments remained as they had been post-1922. With the decision, effective from 1963, to revert to the pre-war practice of voluntary enlistment, and the subsequent need for further economies in the defence budget, more amalgamations were demanded, including the Household Cavalry and

Standard and escort of the 2nd Dragoon Guards (Queen's Bays) in review order, 1911, with the 1871 pattern brass helmet with black plume. The facings, though officially buff, were cream-coloured. The standard, with crimson ground, is of the type approved in 1858. Once the responsibility of a cornet, cavalry standards and guidons had been carried by troop-sergeant-majors since 1822.

---

[9] Although the 5th Lancers ranked above the 9th, the 82-year gap in their existence counted against them, and not only were they amalgamated with the 16th, but the latter's number took precedence, as in 16th/5th Lancers.

the Royal Armoured Corps. Between 1958 and 1971 the Cavalry regiments were reduced from 22 to 15 (the Royal Tanks also being reduced to four regiments). In 1958, the 4th and 8th Hussars formed the Queen's Royal Irish Hussars; in 1959, the 1st King's and 2nd Dragoon Guards (Bays) became the Queen's Dragoon Guards, while the 3rd and 7th Hussars became the Queen's Own Hussars; in 1960, the 9th and 12th Lancers became the 9th/12th; and in 1969, the 10th and 11th Hussars became the Royal Hussars. Although the Royal Horse Guards, unlike the Life Guards, had survived the 1922 amalgamations, in 1969 they were joined with the 1st Royal Dragoons to form the Blues and Royals. Although the Household Cavalry remains at two regiments (both having an armoured role) there is in effect a third, formed of one mounted squadron of each, known as the Household Cavalry Regiment (Mounted). The principle adopted when choosing regiments for amalgamation had been to spare those who had faced amalgamation in 1920–1922, but this did not avail the 3rd Carabiniers (formerly 3rd and 6th Dragoon Guards) who were amalgamated with the Greys (2nd Dragoons) in 1971 to form the Royal Scots Dragoon Guards. Thus, today, there is no one regiment of Cavalry (as constituted at the turn of the century) that has not suffered amalgamation.

The basic organisation of a Cavalry regiment, whether horsed or armoured, has remained essentially at a headquarters element plus three, sometimes four, 'sabre' or fighting squadrons, each with a similar number of troops; although changing needs of modern warfare, and advances in weapon technology, have seen variations to this number. Between the end of the South African War and the outbreak of hostilities in 1914, considerable debate ensued as to the future role of cavalry; whether they should become mere mounted infantry, looking upon the rifle as their primary weapon, or whether their main function should continue, as in the past, to be shock action with the 'arme blanche', sword or lance. Although musketry received greatly increased attention in the Cavalry, with commendable results both on the peacetime rifle ranges and the battlefields of 1914, the protagonists of the arme blanche had powerful support from senior Cavalry officers holding high positions in the Army. It is indicative of the power of the latter that, although the lance had been abolished in South Africa after 1900, and was to be retained from 1903 only for escorts and ceremonial purposes, it was resumed

as an offensive weapon in 1909 and all lancers went to war in 1914 armed with rifle, sword and lance. Not until 1928, when mechanisation began, was the lance once more relegated to ceremonial use only. As things turned out much of the pre-war argument proved fruitless for, apart from the opening months of the war and again late in 1918 when the Cavalry acted in a traditional role which included a few opportunities for shock action though on a limited scale, the mounted regiments never got their chance, and their war was spent either in training for exploitation of a breakthrough that eluded the trench-bound armies, or fighting dismounted as Infantry in the trenches. Only in Palestine and Mesopotamia did the opportunity for mounted action arise.

This is not the place to discuss the role of armoured cavalry or differing types of armoured fighting vehicles, except to say that during the inter-war years the tank remained the preserve of the Royal Tank Corps, until the introduction of the light tank in the late 1930s afforded cavalry regiments an alternative to their armoured-car role. During World War 2 some regiments remained with armoured cars throughout, while others were equipped with the battle tank of the day. In 1942, for example, the 12th Lancers had Humber armoured cars, while the 9th used Sherman tanks. Today the roles of armoured regiment and armoured reconnaissance regiment are interchangeable, both between the old Cavalry regiments, and between such regiments and the Royal Tank Regiment. While in Northern Ireland, modern cavalrymen have found themselves acting, not for the first time, in an infantry role.

Dress 1902–1918

After the South African War full dress became reserved for ceremonial occasions and for walking-out, in the latter case with a forage cap. The pouch-belt, for so long an important piece of the cavalryman's accoutrements, was abolished for all ranks, except in the Household Cavalry, and there were a number of minor changes to insignia, like a new Royal cypher and crown following Queen Victoria's death. Otherwise the full dress of all types continued as in the previous period until the outbreak of war in 1914 when full dress was withdrawn. In the intervening years the different types of Cavalry were still easily identifiable at reviews, on the main-gate guards of barracks and in the streets of garrison towns, but on all other occasions a knowledge of regimental cap badges was necessary if a dragoon was to be distinguished from a lancer or hussar. Furthermore, in 1902 the former undress uniform was abolished and was replaced by a khaki service dress for all occasions other than those requiring full dress. Since the new dress was universal for all regiments, the uniform will now be considered as a whole, and not by separate types as hitherto.

The khaki tunic for the men was of 'drab-mixture' serge, with turned-down collar, reinforcing patches at the shoulder, two patch breast pockets with pleats, two side pockets with flaps; the whole fastening with brass buttons, five large size down the front, small size for the pockets. The first issues had detachable shoulder straps, which changed to shoulder cords in 1904 and changed again to fixed straps in 1907. No collar badges were to be worn but the wearer's regiment was to be denoted by an embroidered title on a curved strip of material sewn one inch below the sleeve seam; for Cavalry these had blue lettering on a yellow ground. To what extent they were actually worn is uncertain and, in 1907, a brass, abbreviated title was ordered to be worn on the shoulder straps. A white, plaited lanyard was worn round the left shoulder. For mounted duties Bedford cord pantaloons with khaki puttees tied at the bottom over laced ankle boots and spurs strapped on, provided the nether garments. The headdress ordered for this uniform was the short-lived 'Brodrick', a coloured, broad-crowned, peakless cap with a patch in the facing (or busby-bag) colour in front, on which was set the badge; the body of the cap was coloured crimson in the 11th Hussars, red or scarlet for other Hussars, 12th and 16th Lancers, and blue for the remainder. From 1903 the 13th Hussars had white caps, with Royal blue patch and dark blue piping round the bottom. However, photographs of Army manoeuvres in 1903 and 1904 show the slouch hat used for field service. In 1905 both were replaced by the stiff khaki cap with peak, chin-strap and badge on the front. If the chin-strap was actually used to keep the cap on, a duplicate was added to avoid spoiling the appearance of the cap. A similarly shaped, coloured forage cap, with black leather peak, was introduced for walking out in full dress.

The pouch-belt was now permanently replaced as an ammunition carrier by the leather bandolier used in South Africa. In 1903 this gave way to a new bandolier, also in brown leather, which had five pouches each containing ten rounds in two chargers of five. Later four more pouches were added to the back strap, giving a total of 90 rounds carried. A canvas haversack and felt-covered rectangular water bottle with brown leather carrier and strap went over the right shoulder. The circular mess-tin was strapped to the rolled cloak on the front of the saddle. The cloak was replaced by a khaki greatcoat in 1904. The sword continued to be carried on the saddle, thus dispensing with the need for a sword belt when mounted.

By the later stages of the Boer War many regiments had discarded the sword altogether, relying solely on a rifle, a practice which continued after the war on home manoeuvres. However, the War Office memorandum of 1903, which named the rifle as the cavalryman's primary weapon, also stipulated a requirement for the sword. The 1890 and 1899 patterns having proved unsatisfactory, numerous experimental swords were tried out from 1904 onwards. This eventually resulted in what has been described as 'the finest sword ever produced for the British Army'—the 1908 pattern, with straight blade,

---

PLATE 27: 1902–1918

75. Trumpeter, 2nd Dragoons (Royal Scots Greys), 1910.
76. Sergeant, 5th (Royal Irish) Lancers, 1910.
77. Officer, 13th Hussars, 1910 (India).

From 1902 khaki service dress (see next plate) was introduced for most occasions, but full dress continued in use for ceremonial duties (as in Figures 75 and 77, both from photographs). Except for minor changes of insignia and the adoption of collar badges, uniforms were largely as before. Pouch-belts were still worn by officers, trumpeters and bandsmen but were now discontinued for the remainder, as can be noted from Figure 76. Figure 75's rank is denoted by his arm badge, aiguillettes and by the use of a curling red plume instead of an upright white one; similar embellishments distinguished the bandsmen. Figure 76's green plume distinguishes his regiment from the similarly uniformed 9th and 12th Lancers. In contrast, Figure 77 wears the tropical version of the new service dress, together with the Wolseley helmet with regimental flash and badge, replacing the old helmet. Officers' tunics, at first, had a closed collar like the men's but this changed to that shown here. From 1913 the shirt and tie became khaki. Whereas rank badges were worn on the cuff in the home service dress, in the tropical version they were placed on the shoulder straps.

75. Tptr, 2nd Dragoons, 1910.

76. Sgt, 5th Lancers, 1910.

77. Offr, 13th Hussars, 1910.

Left: *Officer, 6th Dragoon Guards (Carabiniers) in review order, 1910. Apart from the white plume, the 1871 helmet, the pantaloons and knee-boots, the uniform has changed little since that shown on page 132 for 1870. Painting by Harry Payne.*

Below: *Squadron-sergeant-major, 14th (King's) Hussars in review order, 1910. The pouch-belt had been abolished following the introduction of the bandolier, and collar badges were now worn, otherwise the uniform is as before. Plume white, busby-bag yellow.*

sheet steel bowl guard and steel scabbard. A basically similar but more ornamental pattern was approved for officers in 1912. The Household Cavalry adopted these swords for field use but retained their former weapons for ceremonial.

When armed with the Infantry Lee-Metford or Lee-Enfield rifle, cavalrymen carried the weapon in a low butt bucket on the rear off-side, the muzzle being steadied by a short sling round the rider's arm. However, when the Short Lee-Enfield was introduced after 1902 to replace all former rifles and carbines, it was carried muzzle down in a long, wide-mouthed bucket as formerly.

The service dress ordered for officers was broadly similar to that of the men, but of superior materials and with large, expanding pockets in the skirts, which in the Cavalry were cut long. The shoulder straps followed the same changes as described for the men except that the detachable variety had a coloured edging, which for Cavalry was yellow. These edged straps were

also worn on the khaki greatcoat. The high tunic collar gave way, around 1908, to an open, step collar, revealing a white shirt and black tie, changed in 1913 to khaki. Rank was at first distinguished by a graduated arrangement of khaki braiding on the cuffs, but this soon changed to a cuff slash outlined in drab lace wherein were sewn the same rank badges as on the tunic but in worsted, with rings of drab lace and tracing braid, varying according to rank, passing round the cuff from the centre point of the slash. Breeches were cut wide at the thigh and close at the knee, being accompanied at first by Stohwasser leggings, later by other leggings (without the former's spiral straps), or brown butcher boots. From 1905, headdress was the peaked khaki cap with badge, which was bronzed in most regiments, as were the collar badges. Prior to this a coloured forage cap with wide crown and black patent leather peak was worn, having been introduced in 1902. The colour varied between regiments; the 4th Dragoon Guards, for example, having an all-blue cap;

the 17th Lancers having a blue crown, white band, white welts and quarter welts; while the 17th's colouring was reversed for the 13th Hussars, but without welts. All-scarlet caps were common among other Hussars, except for the 11th's crimson.

The blue serge frock was reintroduced on an optional basis in 1911, officially without shoulder chains although these continued to be worn by some regiments in India.

The coloured forage cap was also worn with the only surviving officers' undress uniform other than mess dress: a plain, double-breasted blue frock coat with collar badges and gilt buttons, over blue overalls with regimental striping. Mess dress consisted of the same overalls and a short jacket which derived from the old stable jacket but was worn open to display a waistcoat of regimental pattern.

The Household Cavalry did not at first receive the khaki service dress and it was not until the 1912 Army manoeuvres that its regiments first

Left: The universal khaki service dress introduced in 1902, worn here by a private of the 12th (Prince of Wales's Royal) Lancers in 1910. He is equipped with the 1903 pattern 50-round bandolier and is armed with sword, lance and .303-in. Short Magazine Lee-Enfield rifle.

Right: In contrast, a trumpeter of the 5th (Royal Irish) Lancers at the same date in full dress. Facings scarlet, plume green. Trumpeters carried both trumpet and a bugle, the latter in use here, for sounding field calls.

appeared in khaki. When the pillbox forage cap was replaced by the wide-crowned type in 1902, no cap badge was worn on the scarlet band until a common badge was authorised for all three regiments in 1913; however, this was not issued until after the war. Each regiment wore its own badge on the peaked khaki cap, which differed from the common type in having the regimental title on the circle instead of the Garter motto.

Officers and men of the 4th (Queen's Own) Hussars, 1902, in the summer review order worn in India of white tunic and home service pantaloons. The old foreign service helmet shown here was soon to be replaced by the Wolseley pattern.

For regiments on foreign service, as in India, a similar service dress to the home pattern was authorised for all duties other than ceremonial, but in khaki drill or twill. The Wolseley helmet was adopted for all ranks. In service dress the helmet was khaki, usually with some regimental flash on the side, but for ceremonial it was white with a brass spike and the regimental badge on the front. The white helmet was worn all the year round, with home service review order (full dress) in the cold weather; in the hot season, with a white tunic cut similarly to the khaki drill pattern, with home service blue pantaloons with knee-boots if mounted, white overalls if dismounted. As was the practice at home, the men in review order wore only the white sword belt with slings and snake clasp, over the tunic for the Heavies, under it for Hussars and Lancers, the latter also wearing their girdles.

The Cavalry of the Line appeared for the last time in the splendour of full dress in the Royal Review at Aldershot in the summer of 1914. A few weeks later it was all set aside and the regiments went off to war in the khaki described

PLATE 28: 1902–1918

78. **Lance-Corporal, 18th (Queen Mary's Own) Hussars, 1914 (France).**
79. **Lieutenant, 4th Royal Irish Dragoon Guards, 1914 (France).**
80. **Private, 14th (King's) Hussars, 1917 (Mesopotamia).**

Figures 78 and 79 illustrate khaki service dress as it had developed since its introduction in 1902, worn with the khaki cap authorised from 1905. The neck curtain shown for Figure 78 was worn by many troops during the intense heat of the retreat from Mons in 1914. His arm badge denotes a regimental scout. He wears the 1903 bandolier, which had another four pouches on the back, webbing haversack and water bottle. He is armed with the universal SMLE rifle and both he and Figure 79 would have swords, of the 1908 and 1912 patterns respectively, attached to their saddles. Figure 79's badges are bronzed, and his rank badges are visible on the cuff. His equipment includes revolver holster, binocular case and haversack. The 14th Hussars went to the Mesopotamia campaign direct from India and Figure 80 thus wears the Wolseley helmet and Indian pattern khaki drill, which sometimes had a greenish tinge, and has the old canvas haversack instead of the webbing type. He carries the Hotchkiss light machine-gun issued to cavalry regiments from 1916 and wears the special bandolier issued for this weapon. Machine-gunners were armed with revolvers as their personal weapon. The gun, its ammunition and associated stores were transported on pack horses. This figure is based on drawings by a soldier of the 14th, Figures 78 and 79 are based on photographs.

78. L/Cpl, 18th Hussars, 1914.

79. Offr, 4th Dragoon Guards, 1914.

80. Pte, 14th Hussars, 1917.

Private of the 16th (The Queen's Own) Lancers, in review order, as he would have appeared for the last time before full dress was returned to store on the outbreak of war in 1914. Painting by Harry Payne.

Opposite left: *The same regiment on active service in France during the advance from the Marne to the Aisne, September 1914. The 50-round bandoliers now have an additional four pouches, giving 90 rounds carried. Haversacks are slung over the right shoulder, water bottles over the left. The lance-flags have been removed.*

Opposite right: *A fully equipped cavalryman in fighting order as worn in World War 1 after the introduction of the steel helmet in 1916, and the respirator, which was slung on the back. For fighting dismounted in trenches, a bayonet was also issued, suspended from a brown leather waistbelt.*

above. In the Near and Middle East campaigns Wolseley helmets and khaki drill were worn. Certain changes and additions were made as the war progressed. The long greatcoat was changed for a knee-length pattern and the canvas haversack for one of webbing, and the caps lost the stiffening wire in the crown.

As the cavalryman came to act more and more as infantry, a brown leather waistbelt (from the 1903 Infantry equipment) was added to support a bayonet and additional 10-round pouches. In 1915 the anti-gas respirator was issued—at first a small satchel type, later the box pattern—which was carried behind the right shoulder so as not to interfere with the bandolier. 1916 saw the issue of the steel helmet. The horse's load now included an extra 90-round bandolier round its neck, two blankets, the saddle, with a pair of wallets containing spare boots, iron rations and two hand grenades. On the near side of the saddle were the sword, shoe-case, picketing-peg, haynet and a day's ration of oats; on the off side were the rifle bucket, mess-tin and canvas water bucket; while across the rear arch was the rolled greatcoat. When acting dismounted in the trenches, a role

for which the cavalryman's personal equipment was ill-suited, the trooper had to carry his greatcoat and groundsheet, and perhaps a blanket, in a roll with the mess-tin strapped to it, two grenades and rations in his haversack, and a couple of cotton badoliers of extra ammunition. Each regiment had gone to war with two Maxim machine guns mounted on carriages; these were withdrawn in early 1916, but were replaced by light Hotchkiss guns carried on pack horses at a scale of four per squadron. Hotchkiss gunners had special bandoliers (see Fig. 80, Plate 28).

Officers appear to have given up the double braces of the Sam Browne, using only a cross brace to support the revolver and ammunition pouch. Binoculars, compasses, and map cases were slung from separate straps. Their caps too lost the pre-war uniform appearance, and legwear varied according to taste. In a photograph of the 17th Lancers' officers, in 1915, butcher boots, canvas and leather leggings, and puttees all appear.

Contrasting types of the pre-war and wartime Cavalry are shown in Figures 75–80, Plates 27 and 28.

Dress 1919–1939

Full dress was resumed by the Household Cavalry after the war. Essentially this remained as pre-war, although the amalgamation of the 1st and 2nd Life Guards required some small modifications: the red flask cord and lace patterns of the 1st Regiment were retained, as were the overalls of the 2nd, but buttons and officers' shabraques were re-designed. Officers resumed

Troopers of the Royal Horse Guards (The Blues) in service dress, with steel helmet, and full dress, resumed by the Household Cavalry only, after the end of World War 1.

their undress frock coats and mess dress, but for all occasions other than those needing full dress, the Household Cavalry wore khaki service dress like the rest of the Army.

For the Line cavalry the wearing of full dress was now confined to officers attending levées, and to bands, standard and guidon parties and detachments on special occasions like the Royal Tournament or the Aldershot Tattoos of the 1930s. Though no longer generally worn, full dress was never formally abolished and the amalgamation of regiments from 1920 called for some changes of headdress plumes and facings as listed in Appendix 8. Notable among these changes were the disappearance of the blue tunic formerly worn by the Carabiniers (6th Dragoon Guards) and the adoption by the new 5th Inniskilling Dragoon Guards (briefly titled 5th/6th Dragoons, 1922–1927) of dark green overalls, pantaloons, and the white metal helmet of the former 6th Dragoons.

For the Coronation of King George VI in 1937 certain mounted detachments in the procession wore full dress, but a dark blue uniform was issued for the remainder, based on the optional 'patrol' dress that soldiers had been permitted to purchase for walking-out. This had a coloured forage cap, generally blue with a distinctive band,

---

PLATE 29: 1919–1939

81. Trooper, 1st King's Dragoon Guards, 1937 (India).
82. Lance-Corporal, 7th Queen's Own Hussars, 1932.

This plate represents the last years of horsed cavalry at home and abroad. Figure 81's uniform is as worn by the regiment in India at its last mounted parade before mechanisation. The upper fold of the helmet puggaree is edged with the facing colour and the red hackle at the side recalls the plume of the full dress helmet. The collar badge is that worn before the resumption of the double-headed eagle in 1938. The sword is the 1908 pattern. In India, the Wolseley helmet was reserved for ceremonial by this time, the flat-topped pith topee being worn for training and other duties, and subsequently for parades as well. Figure 82 is in field service marching order as worn at home, less the steel helmet. It has changed little since 1914, except for a respirator slung on the back in the cavalry fashion to keep it clear of the bandolier. The haversack hangs on the left side. On the horse are the waterproof cape in front, rifle in its bucket, with mess-tin attached, and sword on the far side. Figure 81 is based on a Snaffles painting and photographs, Figure 82 on a photograph.

82. L/Cpl, 7th Hussars, 1932.

81. Tpr, 1st King's Dragoon Guards, 1937.

Major D Bowes Daly and officers of the Royal Horse Guards (The Blues) in khaki service dress at Windsor, September 1939. Second from left has a respirator slung over his right shoulder.

but all scarlet for the 3rd, 10th and 15th/19th Hussars and 12th Lancers, crimson for the 11th, and dark green with a primrose band for the 5th Dragoon Guards. The two latter regiments had overalls in these colours, but overalls for the remainder were blue with regimental stripes. Jackets were similar to the old serge frocks but with patch breast pockets. Shoulder chains were worn by some regiments. Officers wore dress pouch-belts, the men white sling waistbelts with snake clasp.

Other than these uniforms, khaki service dress was worn for all occasions, including ceremonial. After the war the khaki dress became smarter and better tailored but its components and accoutrements remained unchanged. Officers' rank badges were now placed on the shoulder straps and the amalgamation of regiments required some changes to the brass shoulder titles. A leather bandolier, rather than his sword belt, became the hallmark of a cavalryman; although the latter, of the old buff leather type with slings, was worn for

Drum horses and drummers in full dress at the Aldershot Tattoo of 1933. It was only on such occasions that full dress was still worn by the Cavalry of the Line. From left: 3rd Carabiniers (Prince of Wales's Dragoon Guards), Royal Artillery, 5th Inniskilling Dragoon Guards, with drum banners of the 6th (Inniskilling) Dragoons, 7th Queen's Own Hussars, 5th Inniskilling Dragoon Guards, with drum banners of the 5th Dragoon Guards (Princess Charlotte of Wales's) and shabraque of the 6th Dragoons.

Above: *NCOs and troopers, 13th/18th Royal Hussars (Queen Mary's Own), in Wolseley helmets and khaki drill service dress in India, c 1930.*

The last days of horsed cavalry: the 7th Queen's Own Hussars, still a mounted regiment as shown by the trooper in fighting order, but the motor cycle despatch rider and the Austin 7 are indicative of increasing mechanisation.

dismounted parades when the sword, still of the 1908 pattern, was carried on the man instead of on the horse. On foreign service the Wolseley helmet and khaki drill was likewise worn for all purposes. There was no return to the hot weather white uniform in India, while in Mediterranean stations, like Egypt and Palestine, home service khaki was worn in the winter months. In India a light flat-topped pith topee began to be worn for training and ordinary duties instead of the Wolseley helmet, and by the late 1930s the topee was in use for all occasions, even after the regiments had been mechanised. At the same time shirt-sleeve order became customary for training, the drill tunics being reserved for ceremonial.

Mechanisation and the phasing out of horsed cavalry saw the gradual disappearance of those things—the bandolier, breeches, puttees and spurs—that, alone in this period, distinguished the cavalryman from the infantry soldier. These were hardly best suited for clambering in and out of a tank or armoured car. Even the service dress cap had its disadvantages, a fact discovered by the 11th Hussars (the first to be mechanised), who were henceforth permitted a brown beret with crimson brow-band for wear in armoured cars, a type of headgear pioneered, in 1924, by the Royal Tank Corps who adopted a black beret for all forms of dress (even though their service dress followed the infantry, rather than cavalry style). One-piece overalls were issued to protect clothing in armoured vehicles. Another sign of the times was a brass badge, of a Rolls-Royce armoured car, worn on the tunic sleeve by such crewmen of the 12th Lancers after they were mechanised in 1929. As the horse disappeared, so too did the sword and rifle with their accompanying accoutrements, the revolver taking their place as the cavalryman's personal weapon. This was carried in a leather holster, with a small leather ammunition pouch, supported by a modified set of the Infantry 1908 web equipment.

By the late 1930s a major change of dress was on the way, a change that not only finally deprived the cavalryman of his distinctive appearance but also rendered all Arms of the service and all ranks indistinguishable from one another, except for cap badges and rank insignia. This change was the introduction of battledress: a shapeless costume of short khaki blouse and wide trousers, furnished with many pockets and devoid of all brass buttons and shoulder titles; approved in 1938 for all purposes. The folding field service cap of the 1890s was resurrected in a khaki version as headdress, though in some regiments officers adopted the coloured pattern. Short webbing anklets were issued, to close the trouser bottoms round the ankle boots.

A new web equipment, the Braithwaite pattern, had been approved in 1937 for all Arms as a replacement for the 1908 type. This had a narrower belt and braces, for which special attachments were provided for fastening to the belt, since the large pouches to which the braces were attached by the Infantry, were not required by armoured vehicle crews. Their revolvers were carried in open-ended web holsters, which were attached to the belt by a long strap, so as to rest against the thigh. The water bottle was the same as the 1908 pattern, and the equipment was completed by a large pack, also of the 1908 type, and a haversack, or small pack. However, since the cavalryman now had a vehicle in which to stow such receptacles, he was seldom encumbered by more than his skeleton equipment, if that. No longer was he a mounted swordsman, lancer or even rifleman, but a driver, gunner or wireless operator. Cavalrymen of the inter-war years are shown in Figures 81–85, Plates 29 and 30.

PLATE 30: 1919–1939

83. **Trooper, 11th Hussars (Prince Albert's Own), 1937 (Egypt).**
84. **Corporal, 12th Royal Lancers, 1938.**
85. **Sergeant, 13th/18th Royal Hussars (Queen Mary's Own), 1939.**

This plate illustrates mechanised cavalry regiments up to and including the outbreak of war in 1939. Figures 83 and 85, from photographs, show men of the first two regiments to be converted to armoured cars, the former in the dress worn for ceremonial parades in Egypt, the latter dressed for manoeuvres at home. The revolver had replaced sword and rifle as the cavalryman's personal weapon, hence the bandolier and sword slings gave way to the Infantry 1908 web equipment as modified for pistol-armed troops. Besides the steel helmet and respirator worn in the Infantry manner, Figure 84 is dressed in overalls as more suited for work inside vehicles. The equipment of these two figures was soon to be replaced by the 1937 pattern webbing, as illustrated in Figure 85, with the pistol now carried in a thigh holster. He also wears overalls and the khaki field service cap, authorised for use with the introduction of battledress from 1938; a headdress which made up in practicality (particularly in the light tanks, with which the 13th/18th were then equipped) what it lacked in smartness.

83. Tpr, 11th Hussars, 1937.

85. Sgt, 13th/18th Hussars, 1939.

84. Cpl, 12th Lancers, 1938.

Dress 1940–1962

On the outbreak of World War 2 in 1939 battledress had yet to reach all troops, but by the time fighting started in earnest in 1940 it was almost universal and the old service dress was only occasionally to be seen. Nevertheless, officers continued to have service dress throughout this period but, as a rule, only when not on parade or duty with troops. Except in tropical climates, battledress would remain the standard uniform of all arms and services throughout the war and for more than a decade and a half thereafter. Its basic design of blouse and trousers continued unchanged, though with various small modifications and economies, which it is not proposed to detail

Armoured cars of the 1st The Royal Dragoons, one of the last regiments to be mechanised, in Syria 1941. The crewmen wear khaki drill shirts and shorts, hose-tops and short puttees, with the grey berets adopted by this regiment between 1941–1944. Except for the 11th Hussars, the black beret was universal for all Cavalry from 1942–1948.

here[10]. Since battledress had to serve the soldier for parades as well as work and training, it became better tailored after the war, as had service dress after 1918. Officers had always worn the neck of the blouse open to reveal collar and tie, and, in 1945, this concession was extended to the men for

[10] These are considered in detail in the companion work to this volume: *British Infantry Uniforms Since 1660*, Blandford Press, 1982.

walking-out. The inside of the collar was faced with serge material, and the neck was later re-designed to permit the wearing of a collar and tie on all occasions.

The very utilitarian appearance of the blouse was brightened during the war by the wearing of formation signs on the upper arm, a device first employed in 1914–1918. To these was added an arm-of-service flash which for the Royal Armoured Corps was a cloth strip in red and yellow. Later on during the war, embroidered shoulder titles were introduced, including one for the RAC with red letters on yellow; but most cavalry regiments resumed the brass titles on their shoulder straps as worn pre-war. The Household Cavalry wore no arm-of-service strip in battle-dress but had embroidered titles, with blue letters on scarlet for the Life Guards, the reverse for the Blues.

The chief change affecting the Cavalry concerned headdress. The khaki field service cap continued as the official headgear for a while, though officers usually wore their peaked service dress caps or else the coloured field-service cap. From 1942 all Royal Armoured Corps regiments were to wear the black beret of the Royal Tank Regiment, though with their own cap badges. The 11th Hussars were excepted from this ruling, retaining their brown berets. Another exception, though unofficial, was the grey beret adopted by the Royal Dragoons in 1941 after they were mechanised. This was formally approved, in June 1943, by King George VI, but when he was reminded that black was now regulation for the RAC, his decision had to be reversed and in 1944 the Royals relinquished the grey beret. Another unique headdress was that worn by officers of the 8th Hussars: a green cap, laced gold, of French or Belgian style, known as a 'tent-hat'. When the blue beret was introduced in 1948 for most of the Army, the black beret again became the sole prerogative of the Royal Tank Regiment, and the Cavalry, except the 11th Hussars, assumed blue. However, officers used the peaked khaki service dress cap for most occasions.

Turning to tropical clothing, a photograph of the Royal Horse Guards in Palestine in 1940, still horsed, shows them in Indian-type topees, shirt-sleeve order, breeches and puttees. One of the most surprising lessons of the fighting in North Africa, in which many Cavalry regiments took part, was the realisation that the tropical helmet, for so long considered essential in hot climates, was quite unnecessary. The field-service cap or

beret was therefore worn by tank and armoured car crews with no ill effects under the hottest sun. Khaki drill shirts or bush-jackets and shorts with woollen hose-tops and short puttees or anklets were the most usual dress in the hot season, though long khaki drill trousers were also worn, being preferred by most officers. In the desert campaign, officers' dress, and to some extent that of their men, became anything but uniform and a variety of civilian articles, neck scarves, pullovers, golfing jackets, corduroy trousers and suede desert boots, were added or substituted for military clothing, both in the hot weather and the cold, when battledress replaced khaki drill.

After the war the usual smartening-up process was applied to tropical uniforms, both to the khaki drill worn in the Middle East and its equivalent for regiments in the Far East, jungle (later olive) green. In tropical stations post-war the headdress was as worn at home.

In 1944 armoured vehicle crews were issued with a one-piece 'tank suit' in heavy, lined canvas to afford extra warmth. This garment survived the war and remained in use up to the end of this period. Personal equipment was usually stripped down to the 1937 pattern belt, revolver holster and ammunition pouch. The practice of support-ing the holster on the thigh was abolished after 1943, though sometimes continued unofficially, and the holster, either the open type or officers' pattern with flap, was hooked directly on to the belt or suspended from the pouch. After the war the braces and attachments were again fastened to the belts for dismounted parades, though the system varied between regiments. The equipment was kept clean with blanco, which, for the Royal Armoured Corps, was of a buff shade, although some regiments preferred to blacken their web-bing. In the Far East a modified version of the Infantry's 1944 equipment was issued, in per-manently dyed green webbing.

In the post-war period full dress was resumed by the Household Cavalry Mounted Regiment for public duties, as was State dress by the bands of both Life Guards and Blues. Economic considera-tions precluded its return for other Cavalry, but in 1947 a new uniform was approved for all ranks to be worn on occasions demanding something smarter than battledress. Called No. 1 Dress, it was based on the pre-war blue patrol uniform worn at the 1937 coronation. The jacket had a standing collar with collar badges, 5-button fas-tening, pleated breast pockets, flapped skirt pockets and shoulder chains. Blue trousers with regimental striping, cut on civilian lines, were authorised initially, but for Cavalry these came to resemble the pre-war overalls, the latter actually being worn by officers: the 5th Dragoon Guards and 11th Hussars being permitted green with primrose stripe and crimson respectively. The headdress was the peaked forage cap in regimental colours (those worn after the 1958 amalgamations are given at Appendix 9, as are the trouser stripes, and distinctive collars where applicable). Quarter welts were a particular feature of Lancer caps.

For officers a white patent leather pouch-belt with black pouch was approved but most regiments preferred to wear the old full dress patterns. To avoid interfering with medals when these were ordered, the pouch-belt was allowed to be worn over the right shoulder. When swords were resumed by officers for ceremonial, these were suspended from slings attached to a web belt worn under the jacket. The men's jackets had a blue cloth belt for walking-out and it had been intended that a coloured girdle would be worn for parade instead of a waistbelt, but in the event a white waistbelt became customary for ceremonial. Personal weapons carried by the men on dismounted parades were the revolver, later the sub-machine-carbine. Standard and guidon parties were usually provided with the 1908 sword. Practice, in fact, varied between regiments, even within regiments. Photographs of the 15th/19th Hussars bicentenary parade in 1959 show the regiment all in No. 1 Dress, one squadron being armed and accoutred with swords and white pouch-belts, the remainder having white-blancoed 1937 pattern web belts, revolver holsters and pouches, with the band wearing pre-war dismounted full dress. Some Lancer regiments paraded dismounted in No. 1 Dress with lances.

No. 1 Dress had to be purchased by officers and was issued to warrant officers, sergeants and bands, but in a large conscript service (as the Army was at this time), it was not practicable to issue it permanently to the rank and file. Its issue was therefore confined to special occasions, chief of which in this period was the Coronation of Queen Elizabeth II in 1953, when this dress was seen for the first time in large numbers.

The Household Cavalry also had No. 1 Dress, worn with pouch-belts, but more for undress than parade purposes. The forage cap was blue with a scarlet band and, peculiar to these regiments only, had the ranks of warrant officers, NCOs and musicians indicated by rows of Russia braid on the peak: warrant officers I, had five; warrant officers II, trumpet-majors and band-corporals of horse had four; staff corporals and squadron-quartermaster-corporals had three; corporals of horse had two; corporals, musicians and trumpeters had one.

For ceremonial in tropical climates, an equivalent uniform in white drill, No. 3 Dress, was authorised. Being of less expensive material and cheaper to manufacture locally, its use was more widespread than the use of No. 1 Dress at home.

The inferiority of battledress as a parade uniform had long been evident and the bitter winters of the Korean War emphasised its inadequacy as a fighting dress. In the later stages of that war a new combat clothing was produced. Made of windproof and water repellent greyish-green gaberdine material, the jacket had numerous inner and outer pockets, zip and button fastenings, and, to remedy one of the battledress blouse's chief defects, an all-round skirt with draw-strings at waist and hip. Trousers of the same material were closed round the ankles by short puttees. For really cold

---

PLATE 31: 1940–1962

86. Captain, 11th Hussars (Prince Albert's Own), 1942 (Middle East).
87. Trooper, Royal Scots Greys (2nd Dragoons), 1944 (North-West Europe).
88. Corporal, 14th/20th King's Hussars, 1950.

This plate is representative of World War 2 and the battledress period. Officers' dress in the desert campaigns was frequently anything but uniform, but Figure 86's jersey, khaki drill shirt and trousers (sometimes corduroy) with suede desert boots are fairly typical. The distinctive beret of the 11th Hussars had been adopted before the war as more practical for use in armoured cars than the then regulation cap, shown in Figure 82. From 1942 all regiments of the Royal Armoured Corps, except the 11th and briefly (with grey berets) the Royal Dragoons, adopted the black beret of the Royal Tank Regiment instead of the field service cap, but with their own regimental cap badges, as in Figure 87. This soldier also wears the special 'tank suit' issued to armoured crewmen in 1944. Both he and Figure 86 are equipped with stripped-down 1937 pattern equipment to carry their revolvers. Figure 88 illustrates how this equipment and battledress were smartened up after the war for parade purposes; now to be worn with the blue beret approved in 1948 for all except the 11th Hussars and the Royal Tanks. The crossed kukris between the brass regimental shoulder title and the formation sign denote an affiliation between the 14th/20th and the 6th Gurkha Rifles.

86. Offr, 11th Hussars, 1942.

87. Tpr, Royal Scots Greys, 1944.

88. Cpl, 14th/20th Hussars, 1950.

Above: *Tank crew of the 5th Royal Inniskilling Dragoon Guards in North-West Europe, 1944. They wear 'denims' of the battledress pattern, anklets, 1937 web equipment with revolvers and steel helmets of the Royal Armoured Corps type.*

Left: *Officer of the 8th King's Royal Irish Hussars in battledress of the improved post-war pattern and the green and gold 'tent hat', peculiar to officers of this regiment. Note the collar badges, leather buttons, the 7th Armoured Division sign on the sleeve, and the light khaki shirt and tie affected by cavalry officers.*

weather a 'parka', with synthetic fur lining and hood, was also available. The old style of ankle boot with studded leather soles gave way to a new pattern with thick moulded rubber soles. Towards the end of this period combat clothing began to be issued generally for wear on operations and training in all temperate climates.

When manning an armoured vehicle there was naturally little need for a steel helmet. However there were occasions when one was necessary and in the later stages of World War 2 troops from the Royal Armoured Corps were issued a helmet of the same pudding-basin shape worn by the Parachute Regiment but with an ordinary chin-strap. This continued in use after the war.

Uniforms of this and the final period—the era of total mechanisation—are shown in Figures 86–91, Plates 31 and 32.

Dress 1963 to date

The ending of national service and the return to a smaller Army of regular soldiers afforded the opportunity to replace the unsightly and unpopular battledress with a more soldierly costume. No. 1 Dress had been an attempt in this direction, not altogether successful, but economic factors had precluded its becoming a general issue; in any case its cut and colour were not that different from uniforms worn by non-military organisations and services, although dark blue as a uniform colour was not as inappropriate for the Cavalry (or at least its hussars and lancers) as it was for the Infantry. It was also clear that a uniform that enhanced a soldier's appearance on parade was no longer suitable for field use, and that the two functions required quite separate uniforms. Initially, the combat clothing described in the previous section fulfilled the second purpose, while for the first a costume resembling officers' service dress was decided upon. This was

to be in khaki, which had now assumed a traditional aspect as it was the colour most closely associated with the Army since the beginning of the century. Together with the officers' service dress, which was retained, it was to be known as No. 2 Dress.

The blue beret, or its variations, remained as the working headdress, while the coloured forage cap, as worn with No. 1 Dress, was authorised for smarter occasions. Among the inevitable exceptions, so characteristic of the British Army, was

H R H Princess Alice, Duchess of Gloucester, as Colonel-in-Chief, inspecting a guard of honour, with the guidon of the Royal Hussars (Prince of Wales's Own), in No. 1 Dress. The forage caps, overalls of the officers and senior NCOs, and trousers of the men are the crimson of the former 11th Hussars. The Prince of Wales's feathers in the badge are of the former 10th Hussars. The guidon escort are armed with the 1908 sword; the men with Sterling sub-machine-guns. Guidons were approved for all Hussars and Lancers from 1956.

the green tent hat of officers of the Queen's Royal Irish Hussars. Officers were also permitted coloured field service (or side) caps, instead of berets; or for wear with mess dress in accordance with regimental custom. The Royal Scots Dragoon Guards and Royal Hussars adopted the tent hat pattern; in blue with yellow vandyke for the former, in crimson with gold lace for the latter.

In 1969 the first officers dress regulations to be published since 1934 were issued, and these, with subsequent amendments, remain the basis of the dress worn today. The variations on the new uniform were codified into twelve different orders of dress, expanded from 1971 into fourteen (however, No. 5 Dress, battledress, has now been deleted). Although not all of these orders are applicable to soldiers, as opposed to officers, they will be used here to describe the uniform of this final period. This can only be done in general terms but some of the regimental peculiarities can be found in Appendix 9. These orders of dress—less those for tropical, or warm weather climates—can be seen in the accompanying black and white illustrations of officers and men of the Queen's Own Hussars.

No. 1 Dress—Temperate Ceremonial

As described in the preceding section but from 1969 'not now in normal use for parade wear'. Officers' jackets of the Queen's Royal Irish Hussars are of a special pattern, the breast pockets having no pleats and a V flap, all buttons being plain and domed, and the rank badges of a small size. Officers' pouch-belts are of white plastic, worn over the left shoulder, and have a silver flap to the pouch; both Royal Scots Dragoon Guards and Royal Hussars have a special regimental pattern. Officers' sword slings are of gold lace on crimson leather for 4th/7th Dragoon Guards, 5th Inniskilling Dragoon Guards, Queen's Own, Queen's Royal Irish, Royal and 14th/20th Hussars, and 9th/12th Lancers; on blue leather for other regiments. Field officers and all officers of the Royal Hussars are permitted $\frac{3}{4}$-in. gold embroidery on the forage cap peak.

No. 2 Dress—Temperate Parade and Ceremonial

Forage cap, service dress, brown shoes for officers (black for 5th Dragoon Guards), black boots for men. Belts are as shown in Appendix 9. On ceremonial parades soldiers are usually armed with the Sterling sub-machine-gun, officers with swords. For less formal parades and duties officers

may wear the khaki service dress cap. An improved pattern No. 2 Dress, still in khaki, is to be issued to soldiers in the late 1980s.

No. 3 Dress—Warm Weather Ceremonial

This is the white version of No. 1 Dress.

No. 4 Dress—Warm Weather (Service Dress)

Only applicable to officers, this dress is the same as No. 2 but in stone-coloured polyester and wool worsted.

No. 5 Dress

This was listed as battledress but has now been deleted from the regulations.

No. 6 Dress—Warm Weather Parade

This dress, in stone-coloured twill polyester and cotton, is similar for officers and soldiers and consists of bush-jacket and trousers; headdress as for No. 2 Dress.

PLATE 32: 1963 to date

89. Trooper, 17th/21st Lancers, 1975.
90. Trooper, Royal Scots Dragoon Guards (Carabiniers and Greys), 1978.
91. Trooper, Queen's Royal Irish Hussars, 1983.

This final plate shows a lancer, dragoon and hussar of modern times in three different orders of dress. Figure 89 illustrates the No. 1 Dress of the 17th/21st, the uniform devised in 1947 for ceremonial, but from 1969 no longer in normal use for such occasions. The lancer girdle, formerly worn with the tunic, is retained. The jacket is embellished with chain-mail shoulder straps and cap-lines of the type attached to the full dress lance-cap, the shape of which is recalled by the quarter-welts on the forage cap. Parade dress is now normally No. 2 Dress with forage cap, as in Figure 90. The distinctive cap-band is a combination of the yellow band formerly worn by the 3rd Dragoon Guards and, from 1922, the 3rd Carabiniers, and the white vandyke of the Greys. The cap and collar badges are a union of the crossed carbines of the Carabiniers and the Napoleonic eagle of the Greys. The arm badge, perpetuating the Prince of Wales's feathers of the 3rd Dragoon Guards, is worn by all ranks, as is the brown leather pouch-belt. Figure 91 is in No. 8 Dress with the latest type of boot and the distinctive green beret of this regiment. He carries the modern cavalryman's personal weapon, the Sterling SMG, and holds a crewman's helmet worn in armoured vehicles. The cap badge combines the crowned circle of the 4th Hussars with the harp of the 8th.

89. Tpr, 17th/21st Lancers, 1975.

91. Tpr, Queen's Royal Irish Hussars, 1983.

90. Tpr, Royal Scots Dragoon Guards, 1978.

Officers of the Queen's Royal Irish Hussars. Left, in No. 1 Dress with scarlet forage cap, right, in No. 2 Dress with the 'tent hat' of the former 8th Hussars.

No. 7 Dress—Warm Weather Working

For daily routine, consisting of shirt and lightweight olive green trousers, with service dress cap (or equivalent) for officers, berets for men. Web belt or regimental stable belt.

No. 8 Dress—Temperate Combat (Cold/Wet)

For operations and training, it consists of smock with liner and trousers in 'Disruptive Pattern Material' (DPM), worn with a beret, 'boots DMS' (direct moulded soles), and short puttees. A higher boot, which dispenses with the puttees, was issued generally from 1982.

No. 9 Dress—Warm Weather Combat (Jungle/Desert).

The tropical equivalent of No. 8, also in DPM.

No. 10 Dress—Temperate Mess Uniform

This and No. 11 are only applicable to officers. Mess jackets, worn with No. 1 Dress overalls, are of regimental pattern; scarlet for Dragoon Guards and 16th/5th Lancers, blue for Hussars and other Lancers. The design, of the 1902 pattern, derives from the old stable jacket, with standing collar and worn open to reveal a regimental pattern waistcoat.

No. 11 Dress—Warm Weather Mess Uniform

White jacket and cummerbund in regimental colours with No. 1 Dress overalls.

No. 12 Dress—Coveralls

A working dress with overalls to protect the under garments.

No. 13 Dress—Barrack Dress

The temperate equivalent to No. 7: shirt, 'jersey, wool heavy', trousers of a dark greenish material, service dress cap or equivalent, beret. Jerseys are olive-green, except for officers of the Queen's Own Hussars who have lovat-green, and for the Queen's Royal Irish, Royal, 13th/18th and 14th/20th Hussars who have dark green. The Royal Hussars have crimson shoulder straps.

No. 14 Dress—Shirt Sleeve Order

As for No. 13, but without the jersey, with shirt sleeves rolled one inch above the elbow, and regimental stable belt.

The 1937 pattern web equipment was replaced from 1958 by a new and improved pattern in dark green webbing which is still in service though some modifications have been made to it. The modern cavalryman, being mounted in and fighting from his armoured vehicle, has little need to accoutre himself with ammunition and 'kidney' pouches, yoke and water bottle, which would in any case incommode him in the narrow confines of his vehicle. However, when acting in an infantry role, as cavalry regiments have been called upon to do in Northern Ireland, part of this equipment has to be worn, with the cavalryman's usual personal weapon, the Sterling SMG, exchanged for the 7.62 mm self-loading rifle. The possibility of nuclear, biological or chemical warfare has necessitated the development of a NBC suit for wear over No. 8 and No. 12 Dress; a version in DPM is being produced.

The old full dress of the dragoon, hussar and lancer, so familiar before 1914, has been resurrected for use by many Cavalry bands with modifications to take account of amalgamations where necessary. In addition to their military band, the Royal Scots Dragoon Guards (Carabiniers and Greys) have a pipe band in which the pipers wear Highland dress of feather bonnet with vandyke band, dark blue doublet, kilt and plaid of Royal Stewart tartan—a uniform adopted by the Greys in 1953 but previously worn only by Scottish Infantry. However, the Cavalry character of this pipe band is emphasised by its drummers, who wear the Greys' bearskin cap with white plume (in contrast to the crimson plumes of the military band and trumpeters), scarlet tunic with the yellow facings of the 3rd Carabiniers, blue overalls with double yellow stripes (a compromise between the single yellow formerly worn by the Greys and 3rd Dragoon Guards, and the double white of the 6th Dragoon Guards) and spurs. When it is remembered that in the seventeenth and eighteenth centuries, Dragoons were equipped with drums and hautbois instead of

the Horse's trumpets, the use of infantry drums by a cavalry band is not as inappropriate as might first appear. The white bearskin, formerly worn by the Greys' kettle-drummer, is still the head-dress of the bass drummer of the military band, or of the kettle-drummer if mounted on the black drum horse, recently presented by HM the Queen.

The provision of full dress for regiments of the old Line Cavalry is dependent on regimental funds. It is now only supplied at the public expense for the mounted squadrons of the Household Cavalry Regiment, and then only for wear as follows: by the Queen's Life Guard; on all state occasions when ordered by the Sovereign; on public duties; in the Lord Mayor's procession; or musical rides and recruiting displays; and by the two bands as ordered. The plumed and polished steel helmets, the back-and-breast cuirasses, the scarlet or blue tunics, white leather breeches and jack-boots all remain essentially as worn since the latter half of the nineteenth century, while the black caps and gold-laced crimson coats of the musicians' and trumpeters' State dress display a much longer lineage, having changed little since the seventeenth century. Though the Blues were amalgamated with the Royal Dragoons, the full dress of the Blues and Royals remains that of the senior regiment, with only a gold-embroidered Napoleonic Eagle on the upper left arm to recall the distinctions of the oldest Line Cavalry regiment—the onetime Tangier Horse.

Other than these glittering squadrons with their black horses, the splendid finery of the British Cavalry is now a thing of the past, and some might say not before time. As long ago as 1853 Captain Lewis Nolan, of Balaclava fame and the 15th Hussars, was inveighing against what he saw as 'too much frippery, too much toggery, too much

Opposite above and right: *Orders of Dress, 1980, as worn by the Queen's Own Hussars.*

Above: *Officers, from left: No. 8 Dress (temperate combat dress), No. 10 (temperate mess dress), No. 13 (barrack dress), No. 2 (temperate parade uniform), No. 1 (temperate ceremonial uniform), No. 12 (coverall clothing).*

Right: *Soldiers, from left: No. 13 (barrack dress), No. 2 (temperate parade uniform), No. 14 (shirt-sleeve order), No. 8, (temperate combat dress), No. 12 (coverall clothing).*

weight in things worse than useless ... I can never believe that our hussar uniform is the proper dress in which to do a hussar's duty in war'. A few years later Valentine Baker, a distinguished officer of the 12th Lancers and the 10th Hussars, remarked, 'A tight well-fitting jacket is all very well for a dragoon to walk about a country town and make love to nursery maids; but this is not for which the soldier is intended'. There was much justice in these observations, yet it was in similar clothing that the Union and Hussar Brigades charged at Waterloo, the Heavies at Balaclava won their glory which has been so overshadowed by the Light Brigade, and the Lancers marched and fought under blistering suns in India, Afghanistan and South Africa. The British Cavalry has often been criticised for its lack of professionalism in the past but it has never been found wanting for dash and spirit, the mainspring of which has been pride in its regiments and its horses. A contributory factor to this pride was Nolan's 'frippery and toggery' which each regiment jealously preserved and cherished despite its cost and impracticality, and which marked out a man and his horse as an Inniskilling Dragoon, an 11th Hussar or a Scarlet Lancer. Now this has gone: the plumed helmets, the busbies, the lance-caps, the tunics, jackets and pelisses, the shabraques and the sabretaches, all have gone, along with the horses. Yet the tradition, the significance of it all lingers on, so that, though clad in universal DPM and enclosed within his Chieftain, Scorpion or Scimitar, the armoured soldier, be he Household Cavalryman, dragoon, hussar or lancer, remains the inheritor and exemplar of the old cavalry spirit.

Appendices

1 *The following nine appendices list in note and tabulated form the individual regimental distinctions of the Household and Line Cavalry from 1742 to the present.*

2 *In the following list of regimental abbreviations used in the appendices, the letter H is used for both Horse and Hussars, but the two types do not appear in any one appendix, Horse being shown in Appendices 2–4 only, Hussars in 5, 7–9.*

1 Tp HG/1 LG = 1st Troop, Horse Guards/1st Life Guards
2 Tp HG/2 LG = 2nd Troop, Horse Guards/2nd Life Guards
3 Tp HG = 3rd Troop, Horse Guards
4 Tp HG = 4th Troop, Horse Guards
1 Tp HGG = 1st Troop, Horse Grenadier Guards
2 Tp HGG = 2nd Troop, Horse Grenadier Guards
RHG = Royal Horse Guards (Blues)
King's H/1 DG = King's Regiment of Horse/1st King's Dragoon Guards (Queen's H, 1685–1715)
Queen's H/2 DG = Queen's Regiment of Horse/2nd Dragoon Guards (Queen's Bays)
4 H/3 DG = 4th Horse/3rd (Prince of Wales's) Dragoon Guards
5 H/1 H/4 DG = 5th Horse/1st Horse/4th Royal Irish Dragoon Guards
6 H/2 H/5 DG = 6th Horse/2nd Horse/5th (Princess Charlotte of Wales's) Dragoon Guards
7 H/3 H/6 DG = 7th Horse/3rd Horse/6th Dragoon Guards (Carabiniers)
8 H/4 H/7 DG = 8th Horse/4th Horse/7th (Princess Royal's) Dragoon Guards
QDG = 1st The Queen's Dragoon Guards
3 Carabiniers = 3rd Carabiniers (Prince of Wales's Dragoon Guards)
RSDG = Royal Scots Dragoon Guards (Carabiniers and Greys)
4/7 DG = 4th/7th Royal Dragoon Guards
5 RIDG = 5th Royal Inniskilling Dragoon Guards
1 D = 1st Royal Dragoons
2 D = 2nd Royal North British Dragoons/Royal Scots Greys (2nd Dragoons)
3 D/LD/H = 3rd King's Own Dragoons/Light Dragoons/Hussars
4 D/LD/H = 4th Queen's Own Dragoons/Light Dragoons/Hussars
5 D/L = 5th (Royal Irish) Dragoons/Lancers
6 D = 6th (Inniskilling) Dragoons
7 D/LD/H = 7th Queen's Own Dragoons/Light Dragoons/Hussars
8 D/LD/H = 8th Dragoons/(King's Royal Irish) Light Dragoons/Hussars
9 D/LD/L = 9th Dragoons/Light Dragoons/(Queen's Royal) Lancers

10 D/LD/H = 10th Dragoons/Prince of Wales's Own Light Dragoons/Hussars
11 D/LD/H = 11th Dragoons/Light Dragoons/(Prince Albert's Own) Hussars
12 D/LD/L = 12th Dragoons/(Prince of Wales's) Light Dragoons/Lancers
13 D/LD/H = 13th Dragoons/Light Dragoons/Hussars
14 D/LD/H = 14th Dragoons/(King's) Light Dragoons/Hussars
15 LD/H = 15th (King's) Light Dragoons/Hussars
16 LD/L = 16th Light Dragoons/(Queen's) Lancers
17 LD/L = 17th Light Dragoons/Lancers (Duke of Cambridge's Own)
18 LD/H = 18th Light Dragoons/Royal Hussars (Queen Mary's Own)
19 LD/L/H = 19th Light Dragoons/Lancers/Hussars (Queen Alexandra's Own)
20 LD/H = 20th Light Dragoons/Hussars
21 LD/H/L = 21st Light Dragoons/Hussars/Lancers (Empress of India's)
22 LD = 22nd Light Dragoons

23 LD/L = 23rd Light Dragoons/Lancers
24 LD = 24th Light Dragoons
25 LD = 25th Light Dragoons
13/18 H = 13th/18th Royal Hussars (Queen Mary's Own)
14/20 H = 14th/20th King's Hussars
15/19 H = 15th/19th King's Royal Hussars
16/5 L = 16th/5th Queen's Royal Lancers
17/21 L = 17th/21st Lancers
QOH = Queen's Royal Hussars
QRIH = Queen's Royal Irish Hussars
9/12 L = 9th/12th Royal Lancers (Prince of Wales's)
RH = Royal Hussars (Prince of Wales's Own)

Colours / Metals

bf	= buff	lt	= light
bl	= blue	or	= orange
blk	= black	p	= pink
br	= brown	r	= red
c	= crimson	sc	= scarlet
g	= gold	s	= silver
gr	= green	w	= white
gy	= grey	y	= yellow

APPENDIX 1

Distinctions, Troops of Horse Guards & Horse Grenadier Guards 1742–1787

Troop	Facings	Waistcoat & breeches	Lace	Cloak & lining	Flask cord	Carbine belt stripes	Housing & holster caps[1]	Caps[2]	Remarks
1 Tp HG	bl	bf	g	r/bl		3g, 2r	r		from 1788 1 LG
2 Tp HG	bl	bf	g	r/bl		3g, 2w[3]	w[3]		from 1788 2 LG
3 Tp HG	bl	bf	g	r/bl		3g, 2y	y		disbanded 1746
4 Tp HG	bl	bf	g	r/bl		3g, 2bl	bl		disbanded 1746
1 Tp HGG	bl	bf	w	r/bl	bl		bl	bl/r/r/bl[4]	from 1788 1 LG
2 Tp HGG	bl	bf	w	r/bl	r		r	r/bl/bl/bl[5]	from 1788 2 LG
		6			7				

Notes

[1] HG edged double gold lace. HGG edged double yellow lace, red stripe for 1 Tp, blue for 2 Tp. All embroidered with GR in gold on red within the garter, surmounted by the crown.

[2] Colours in order represent: front/flap/bag/turn-up. Both with crown, cypher and garter. From c 1763, caps in fur with metal plate bearing Royal arms.

[3] From 1751 blue.

[4] From 1751 bl/r/r/r. Grenade on flap.

[5] From 1751 r/bl/r/bl. Thistle on flap.

[6] From c 1764 white.

[7] From 1829 flask cords re-introduced on pouch belts: 1 LG crimson, 2 LG blue.

APPENDIX 2

Distinctions, Horse & Dragoons, 1742

Regt	Facings	Waistcoat & breeches	Cloak & lining	Flask cord	Hat lace	Housings & holster caps	Embroidery on housings[1]	Remarks
RHG	r	r/bl	bl/r	r	y	r	w & y	
King's H	bl	bl	r/bl	bl	y	r	y & w	1746 1 DG
Queen's H	bf	bf	r/bf	bf	y	r	y & w	1746 2 DG
4 H	w	w/r	r/w	w	w	w	w & r	1746 3 DG
5 H	bl	bl	r/bl	bf	y	y	r & w	1746 1 H
6 H	gr	gr	r/gr	bf	w	w	w & y	1746 2 H
7 H	y	y	r/y	y/bf	w	w	r & bl	1746 3 H
8 H	blk[2]	bf	r/bf	bf	y	y	r,w,blk[3]	1746 4 H
1 D	bl	bl/r	r/bl	bl	y	bl	w & y	
2 D	bl	bl	r/bl	r	y	r	y & gr	Grenadier caps
3 D	lt bl	lt bl	r/lt bl	bl	y	r	y	
4 D	gr	gr	r/gr		w	gr	w & r	
5 D	bl	bl	r/bl	bf	y	bl	r & w	
6 D	y	y/r	r/y		w	y	r & blk	
7 D	w	w	r/w	w	w	w	r,bl,y	
8 D	or	or	r/or		w	or	w	cross-belts
9 D	bf	bf	r/bf		w	bf	r & blk[3]	
10 D	y	y	r/y		w	y	r & blk[3]	
11 D	w[2]	w/r	r/bf		w	bf	r & blk[3]	
12 D	w	w/r	r/w		w	w	r,y,blk[3]	
13 D	gr[2]	w	r/w		w	bf	r & bl	
14 D	y[4]	w	r/y		w	y	r & bl	
15 D	gr	bf	r/gr		y	gr	y & gr	raised 1745 as Kingston's Light Horse disbanded 1749

Notes

All coats red except for RHG blue.

[1] *Devices*

  i. RHG, King's H, 5 H: Royal arms in full colour, scroll border.

  ii. Remaining H: trophy of arms, standards, trumpets and drums with similar border.

  iii. 1 D, 2 D, 3 D, 5 D and 7 D: Royal cypher within the garter, surmounted by the crown, scroll border.

  iv. Remaining D: knight's helmet above a trophy of colours, drums and trumpets, scroll border; 6 D, diamond pattern, r/y/blk.

[2] Buff linings.

[3] Blk may be dark Blue.

[4] White cuffs.

APPENDIX 3

Distinctions, Dragoon Guards, Horse & Dragoons, 1751

1. Coats red except RHG blue.
2. Facings, waistcoats and breeches unchanged from 1742 except for:
RHG breeches red.
3 DG (formerly 4 H) breeches white.
1 H (formerly 5 H) all pale blue.
1 D breeches blue.
6 D breeches yellow.
11 D all buff.

13 D facings light green.
3. Coats of DG lapelled to waist, of RHG and H to bottom of skirt, of D no lapels.
4. Housings and holster caps matched facings except 1 DG and 1 D both red, and 4 H buff. Scroll border replaced by lace edging in same colours as trumpeters' lace (see below), except in RHG double gold. Holster caps bore Royal cypher above rank of regiment.

Regt	Buttonholes & how set on	Hat lace	Trumpeters, Drummers, Hautbois coat/facing	waistcoat/ breeches	Lace	Housing devices	Remarks
RHG	y, 2 & 2	g	r/bl	bl	royal (y & bl)	crown, cypher, garter	r flask-cord, carbine belt. 1758 cuirasses issued
1 DG	y, 2 & 2	g	r/bl	bl	royal	crown, cypher, garter	1756 light tp added
2 DG	y, 3 & 3	g	r/bl	bl	royal	crown, queen's cypher, garter	1756 light tp added
3 DG	y, 2 & 2	g	w/r	r	y, r stripe	III DG, union wreath	1756 light tp added
1 H	w, 2 & 2	s	pl bl/r	r	w, r stripe	I H, union wreath	
2 H	y, 2 & 2	g	gr/r	r	w, r stripe	II H, union wreath	
3 H	w, 2 & 2	s	y/r	r	w, r stripe	III H, union wreath	1760 cuirasses issued
4 H	y, 2 & 2	g	bf/r	r	w, blk stripe	IV H, union wreath	1760 cuirasses issued
1 D	y, 2 & 2	g	r/bl	bl	royal	crest of England, garter	1756 light tp added
2 D	w, 2 & 2		r/bl	bl	royal	thistle, St Andrew's circle	grenadier caps. 1756 light tp added
3 D	y, 3 & 3	g	r/bl	bl	royal	white horse, garter	1756 light tp added
4 D	w, 2 & 2	s	gr/r	r	w, bl stripe	IV D, union wreath	1756 light tp added
5 D	w, 3 & 3	s	r/bl	bl	royal	harp & crown	
6 D	w, 2 & 2	s	y/r	r	w, bl stripe	castle of Inniskilling, union wreath	1756 light tp added
7 D	w, 3 & 3	s	r/bl	bl	royal	queen's cypher, garter	1756 light tp added
8 D	w, 3 & 3	s	y/r	r	w, y stripe	VIII D, union wreath	
9 D	w, 2 & 2	s	bf/r	r	w, bl stripe	IX D, union wreath	
10 D	w, 3, 4 & 5	s	y/r	r	w, gr stripe	X D, union wreath	1756 light tp added
11 D	w, 3 & 3	s	bf/r	r	w, gr stripe	XI D, union wreath	1756 light tp added
12 D	w, 2 & 2	s	w/r	r	y, gr stripe	XII D, union wreath	
13 D	y, 3 & 3	g	gr/r	r	w, y stripe	XIII D, union wreath	
14 D	w, 3 & 3	s	y/r	r	w, r & gr stripe	XIV D, union wreath	

APPENDIX 4

Distinctions, Dragoon Guards, Horse, Dragoons, Light Dragoons, 1768

1. The regiments RHG to 11 D, 13 D and 14 D were unchanged from 1751 except for:

a. Facings
  1 H blue.
  3 H white.
  13 D deep green.

b. Coats
  All DG and H lapelled to waist; D no lapels.

c. Waistcoats, breeches, coat and cloak linings
  All changed to white, except for 1 DG, 2 DG, 4 H, 3 D, 9 D, 11 D and 13 D who had buff.

d. Trumpeters, drummers and hautbois
  i. Coats and facings
    3 H white/red.
  ii. Waistcoat, breeches and coat linings
  All to white except:
    1 DG, 2 DG, 3 D who had buff.

6 D, 8 D, 9 D, 10 D, 11 D and 14 D who retained their 1751 colours.

  iii. Lace
    3 DG Royal lace.
    3 H yellow, black stripe.
    4 D white, red stripe.

e. Housings and lace
  To match 1. *a* and 1. *d iii.*

f. Housing devices
  3 DG: Prince of Wales's Feathers issuing from coronet.

2. Light Dragoons
  12 D converted 1768. 15 LD–18 LD raised 1759. All red coats lapelled to waist. All white buttons, 2 and 2. All waistcoats, breeches, coat and cloak linings white.

Regt	Facings	Trumpeters' Coats/ facings	Waistcoats, breeches, linings	Lace	Housings & holster caps Colour	Lace	Device
12 LD	blk	r/bl	w	royal	blk[1]	royal	Prince of Wales's Feathers
15 LD	bl	r/bl	w	royal	w	royal	king's crest, garter
16 LD	bl	r/bl	w	royal	w	royal	queen's cypher, garter
17 LD	w	w/r	r	w, blk edge	w	w, blk edge	XVII LD
18 LD	w	w/r	r	r & w	w	nil	XVIII LD

Note
[1] With stripes of white goatskin.

APPENDIX 5

Distinctions, Light Dragoons, 1784–1822

1. All jackets and shells dark blue (jackets only from 1796) except for regiments in India or at the Cape who wore grey.
2. All breeches white except for 9 LD, 11 LD and 13 LD who wore buff.
3. Colours under each date column represent facings/lace.

Regt	1784	1803	1808	1812[1]	Remarks
7 (H 1805)	w/s	w/s	w/s[2]	bl/g	dark bl netherwear 1814
8	sc/s	sc/s	sc/s	sc/g	grey jackets 1796–1812
9 (L 1816)	bf/s	bf/s	bf/s	c/g	
10 (H 1805)	y/s	y/s	y/s[2]	sc/s	1814 bl/g
11	bf/s	bf/s	bf/s	bf/s	
12 (L 1816)	y/s	y/s	y/s	y/s	1817 sc/g
13	bf/g	bf/g	bf/g	bf/g	
14	y/s	or/s	or/s	or/s	
15 (H 1805)	sc/s	sc/s	sc/s[2]	sc/s	
16 (L 1816)	sc/s	sc/s	sc/s	sc/s	
17 (L 1822)	w/s	w/s	w/s	w/s	grey jackets 1810–1812
18 (H 1807)	w/s	w/s	w/s[2]	w/s	disbanded 1821
19 (L 1816)		y/s	y/s	y/g	disbanded 1821
20		y/s	or/g	or/g	disbanded 1818
21		y/s	p/g	p/g	disbanded 1819
22		sc/s	p/s	p/s	1815 r/s. disbanded 1820
23 (L 1816)		bl/s	c/s	c/s	disbanded 1817
24		w/s	lt gy/g	lt gy/g	disbanded 1819
25		y/s	lt gy/s	lt gy/s	disbanded 1819
3 (LD 1818)					1818 sc/g
4 (LD 1818)					1818 y/s

Notes

[1] New dress.

[2] Hussar details
a. Fur caps. All brown fur, except officers of 10 H who had grey (1805–08), officers 15 H and 18 H having black. Plumes, white over red. Bags, red except 18 H pale blue.
b. Shakos 7 H blue (1812–14). 10 H black (1809–14), scarlet (1815–18), black (1819–22). 15 H scarlet (1813–14) and (1819–22). 18 H nil.
c. Pelisse fur. 7 H officers brown, men white, 1819 all black. 10 H officers grey, men white, 1815 both black. 15 H both black. 18 H both white, 1819 both grey.

APPENDIX 6

Distinctions, Life Guards, Royal Horse Guards, Dragoon Guards & Dragoons, 1788–1920

1. Coats and tunics (post–1855) scarlet throughout except where noted. Facings unchanged after 1812, except where noted. From 1822–1828 buttons in pairs for DG, regular for D; thereafter regular for all.

2. Trumpeters
From 1812 coats only distinguished from the men's by special lace on active service.

From 1834 all trumpeters and bandsmen in red, except RHG in blue.

3. Shabraques
From 1827 blue for all regiments (officers only) with double gold lace for DG, single for D. Introduced for men in 1857, but abolished in 1872; for officers in 1897.

Regt	1788 Facings	Buttons	Hat lace	1812[1] Facings	Coat lace[2]	1855 helmet plumes[3]	Remarks
1 LG	bl	y	g	bl	g	w[4]	
2 LG	bl	y	g	bl	g	w[4]	
RHG	r	y, 2s	g	r	g	r	Household Cavalry from 1820. coats/tunics bl
1 DG	bl	y, 2s	g	bl	g	r	
2 DG	blk	y, 3s	g	blk	s	blk	facings 1855 bf
3 DG	w	y, 2s	g	w	g	blk/r	facings 1815 bl. 1819 y/s
4 DG	bl	w, 2s	s	bl	s	w	
5 DG	y	w, 2s	s	gr	g	r/w	
6 DG	w	w, 2s	s	w	s	blk (1873 w)	1851–1861, dressed as LD except helmet[5]
7 DG	blk	y, 2s	g	blk	g	blk/w	
1 D	bl	y, 2s	g	bl	g	blk	
2 D	bl	w, 2s	nil	bl	g		bearskin caps, w plume
3 D	bl	y, 3s	g	bl	g		1818 LD (see appx 5 & 7)
4 D	gr	w, 2s	s	gr	s		1818 LD (see appx 5 & 7)
5 D	bl	w, 3s	s				disbanded 1799. 1858 5 L (see appx 7)
6 D	y	w, 2s	s	y	s	w	

Notes

[1] New dress.

[2] Gold for all from 1830.

[3] Helmets: Household Cavalry polished steel. DG and D gilt/brass, black plumes until 1854. From 1855 DG gilt/brass; 1 D & 6 D white metal.

[4] Trumpeters and musicians had red. Farriers black (blue tunics).

[5] Blue tunics thereafter.

APPENDIX 7

Distinctions, Light Dragoons, Hussars & Lancers, 1830–1920

1. Jackets, pelisses, tunics (post–1855) and netherwear dark blue throughout, except where noted. Facings unchanged after 1861. All lace gold/yellow.

2. From 1834 all trumpeters and bandsmen dressed as the men.

3. Shabraques
LD and L blue, Royal cypher above badge and motto of regiment, with crossed lances for L. 7 H and 8 H blue, 10 H and 15 H scarlet, 11 H crimson, Royal cypher and regimental devices. Abolished 1872 for men; 1897 for officers.

Regt	1830[1] Facings	1841 Facings	1855 Headdress plumes[2]	1861 Facings	Plume/ busby bag	Remarks
3 LD (H 1861)	bl	sc	blk & w	sc[3]	w/garter bl	
4 LD (H 1861)	y (1836 gr)	sc	sc	bl	sc/y	
5 L (1858)				sc	gr	
7 H	bl	bl	w	bl	w/sc	
8 H	bl	bl	w & sc	bl	w & sc/sc	
9 L	bl	sc	blk & w	sc	blk & w	special cap, black top
10 H	bl	bl	w & blk	bl	w & blk/sc	netherwear double stripes. blk shako 1846–56
11 LD (H 1840)	bf	bl	w & c	bl	w & c/c	netherwear crimson, double stripes from 1840
12 L	bl	sc	sc	sc	sc	
13 LD (H 1861)	bf (1836 gr)	bf	w	bf[3]	w/bf	netherwear buff stripe
14 LD (H 1861)	bl	sc	r & w	bl	w/y	
15 H	bl	bl	sc	bl	sc/sc	scarlet shakos until 1856
16 L	bl	bl	sc	bl	sc & w	red jacket/tunic throughout. blk plume from 1881.
17 L	w	w	w	w	w	netherwear white stripes. blk plume 1874–83
18 H (1858)				bl	gr/gr	1878 scarlet facings, white plume, blue busby bag
19 H (1861)				bl	w/w	from Hon. East India Coy
20 H (1861)				bl	c/c	from Hon. East India Coy
21 H (1861)				bl	w/french gy	from Hon. East India Coy. 21 L from 1897
21 L (1897)				french gy	w	

Notes

[1] Period of red jackets for LD and L; red pelisses for H.

[2] Hussar busby bags (from c 1841) all red, except for 11 H crimson.

[3] Collar only.

APPENDIX 8

Distinctions, Full Dress, Post–1922

1. Apart from the Household Cavalry, the wearing of full dress in the period following the 1922 amalgamations of regiments was largely confined to officers attending levees, and bands.

2. Scarlet tunics for LG, all DG and D, and 16/5 L. The remainder wore blue tunics.

Regt	Plumes[1]	Busby bags or lance-cap tops	Facings	Netherwear stripes
LG	w[2]		bl	2 sc + welt[3]
RHG	r		r	sc[3]
1 DG	r		bl	y
2 DG	blk		bf	w
3 Carabiniers[4]	blk & r		y	2 w
4/7 DG[5]	w		bl	y
5 RIDG[6]	r & w		y (1937 bl)	y[7]
1 D	blk		bl	y
2 D	w[8]		bl	y
3 H	w	garter bl	sc[9]	y
4 H	sc	y	bl	y
7 H	w	sc	bl	y
8 H	w & sc	sc	bl	y
9 L	sc	blk	sc	2 y
10 H	w & blk	sc	bl	2 y
11 H	w & c	c	bl	2 y[10]
12 L	sc	sc	sc	2 y
13/18 H	w	bf	bf[9]	bf
14/20 H	w	y	bl	y
15/19 H	sc	sc	bl	y
16/5 L	blk	bl	bl	2 y
17/21 L	w	w	w	2 w

Notes

[1] Helmets, LG & RHG white metal, 1 DG–4/7 DG brass, 5 RIDG & 1 D white metal.

[2] Trumpeters & musicians red, farriers black (blue tunics).

[3] On dark blue overalls only.

[4] Formerly 3 DG and 6 DG.

[5] Formerly 4 DG and 7 DG.

[6] Formerly 5 DG and 6 D.

[7] Overalls and pantaloons, dark green (yellow = primrose).

[8] Bearskin caps.

[9] On collar only.

[10] Overalls and pantaloons crimson.

APPENDIX 9

Distinctions, RAC Cavalry Regiments From 1958

Regt	Forage cap crown/band/welts	No. 1 Dress collar	trouser stripe	Sgts arm badge	Stable belt	Belt No. 2 Dress[1] offrs	men
QDG	all bl		single w	old 2 DG badge	all bl		
RSDG	bl/y vandyke/y[2]		double y	eagle on carbines[3]	bl/gy/y/sc/bl	br p/b	br p/b
4/7 DG	all bl		single y	as cap badge	r/y/bl	br p/b	br w/b
5 RIDG	gr/y/y		single y[4]	w horse of Hanover	r/gr/y		
QOH	all sc	sc	double y	QOH cypher	bl/y/bl[5]	br p/b	nil
QRIH	all sc[6]		double y	harp	gr/y/bl/gr	br p/b	gr w/b
9/12 L	sc/–/bl[7]	sc[8]	double y	PoW feathers	r/y/r/y/r		
RH	all c[9]		nil[10]	PoW feathers	bl/y/r/y/bl		
13/18 H	w/bl/–	w[8]	double w	Queen Mary's cypher	bl/w/bl/w/bl		
14/20 H	all sc[11]		double y	cap badge on s oval[13]	bl/y/bl		nil[12]
15/19 H	all sc		double y	royal crest	bl/y/r/bl		
16/5 L	sc/–/bl[7]		double y	harp	r/y/bl		
17/21 L	bl/w/w[7]	w[8]	double w	death's head	w/bl/w/bl/w		

Notes

[1] Other than Sam Browne for officers, white waistbelts for men. p/b = pouch-belt, w/b = waistbelt.

[2] Regimental beret is grey.

[3] All ranks wear the Prince of Wales's feathers badge on left upper arm.

[4] Green trousers, also in No. 2 Dress.

[5] Blue is garter blue with scarlet line through centre.

[6] Officers have 'tent' cap in green, laced gold. Regimental beret is rifle green.

[7] Welts round crown and at quarters.

[8] Gorget patch only.

[9] Regimental beret is brown with crimson backing to badge.

[10] Crimson trousers, also in No. 2 Dress.

[11] Black cap badge.

[12] Warrant officers Sam Browne.

[13] All ranks wear badge of crossed kukris on upper left arm.

Bibliography

Anglesey, Marquess of, *A History Of The British Cavalry, Vol 1, 1816–1850, Vol 2, 1851–1871, Vol 3, 1872–1898*, Leo Cooper, London, 1973, 1975, 1982.

Anglesey, Marquess of (ed.), *Sergeant Pearman's Memoirs*, Jonathan Cape, London, 1968.

Anglesey, Marquess of (ed.), *Little Hodge (Diaries and letters of Colonel Edward Cooper Hodge, 4th DG)*, Leo Cooper, London, 1971.

Atkinson, C T, *The History Of The Royal Dragoons 1661–1934*, Glasgow, 1934.

Barnes, Major R M, *A History Of The Regiments And Uniforms Of The British Army*, Seeley Service, London, 1950.

Barnes, Major R M, *Military Uniforms Of Britain And The Empire*, Seeley Service, London, 1960.

Barrett, C R B, *The 7th (QO) Hussars*, 2 Vols, Royal United Services Institute, London, 1914.

Barrett, C R B, *History Of The XIII Hussars*, 2 Vols, W Blackwood, London, 1911.

Barthorp, Michael, *The Armies Of Britain 1485–1980*, National Army Museum, London, 1980.

Blackmore, Howard L, *British Military Firearms 1650–1850*, Herbert Jenkins, London, 1961.

Carman, W Y, *British Military Uniforms*, Leonard Hill, Glasgow, 1957.

Carman, W Y, *Head Dresses Of The British Army—Cavalry*, privately published, 1968.

Carman, W Y, *A Dictionary Of Military Uniform*, Batsford, London, 1977.

Carman, W Y, *Richard Simkin's Uniforms Of The British Army—The Cavalry Regiments*, Webb & Bower, Exeter, 1982.

Chandler, D G, *The Art Of War In The Age Of Marlborough*, Batsford, London, 1976.

Chappell, M, *British Cavalry Equipments, 1800–1941*, Osprey Publishing, London, 1983.

Chichester, H M, and Burges-Short, G, *The Records And Badges Of Every Regiment And Corps In The British Army*, William Clowes, London, 1895.

Cooper-King, Colonel C, *The British Army And Auxiliary Forces*, 2 Vols, Cassell, London, 1893.

Delves-Broughton, J, *The Dress Of The First Regiment Of Life Guards In Three Centuries*, privately published, n.d.

Featherstone, Donald, *Weapons And Equipment Of The Victorian Soldier*, Blandford Press, Poole, 1978.

Forbes, Major-General A, *A History Of The Army Ordance Services*, 3 Vols, Medici Society, London, 1929.

Fortescue, Hon Sir John, *History Of The British Army*, 13 Vols, Macmillan, London, 1899–1930.

Fortescue Hon Sir John, and Micholls, Major Gilbert, *A History Of The 17th Lancers*, 2 Vols, Macmillan, London, 1931.

Gander, Terry, *Encyclopaedia Of The Modern British Army*, Patrick Stephens, Cambridge, 1980.

Golding, Harry (ed.), *The Wonder Book Of Soldiers*, Ward Lock, London, various editions, 1905–1940.

Gordon-Brown, A (ed.) *The Narrative Of Private Buck Adams (7th DG)*, Van Riebeeck Society, Cape Town, 1941.

Haswell-Miller, A E, and Dawnay, N P, *Military Drawings And Paintings In The Royal Collection*, 2 Vols, Phaidon, Oxford, 1966 and 1970.

Haythornthwaite, Philip, *Weapons And Equipment Of The Napoleonic Wars*, Blandford Press, Poole, 1979.

Index To British Military Costume Prints, Army Museums Ogilby Trust, 1972.

Kipling, Arthur, and King, Hugh, *Headdress Badges Of The British Army*, Frederick Muller, London, 1972.

Lawson, C C P, *A History Of The Uniforms Of The British Army*, 5 Vols, Peter Davies, Kaye & Ward, London, 1940–1967.

Liddell, Colonel R S, *Memoirs Of The Tenth Royal Hussars (Prince Of Wales's Own)*, Longmans Green, London, 1891.

Luard, Lieutenant-Colonel John, *A History Of The Dress Of The British Soldier*, William Clowes, London, 1852.

Mollo, John and Boris, *Uniforms And Equipment Of The Light Brigade*, Historical Research Unit, London, 1968.

Mollo, John, *Waterloo Uniforms—British Cavalry*, Historical Research Unit, London, 1973.

Mollo, John, *Military Fashion*, Barrie and Jenkins, London, 1972.

Mollo, John, *Uniforms Of The Seven Years War*, Blandford Press, Poole, 1977.

Nevill, Ralph, *British Military Prints*, Connoisseur, London, 1909.

Nolan, Captain L E, *Cavalry; Its History And Tactics*, London, 1853.

Oatts, Lieutenant-Colonel L B, *Emperor's Chambermaids: The Story Of The 14th/20th King's Hussars*, Ward Lock, London, 1973.

Parkyn, Major H G, *Shoulder-Belt Plates And Buttons*, Gale and Polden, 1956.

Pomeroy, Major Hon R L, *5th Princess Charlotte Of Wales's Dragoon Guards*, 2 Vols, Blackwood, 1924.

Robson, Brian, *Swords Of The British Army 1788–1914*, Arms and Armour Press, London, 1975.

Rogers, Colonel H C B, *The Mounted Troops Of The British Army*, Seeley Service, London, 1959.

Rogers, Colonel H C B, *Weapons Of The British Soldier*, Seeley Service, London, 1960.

Rogers, Colonel H C B, *Battles And Generals Of The Civil Wars 1642–1651*, Seeley Service, London, 1968.

Rogers, Colonel H C B, *The British Army Today And Tomorrow*, 1980.

Sheppard, Major E W, *The Ninth Queen's Royal Lancers 1715–1936*, Gale and Polden, 1939.

Simkin, Richard, *Life In The Army*, Chapman & Hall, London, 1889.

Simkin, Richard, *Our Armies*, Simpkin, Marshall, London, 1890.

Simkin, Richard, *Types Of The British Army*, Army & Navy Gazette, 1888–1902.

Stadden, Charles, *The Life Guards, Dress And Appointments, 1660–1914*, Almark, London, 1971.

Stewart, Captain P F, *The History Of The XII Royal Lancers*, Oxford University Press, London, 1950.

Strachan, Hew, *British Military Uniforms 1768–96*, Arms & Armour Press, London, 1975.

Wace, Alan, *The Marlborough Tapestries At Blenheim Palace*, Phaidon, Oxford, 1968.

Walton, Colonel Clifford, *History Of The British Standing Army 1660–1700*, Harrison, London, 1894.

Walton, Lieutenant-Colonel P S, *Simkin's Soldiers—The British Army In 1890*, Vol I, Victorian Military Society, 1981.

Wolseley, Viscount, *The Soldier's Pocket Book*, Macmillan, London, 1869 and 1886.

Official Publications

Horse Guards Circular Memoranda, General and Army Orders.
King's and Queen's Regulations.
Royal Warrants.
Clothing Regulations.
Officers Dress Regulations.

Periodicals

Annual Reports, National Army Museum, London.
The Illustrated London News.
The Graphic.
The Illustrated Naval and Military Magazine.
Journal of the Society for Army Historical Research.
Journal of the Victorian Military Society.
The King and His Army.
The Navy and Army Illustrated.
Soldier Magazine.
Plus various regimental journals.

Manuscripts

Lawson, C C P, and Mollo, John, *A History Of The Uniforms Of The British Army*, Vol 6 (illustrated typescript), John Mollo.

Lawson, C C P, *Notebooks*, National Army Museum, London.

Reynolds, P W, *Military Costume In The 18th And 19th Centuries*, Victoria and Albert Museum.

Collection of Regimental Files, Army Museums Ogilby Trust, Aldershot.

Artists

The artists and illustrators whose military work has proved most valuable in the compilation of text and coloured plates for this book are the following. They are given in roughly chronological order from the seventeenth century to the present: Wenceslas Hollar, Jan Wyck, Louis Laguerre, John Wootton, the anonymous hand of the 1742 Clothing Book, David Morier, Sir Joshua Reynolds, Francis Wheatley, Sir William Beechey, F G Byron, George Morland, George Stubbs, Edward Dayes, Edmund Scott, Henry Edridge, J A Atkinson, Thomas Ellis, Charles Hamilton Smith, the Robert Dightons, Denis Dighton, Alexander Sauerweid, R Reinagle, J Pardon, William Heath, Edward Hull, Henry Alken, A J Dubois Drahonet, L Mansion & S Eschauzier, M A Hayes, J Ferneley Jnr, Henry Martens, R R Scanlan, A de Prades, T W Goodrich, William Sharpe, G H Thomas, Orlando Norie, Richard Simkin, Charles Fripp, G D Giles, Harry Payne, Melton Prior, F A Stewart, P W Reynolds, J Mathews, C C P Lawson, A E Haswell Miller, Charles Stadden.

Picture Credits

Index

REGIMENTAL INDEX

Regiments are listed in order of seniority under their successive titles. Those amalgamated in 1920–22 and post-1958 appear below the former senior regiment.